Writing the Research Paper

A Handbook ● Third Edition

Writing the Research Paper

A Handbook ● Third Edition

With Both the MLA and APA Documentation Styles

Anthony C. Winkler
Jo Ray McCuen
Glendale Community College

HBJ

Harcourt Brace Jovanovich, Publishers
San Diego New York Chicago Austin Washington, D.C.
London Sydney Tokyo Toronto

ISBN: 0-15-598292-3
Library of Congress Catalog Card Number: 89-84377
Printed in the United States of America

Preface

This third edition of *Writing the Research Paper* is still organized as a handbook to be used without being read from cover to cover. Information is discretely packed in clearly labeled and indexed units that the researcher can quickly access at a glance without having to pore over the entire volume. In short, the changes we have made in this new edition are all designed to make the book even more practical and easy to use.

To Chapter 2 we have added a list of possible research paper topics that might not readily occur to the beginning researcher, many from a variety of academic disciplines. In Chapter 4 we have clarified the types of sources a researcher should look for, making distinctions between single-fact information, general information, and in-depth information. In this chapter we have also substantially enlarged the section, "Using the computer in your search" and we have included an actual step-by-step example of a researcher using a database.

Because many beginning writers are uncertain about the particular style a researcher is expected to use, we have added a new section to Chapter 6, "Aiming for a readable style." Here we show how to develop an acceptable research paper style that is neither snobbish nor stuffy. Examples are provided to illustrate the difference between foggy and clear phrasing, and specific suggestions are given as to which voice to use and how to write both with greater precision and with greater conciseness.

It is safe to say that the battle between competing styles of documentation is largely over, with the simplicity of the parenthetical style having clearly won. For the most part, the only issue unresolved is whether to use the parenthetical style of the MLA—the one preferred in the humanities—or that of the APA—the style favored by most social sciences. In this book we teach both parenthetical styles and point out their differences in two annotated student papers, one written to conform to the recently revised MLA style and the other to that of the APA. Marginal notations in each paper clearly demonstrate where and how each style differs in documentation conventions. And because there are those who still use them, we continue to explain documentation by footnotes and endnotes.

Marshall Nunn of Glendale College Library has made less obvious but equally significant changes to the Appendix of General and Specialized References. He has painstakingly reviewed the entire list, bringing every indexed item up to date. Because of his efforts, the annotated references are now more useful and accessible than ever.

In preparing this third edition, we have, as before, benefited from the learned counsel of many people, among them Vicki Adams of Kent State University, Beth Basham of the University of Louisville, Joan Bolden of John C. Calhoun Community College, Therese Brychta of Truckee Meadows Community College, and Delma Porter of Texas A & M University. We are grateful to them for taking the time to help us improve this book.

Anthony C. Winkler
Jo Ray McCuen

Contents

Preface v

1 **Basic Information About the Research Paper** 1

- **1a** Definition of the research paper 2
- **1b** Format of the research paper 2
- **1c** Reasons for the research paper 3
- **1d** Steps and schedule involved in writing a research paper 3
- **1e** The report paper and the thesis paper 4

2 **Choosing a Topic** 7

- **2a** How to choose a topic 8
- **2b** Topics to avoid 8
  - 2b-1 Topics that are too big 8
  - 2b-2 Topics that can be traced to a single source 9
  - 2b-3 Topics that are too technical 9
  - 2b-4 Topics that are too trivial 10
- **2c** Narrowing the topic 10

3 **The Library** 15

- **3a** Layout of the library 16
  - 3a-1 Card catalog 16
  - 3a-2 Microform indexes 16
  - 3a-3 Stacks 16
  - 3a-4 Reference room 19
  - 3a-5 Main desk 19
  - 3a-6 Reserve desk 20
  - 3a-7 Audiovisual room 20
  - 3a-8 Microform room 20
  - 3a-9 Newspaper racks 20

3a-10 Copy room 20
3a-11 Typing room 21
3a-12 Carrels 21
3a-13 The computer 21
3a-14 Interlibrary loan 21
3b Organization of the library 21
3b-1 The Dewey Decimal System 22
3b-2 The Cutter/Sanborn Author Marks 23
3b-3 The Library of Congress System 24
3b-4 Classification of periodicals 25
3b-5 Classification of nonbooks 25
4 Doing the Research 27
4a What information to look for 28
4a-1 Single-fact information 28
4a-2 General information 28
4a-3 In-depth information 28
4a-4 Retrospective and contemporary sources 29
4b Where to look for information 29
4c Using the computer in your search 31
4c-1 Sample subject display 32
4c-2 Sample bibliographic display 33
4c-3 Sample database source display 34
4d Assembling a working bibliography 34
4e Selecting your sources 37
4e-1 Primary and secondary sources of evidence 38
4e-2 Evaluating sources of evidence 39
4f Note-taking 40
4f-1 Format of the note cards 41
4f-2 Kinds of note cards 41
a. The summary 41
b. The paraphrase 42
c. The quotation 43
d. The personal comment 44
4g Plagiarism: what it is and how to avoid it 46
5 The Thesis and the Outline 51
5a The thesis: definition and function 52
5a-1 Formulating the thesis 53
5a-2 Rules for wording the thesis 54
5a-3 Placing the thesis 58
5a-4 Title of the research paper 59
5b The outline 59
5b-1 Visual conventions of the outline 60
5b-2 Equal ranking in outline entries 61
5b-3 Parallelism in outline entries 61
5b-4 Types of outlines 62
a. The topic outline 62
b. The sentence outline 63
c. The paragraph outline 64

5b-5 The decimal notation of an outline 66
5b-6 Which kind of outline should you use? 67

6 Transforming the Notes into a Rough Draft 69

6a Preparing to write the rough draft: a checklist 70
6b Incorporating note-taking into the flow of the paper 71
6b-1 Using summaries and paraphrases 71
6b-2 Using direct quotations 73
a. Overuse of quotations 74
b. Using brief quotations 75
c. Using long quotations 77
d. Using quotations from poetry 78
e. Using a quotation within another quotation 80
f. Punctuating quotations 80
g. Interpolations in quoted material 81
h. The ellipsis 81
6b-3 Using indirect quotations 85
6b-4 How to place and punctuate the page reference parentheses 86
a. Short quotations 87
b. Long quotations 87
c. Quotations ending in an ellipsis 87
6b-5 Using personal comments 87
6c Writing the paper with unity, coherence, and emphasis 89
6c-1 Unity 89
6c-2 Coherence 89
6c-3 Emphasis 93
6d Using the proper tense 94
6d-1 Maintain the present tense except when reporting an event that happened in the past. 94
6d-2 Keep your tense or mood consistent. 94
6d-3 Use the present tense for most comments by authorities because they usually continue to be true and in print. 95
6e Aiming for a readable style 95
6e-1 Understand your sources. 97
6e-2 Be scrupulously accurate. 97
6e-3 Be precise. 97
6e-4 Be concise. 98
6e-5 Use the active voice. 101
6e-6 Take an objective stance. 102
6e-7 Avoid sexist language. 103
6f Writing the abstract 104

7 Systems of Documentation 105

7a When to provide documentation 106
7b Types of documentation 106
7c Guide to systems of documentation 108

7d Parenthetical documentation: author and work (MLA style) 109
- 7d-1 Reference citations in the text 109
  - a. Introducing the authority 109
  - b. Identifying the source 110
  - c. Documenting without mention of authority 110
  - d. Material by two authors 110
  - e. Material by more than two authors 110
  - f. Mentioning both author and work 111
  - g. Anonymous author 111
  - h. No author 111
  - i. More than one work by the same author 111
  - j. Work in a collection 112
  - k. Multivolume works 112
  - l. Double reference—a quotation within a cited work 112
  - m. Short passages of poetry 112
  - n. Using Arabic numerals 113
- 7d-2 Varying your introductions 113

7e Parenthetical documentation: author and date (APA style) 114
- 7e-1 Reference citations in the text 115
  - a. One work by a single author 115
  - b. Subsequent references 116
  - c. One work by two or more authors 116
  - d. One work by up to six authors 116
  - e. Work by six or more authors 117
  - f. Corporate authors 117
  - g. Works by an anonymous author or no author 118
  - h. Authors with the same surname 119
  - i. Two or more works within the same parentheses 119
  - j. References to specific parts of a source 120
  - k. Personal communications 120
  - l. Citation as part of a parenthetical document 121
- 7e-2 Minimizing awkward placement of references 121

7f Parenthetical documentation: numbers 122

7g Traditional documentation: footnotes/endnotes 123
- 7g-1 Format for endnotes 124
- 7g-2 Format for footnotes 124
- 7g-3 Numbering of notes 124
- 7g-4 Proper placement of note numbers 124
- 7g-5 Sample footnotes for books 126
  - a. Book by a single author 127
  - b. Book by two or more authors 127

c. Book by a corporate author 127
d. Book by an anonymous or pseudonymous author 127
e. Work in several volumes or parts 128
f. Collections: anthologies, casebooks, and readers 128
g. Double reference—a quotation within a cited work 129
h. Reference work 129
i. Work in a series 129
j. Edition 129
k. Translation 130
l. Pamphlet 130
m. Government publications or legal reference 130
n. Classical works 132
o. The Bible 133
7g-6 Sample footnotes for periodicals 133
a. Anonymous author 133
b. Single author 133
c. More than one author 133
d. Journal with continuous pagination throughout the annual volume 134
e. Journal with separate pagination for each issue 134
f. Monthly magazine 134
g. Weekly magazine 135
h. Newspaper 135
i. Editorial 135
j. Letter to the editor 135
k. Critical review 135
7g-7 Sample footnotes for special items 136
a. Lecture 136
b. Film 136
c. Radio or television program 136
d. Recording (disc or tape) 137
e. Personal letter 138
f. Interview 138
7g-8 Subsequent references to footnotes/endnotes 138
7h Content notes 139
7h-1 Content note explaining a term 141
7h-2 Content note expanding on an idea 141
7h-3 Content note referring the reader to another source 141
7h-4 Content note explaining procedures 141
7h-5 Content note acknowledging assistance 142
7i Consolidation of references 142
7i-1 Footnote using author-work style (MLA) 142

7i-2 Footnote using author-date style (APA) 142
7i-3 Footnote using numbers style 143
7i-4 Footnote using traditional style 143

8 The Bibliography 145

8a The bibliography 146
8a-1 Alphabetizing bibliographic entries 146
8a-2 Sample bibliography page 148
8b Works Cited (MLA and traditional styles) 148
8b-1 General order for bibliographic references to books in "Works Cited" 149
a. Author 149
b. Title 149
c. Name of editor, compiler, or translator 150
d. Edition (if other than first) 151
e. Series name and number 151
f. Volume numbers 151
g. Publication facts 152
h. Page numbers 153
i. Differences between endnotes and bibliographic entries 154
8b-2 Sample bibliographic references to books 154
a. Book by a single author 154
b. Book by two or more authors 154
c. Book by a corporate author 154
d. Book by an anonymous or pseudonymous author 155
e. Work in several volumes or parts 155
f. Work within a collection of pieces, all by the same author 156
g. Chapter or titled section in a book 156
h. Collections: anthologies, casebooks, and readers 156
i. Double reference—a quotation within a cited work 157
j. Reference works 157
k. Work in a series 158
l. Reprint 158
m. Edition 158
n. Edited work 158
o. Book published in a foreign country 159
p. Introduction, preface, foreword, or afterword 159
q. Translation 159
r. Book of illustrations 159
s. Foreign title 160
8b-3 General order for bibliographic references to periodicals in "Works Cited" 160
a. Author 160

b. Title of the article 160
c. Publication information 160
d. Pages 161
8b-4 Sample bibliographic references to periodicals 161
a. Anonymous author 161
b. Single author 162
c. More than one author 162
d. Journal with continuous pagination throughout the annual volume 162
e. Journal with separate pagination for each issue 162
f. Monthly magazine 163
g. Weekly magazine 163
h. Newspaper 163
i. Editorial 164
j. Letter to the editor 164
k. Critical review 164
l. Published interview 165
m. Published address or lecture 165
8b-5 Sample bibliographic references to nonprint materials 165
a. Address or lecture 165
b. Artwork 165
c. Computer source 166
d. Film 166
e. Interview 167
f. Musical composition 167
g. Radio or television program 167
h. Recording (disc or tape) 168
i. Theatrical performance 169
8b-6 Sample bibliographic references to special items 169
a. Artwork, published 170
b. The Bible 170
c. Classical works in general 170
d. Dissertation 171
e. Footnote or endnote citation 171
f. Manuscript or typescript 172
g. Pamphlet or brochure 172
h. Personal letter 172
i. Plays 173
j. Poems 174
k. Public documents 174
l. Quotation in a book or article used as a source 177
m. Report 177
n. Table, graph, chart, or other illustration 177
o. Thesis 178

8c Reference List (APA style) 178
- 8c-1 General order for bibliographic references to books in "Reference List" 178
- 8c-2 Sample bibliographic references to books 179
  - a. Book by a single author 179
  - b. Book by two or more authors 179
  - c. Edited book 179
  - d. Translated book 180
  - e. Book in a foreign language 180
  - f. Revised edition of book 180
  - g. Book by a corporate author 181
  - h. Multivolume book 181
  - i. Unpublished manuscript 181
- 8c-3 General order for bibliographic references to periodicals in "Reference List" 182
- 8c-4 Sample bibliographic references to periodicals 182
  - a. Journal article, one author 182
  - b. Journal article, up to six authors 182
  - c. Journal article, paginated anew in each issue 183
  - d. Journal with continuous pagination throughout the annual volume 183
  - e. Magazine article, issued monthly 183
  - f. Magazine article, issued on a specific day 183
  - g. Newspaper article 184
  - h. Editorial 184
  - i. Letter to the editor 184
  - j. Review 184
- 8c-5 Sample bibliographic references to nonprint materials 185
  - a. Computer sources 185
  - b. Film 186
  - c. Recording (cassette, record, tape) 186
- 8c-6 Sample bibliographic references to special items 186
  - a. Government documents 187
  - b. Legal references 187
- 8c-7 Sample bibliographic references to a report 189

8d Works Cited (numbers system) 189

9 Finished Form of the Paper 191

9a Finished form of the paper 192
9b Outline 192
9c Title page 192
9d Abstract 194
9e Text 194
9f Tables, charts, graphs, and other illustrative materials 195

9f-1 Tables 195
9f-2 Other illustrative materials 196
9g Content notes and endnotes 197
9h Bibliography 199

10 Mechanics 201

10a Using numbers in the paper 202
10a-1 Numerals 202
10a-2 Percentages and amounts of money 202
10a-3 Dates 202
10a-4 Numbers connected consecutively 203
10a-5 Roman numerals 204
10b Titles 204
10b-1 Italicized titles 205
10b-2 Titles within quotation marks 206
10b-3 Titles within titles 207
10b-4 Frequent reference to a title 208
10c Italics 208
10d Names of persons 209
10e Hyphenating 210
10f Handling foreign-language words 211
10g Abbreviations 211
10g-1 Abbreviations and reference words commonly used 211
10g-2 The Bible and Shakespeare 214
a. The Bible 214
b. Shakespeare 215

11 Sample Student Papers 217

11a Entire paper using the author-work style of documentation (MLA) 218
11b Entire paper using the author-date style of documentation (APA) 243
11c Excerpt from a paper using footnote documentation (traditional) 265

Checklist for Preparing the Final Draft 272

APPENDIX General and Specialized References 273

A A list of general references 274
A-1 Books that list other books 274
a. Books currently in print 274
b. Bibliographies 275
c. Book industry journals 276
d. Books about book reviews 276
A-2 Books about periodicals and newspapers 276
a. Periodical and newspaper directories 276
b. Union lists of periodicals and newspapers 277
c. Indexes of periodicals and newspapers 278

A-3 Books about general knowledge: encyclopedias 279
A-4 Books about words: dictionaries 280
- a. General dictionaries 280
- b. Specialized dictionaries 281
- c. Dictionaries of synonyms and antonyms 281

A-5 Books about places 281
- a. Atlases 281
- b. Gazetteers 282

A-6 Books about people 283
- a. General biography of deceased persons 283
- b. General biography of living persons 283
- c. National biography of deceased persons (American and British) 284
- d. National biography of living persons (American and British) 285
- e. Indexes to biographical material 285

A-7 Books about government publications 286
A-8 Books about nonbooks 287
- a. General guides 287
- b. Indexes of microforms 288
- c. Guides to films 288
- d. Guides to sound recordings: music 289
- e. Guides to sound recordings: speeches, readings, and oral history 290

B A list of specialized references 290
B-1 Art 291
B-2 Business and economics 292
B-3 Dance 294
B-4 Ecology 295
B-5 Education 296
B-6 Ethnic studies 297
- a. General 297
- b. American Indian studies 297
- c. Asian American studies 298
- d. Black American studies 298
- e. Hispanic American studies 299

B-7 High technology 299
B-8 History 301
- a. World history 301
- b. American history 301

B-9 Literature 302
- a. General 302
- b. American literature 304
- c. British literature 304

B-10 Music 305
B-11 Mythology/Classics 307
B-12 Philosophy 308

B-13 Psychology 308
B-14 Religion 309
B-15 Science 310
B-16 Social sciences 312
B-17 Women's studies 312

Index 315

Writing the Research Paper

A Handbook ● Third Edition

1

Basic Information About the Research Paper

1a Definition of the research paper

1b Format of the research paper

1c Reasons for the research paper

1d Steps and schedule involved in writing a research paper

1e The report paper and the thesis paper

1a

Definition of the research paper

The research paper is a typewritten paper in which you present your views and research findings on a chosen topic. Variously known as the "term paper" or the "library paper," the research paper is usually between five and fifteen pages long, with most teachers specifying a minimum length. No matter what the paper is called, your task is essentially the same: to read on a particular topic, evaluate information about it, and report your findings in a paper.

1b

Format of the research paper

The research paper cannot follow a random formula but must conform to a specific format such as the one devised by the Modern Language Association (MLA), a society of language scholars, or the American Psychology Association (APA), a society of scientific scholars. The format governs the entire paper from the placing of the title to the width of the margins, and to the notation used in acknowledging material drawn from other sources.

The format of scholarly writing is simply an agreed-upon way of doing things—much like etiquette, table manners, or rules of the road. For instance, in literary articles published recently you are likely to run across passages similar to this one:

> Brashear considers Tennyson to be at his best when his poetry is infused with "that tragic hour when the self fades away into darkness, fulfilling all of the poet's despairing pessimism." (18)

This citation is in the style of "parenthetical documentation" now being used by the Modern Language Association. The author of a quotation is briefly introduced, the quotation cited, and a page reference supplied in parentheses. In the alphabetized bibliography of the article will appear this listing:

> Brashear, William. *The Living Will*. The Hague: Mouton, 1969.

This sort of standardization is as time-saving to scholars as standardization of pipe fittings is to plumbers. To do research, or even to read articles about it, you must become familiar with the major citation styles used by scholars—all of which are covered in this book.

1c

Reasons for the research paper

One obvious reason for writing a research paper is that the experience will familiarize you with the conventions of scholarly writing. You will learn accepted styles of documentation, the ethics of research, and a great deal about the chosen subject.

A second reason is that you will become familiar with the library through the "learn by doing" method. Even the simplest library is an intricate storehouse of information, bristling with indexes, encyclopedias, abstracts, and gazetteers. How to ferret out from this maze of sources a single piece of needed information is a skill that you learn by doing actual research. The ability to use a library is a priceless skill, because sooner or later everyone needs to find out about something: a mother needs to know how to stop her child from biting his fingernails; a physician, how to treat a rare illness; a lawyer, how to successfully argue an unusual case. Everyone can profit from knowing how to do research.

There are other benefits. Writing the research paper is an exercise in logic, imagination, and common sense. As you chip away at the mass of data and information available on your chosen topics, you learn

- how to think
- how to organize
- how to discriminate between worthless and useful opinions
- how to summarize the gist of wordy material
- how to budget your time
- how to conceive of a research project from the start, manage it through its intermediary stages, and finally assemble the information uncovered into a useful, coherent paper.

1d

Steps and schedule involved in writing a research paper

Generally, there are seven distinct steps requiring you to produce at least five hand-ins over a period of five weeks. With some variations, many instructors will more or less observe this schedule:

WHAT YOU MUST DO	WHAT YOU MUST PRODUCE	WHEN IT'S DUE
1. A topic must be selected that is complex enough to be researched from a variety of sources, but narrow enough to be covered in ten or so pages.	Two acceptable topics, one of which will be approved by the instructor.	At the end of the first week. ________ Date due
2. Exploratory scanning and in-depth reading must be done on the approved topic.	A bibliography of all titles to be used in the paper.	At the end of the second week. ________ Date due
3. The information gathered must be recorded (usually on note cards) and assembled into a coherent sequence. 4. A thesis statement must be drafted, setting forth the major idea of your paper. 5. The paper must be outlined in its major stages.	Note cards, a thesis statement, and an outline. (Papers following the APA format will require an abstract rather than an outline.)	At the end of the third week. ________ Date due
6. The paper must be written in rough draft and the thesis argued, proved, or supported with the information uncovered from the sources. Borrowed ideas, data, and opinions must be acknowledged.	A rough draft of the paper.	At the end of the fourth week. ________ Date due
7. A bibliography must be prepared, listing all sources used in the paper. The final paper must be written.	The final paper, complete with bibliography.	At the end of the fifth week. ________ Date due

1e

The report paper and the thesis paper

The two kinds of papers usually assigned in colleges are the report paper and the thesis paper. The report paper summarizes and reports your findings on a particular subject. You neither judge nor evaluate the findings, but merely catalog them in a sensible sequence. For instance, a paper that listed the opinions of statesmen during the debate over the Panama Canal treaty would be a report paper. Likewise, a paper that chronologically narrated the final days of Hitler would also be a report paper.

Unlike the report paper, the thesis paper takes a definite stand on an issue. A thesis is a proposition or point of view that you are willing to argue against or defend. A paper that argues for the legalization of marijuana would therefore be a thesis paper. So would a paper that attempts to prove that Hitler's political philosophy was influenced by the writings of the philosopher Nietzsche. Here are two more examples of topics as they might conceivably be treated in report papers and thesis papers:

Report paper: A summary of the theories of hypnosis.
Thesis paper: Hypnosis is simply another form of Pavlovian conditioning.

Report paper: The steps involved in passage of federal legislation.
Thesis paper: Lobbyists wield a disproportionate influence on federal legislation.

Teachers are more likely to assign a thesis paper than a report paper, for obvious reasons. Writing the thesis paper requires you to exercise judgment, evaluate evidence, and construct a logical argument, whereas writing the report paper does not.

2

Choosing a Topic

2a How to choose a topic

2b Topics to avoid

2c Narrowing the topic

2a

How to choose a topic

Ideally, you should choose a topic that interests you, that is complex enough to generate several research sources, and that will neither bore nor stultify your reader. We offer the following advice:

- Pick a topic that you're curious about, or that you're either an expert on or are genuinely interested in. For example, if you have always been intrigued by the character of Rasputin, the "mad monk" of Russia, you can learn more about him by using him as the topic of your paper. Similarly, an interest in the career of Elvis Presley might lead to a paper analyzing and evaluating his music.
- If you are utterly at a loss for a topic, have positively no interest in anything at all, and cannot for the life of you imagine what you could write ten whole pages on, then go to the library and browse. Pore over books, magazines, and card catalogs. An encyclopedia can be a veritable supermarket of possible topics. Browse through its entries until you find an appealing subject. Check the two-volume *Library of Congress Subject Headings* (LCSH) for some heading that might appeal to you. Even a general idea can be whittled down to a specific topic (see Section 2c). But you must first arrive at the general idea.
- Take your time as you search for a topic. Don't latch onto the first workable idea that pops into your head. Mull it over. Ask yourself whether you'd really enjoy spending five weeks on that topic. If you have any qualms, keep browsing until you get an idea that really excites you. All of us are or can be excited about something (thankfully, not the same thing). So whatever you do, don't make the mistake of choosing "any old" topic merely for the sake of getting on with it. Choose carelessly now and you'll pay dearly later. But choose carefully and you'll be rewarded with the age-old excitement of research.

2b

Topics to avoid

Some topics present unusual difficulties; others are simply a waste of time. Here is a summary of topics to avoid:

2b-1 Topics that are too big

The research paper, though it may be the longest writing assignment you will receive during the semester, is still scarcely longer than a short magazine article. Obviously, you can neither review the evolution of man nor completely fathom the mysteries of creation in ten pages. Don't even try. Regrettably, we cannot give you a good rule of thumb for avoiding impossibly broad topics. Use your common sense. Check the card catalog. If you find that numerous books have been written about your topic, then it is probably too big. The signs that you may have bitten off more than you can chew usually come only after you're already deeply mired in the research. Reference sources that multiply like flies; a bibliography that grows like a cancer; opinions, data, and information that come pouring in from hundreds of sources—these signs all indicate a topic that is too big. The solution is to narrow the topic without darting to the sanctuary of the trivial. Here are some examples of hopelessly big topics: "The Influence of Greek Mythology on Poetry"; "The Rise and Fall of Chinese Dynasties"; "The Framing of the U.S. Constitution."

2b-2 Topics that can be traced to a single source

Research papers must be documented with a variety of opinions drawn from different authorities and sources. One reason for assigning the research paper in the first place is to expose students to the opinions of different authorities, to a variety of books and articles, and to other reference sources. Consequently, if the topic is so skimpy that all data on it can be culled from a single source, the purpose of the paper is defeated. Choose only topics that are broad enough to be researched from multiple sources.

Biographies are numbered among those topics that must be chosen with care lest they lead to a one-source paper. If you choose to write about a person, use an approach that allows the use of a variety of sources. You might focus on his or her contributions, motivation, or development. For instance, if you were to write about James Monroe you might narrow your focus to an evaluation of the Monroe Doctrine, which would require research of multiple sources. Avoid becoming so charmed by any single account of the person's life that you end up merely parroting that source.

2b-3 Topics that are too technical

A student may have an astonishing expertise in one technical area, and may be tempted to display this dazzling knowledge in a research paper. Resist the temptation. Technical topics often require a technical jargon that the teacher might not understand and might even dismiss as an elaborate "snow job." The skills that a research paper should instill in you are better displayed in a paper on a general topic. Stick to some area broad enough to be understood by any decently educated reader. The following are examples of overly technical topics: "The Use of Geometry in the Perspective of Paolo Uccelo"; "Heisenberg's Principle of Indeterminacy as It applies to Subparticle Research"; Utilitarianism versus Positivism in Legal Rights Cases Involving Minorities."

2b-4 Topics that are too trivial

Obviously, your own common sense and judgment must steer you away from such topics, but here are some that teachers would reject as too trivial: "The Use of Orthopedic Braces for Dachshunds Prone to Backaches"; "The Cult of Van Painting in America"; "The History of the Tennis Ball"; "How to Get Dates When You're Divorced."

2c

Narrowing the topic

Monster-sized topics are easy enough to think of, probably because big issues such as feminism, civil rights, and human aggression are constantly bandied about in the press and in casual talk. But it is a serious mistake to try to corral one of these monsters in a ten-page paper. First, it is difficult to make sense out of the millions of words in the library on such issues. Deluged with innumerable sources, most of which you simply haven't got the time to go through, you will end up choosing a few random sources out of hundreds, with the attendant risk of making a bad, unrepresentative choice. Second, apart from being more difficult to research, the big topic is also more difficult to write about: one never knows quite where to begin, and one never knows how to end without seeming silly. Third, omissions and oversights are nowhere more crudely obvious than in a small paper on a big topic.

The first step, then, once a general subject is found, is to narrow it down to a suitably small topic. There is no easy or set way of doing this. You must simply be guided by the available sources and information; again, common sense must come into play. No python knows the exact dimensions of its mouth, but any python instinctively knows that it cannot swallow an elephant. Experiment with your topic: pursue one train of thought and see where it leads, and whether or not it yields an arguable thesis. Pare down and whittle away until you've got something manageable. Bear in mind that ten pages amount to a very modest length—some books have longer prefaces. Here are a few examples of the narrowing that you'll have to do:

GENERAL SUBJECT	FIRST NARROWING	FURTHER NARROWING
Mythology	*Beowulf*	Courtesy codes in *Beowulf*
Migrant workers	California migrant workers	Major California labor laws and their impact on Mexican migrant workers

GENERAL SUBJECT	FIRST NARROWING	FURTHER NARROWING
Theater	Theater of the Absurd	Theater-of-the-Absurd elements in *Who's Afraid of Virginia Woolf?*
Jack Kennedy	Jack Kennedy's cabinet	The contribution of Averell Harriman as U.S. Ambassador to Russia
Russia	The Bolshevik Revolution of 1917	The role of Grigory Efimovich Rasputin in pre-revolutionary Russia
China	Chinese agriculture	The effect on China of Chinese agricultural policies during the past ten years
Indians	Famous Indian fighters	Major Rogers' Rangers during the Indian wars
Nature's carnivores	Parasites	The ichneumon wasp and its parasitic hosts
Educational psychology	Psychological testing in schools	The Thematic Apperception Test (TAT) and its present-day adaptations
Banking	Restrictions on banking powers	The role of the Federal Reserve in credit management

The first attempt at narrowing a subject is usually easier than the second, which must yield a specific topic. Use trial and error until you've got a topic you're comfortable with. Further narrowing, if necessary, will suggest itself once you're into the actual research. Note that whatever subject you choose must be approved by your instructor. So before you become too involved in narrowing the subject, be sure that in its basic outline your teacher approves of it.

If you have trouble coming up with a particular topic, chances are you might be tempted to try your hand at a standby such as the legalization of drugs, the right to have an abortion, the ethics of euthanasia, the effects of obscenity laws, the existence of UFOs, or the morality of capital punishment. The trouble with these familiar and recurring topics is that instructors typically are weary of them. Moreover, it is hard to have an original opinion on topics that have been so thoroughly and repeatedly thrashed out in public debate. If you wish to try writing about something different but have no idea what, here is a list of new topics, organized by academic discipline, worth investigating:

HUMANITIES

The evolution of children's literature
The decline of Broadway
Contemporary minimalist fiction
Modern fiction with a political message
Fictional protagonists with psychological problems
Classical mythology in modern literature
Themes in Noble Prize winners' speeches
Nihilism as a theme in modern literature
Optimism as a theme in modern literature
Early American films
American literature of minority cultures (Black, Indian, Jewish, Chicano)
Slang or dialect in American literature
Social commentary in rock lyrics
Aspects of modern architecture, sculpture, painting, or music
Ballet in today's culture

LIFE SCIENCES

The moral implications of cloning
The creation of matter in the Big Bang (or attacking the Big Bang theory)
Theories about the extinction of the dinosaurs
The Greenhouse effect
Plastic pollution
Marine organisms and medical research
Parasites—good and bad
Wildlife management
The latest research in predicting inherited diseases
Plate tectonics and earthquakes
Mechanics of the hurricane
The latest in genetic engineering
Disposal of toxic wastes
The latest crazes in exercise (*e.g.*, having your own trainer)
PNI Psychoneuroimmunology (how the mind and body interact)
The inheritance link in alcoholism
Modern diseases (*e.g.*, AIDS, anorexia nervosa, Tourette syndrome, Epstein-Barr, cystic fibrosis)

SOCIAL SCIENCES

Dirty political campaigning
The destiny of Christopher Columbus' ships the *Niña*, the *Pinta*, and the *Santa Maria*

Hitler's medical problems
Adopted children and their real parents
Alcoholism and genetics
Forced military service
Freedom of the press versus gag rules
Nationalized health or car insurance
The psychology of grief
The problem of aging
Alternative life-styles in the last two decades
Hunger and famine in third-world countries
The latest research in the nature/nurture debate
Labor, property, and status
Immigrant women and their contributions
Unraveling America's Hispanic past
Ethnic minorities and urban politics
Feminism: the value of women in a free market
The Soviet Union's *glasnost* or *perestroika*
Satellites and U.S. security
Revolutions in third-world countries
Relations between the U.S. and another world power
The effect of public opinion polls on politics

BUSINESS

Gold as an investment
Women in management
Women police officers (or fire officers, ministers, etc.)
Inside trading on Wall Street
Free market versus fair market
The role of the Securities and Exchange Commission
The role of the Federal Trade Commission
Loan programs for college costs
Career development strategies

TECHNOLOGY

Computer viruses
Causes of aircraft stalling
Solving traffic gridlock in major cities
Modern technology for the blind and deaf
The future of microchips in computers
Applications of Superconductors

3

The Library

3a Layout of the library

3b Organization of the library

3a

Layout of the library

Most of the research for your paper will be done at a library. Basic architectural design varies from one library to another, but certain facilities are standard. All well-organized libraries include the following:

3a-1 Card catalog

The card catalog is an alphabetical index of all books in the library. It consists of 3 × 5 cards that are stored in little drawers, usually near the main entrance of the library. The card catalog lists all books under at least three headings: author, subject, and title. The cards are alphabetized by the first important word in the heading. A book that straddles two or more subjects will be listed separately under each subject. If an editor, translator, or illustrator is involved, the book will also be listed under the name of each, in addition to being listed under the name of the author. A jointly authored book is also likely to be listed under the name of each author.

Basic research generally begins with a search of the card catalog, which literally puts a wealth of information at a researcher's fingertips. On pages 17–19 are examples of index cards that list the same book in different ways.

In combing the card catalog for books and sources on a topic, don't overlook the possibility of finding useful material under separate but related headings. For example, if you are looking for sources on "Pablo Picasso," you should also look under such cross-references as "Modern Art," "French Art," "Abstract Art," and "Cubism."

3a-2 Microform indexes

Many libraries now use microform indexes for periodicals as well as for their permanent book collections. Systems vary from one library to another. Microfilm systems are used by some libraries to index the articles of major periodicals. Most such systems depend on microfilm readers that allow for a fast scan or slow search. A microfiche storage system is also used to catalog articles published in major national newspapers. Either system (or both) may be available in your own library. A few large libraries may even have an on-line computerized system for their permanent collections. Ask the librarian.

3a-3 Stacks

"Stacks" is the name given to the shelves on which the books and periodicals are stored in the library. The stacks may be either *open* or

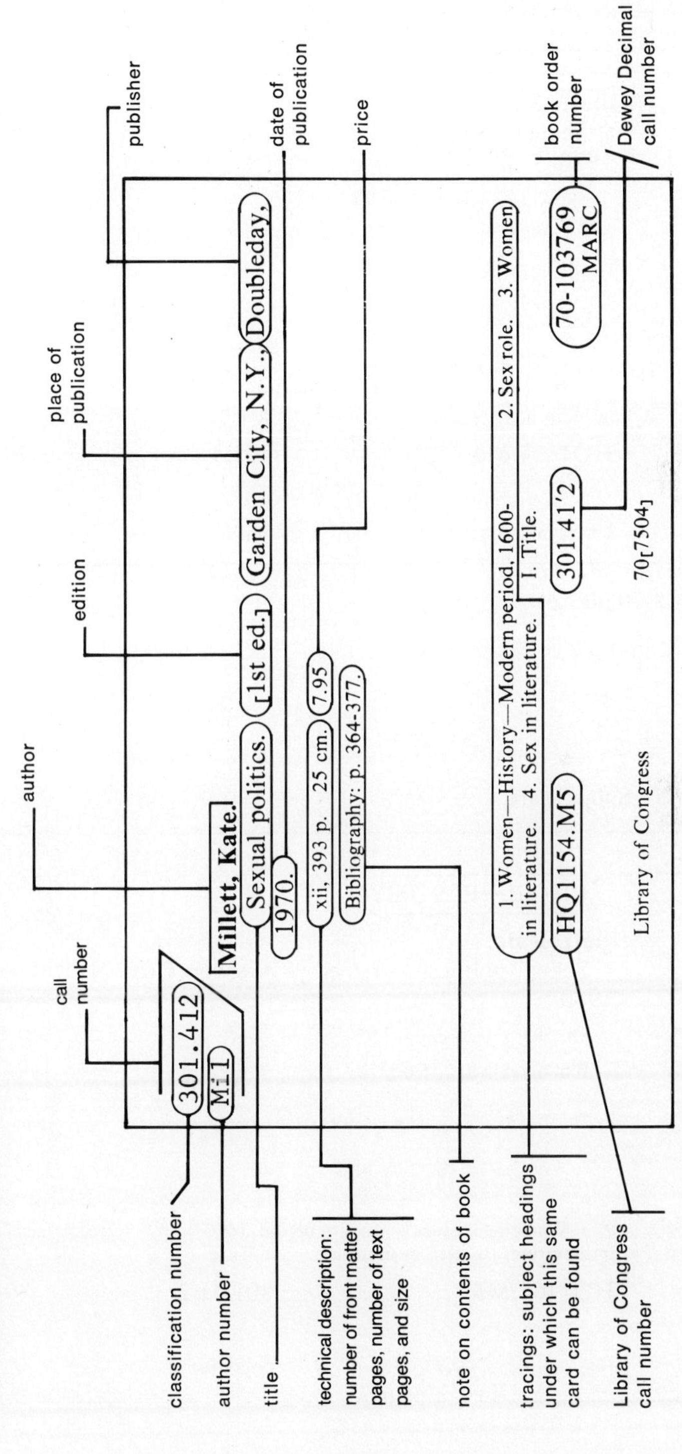

Figure 3-1 Author card (also called "Main entry")

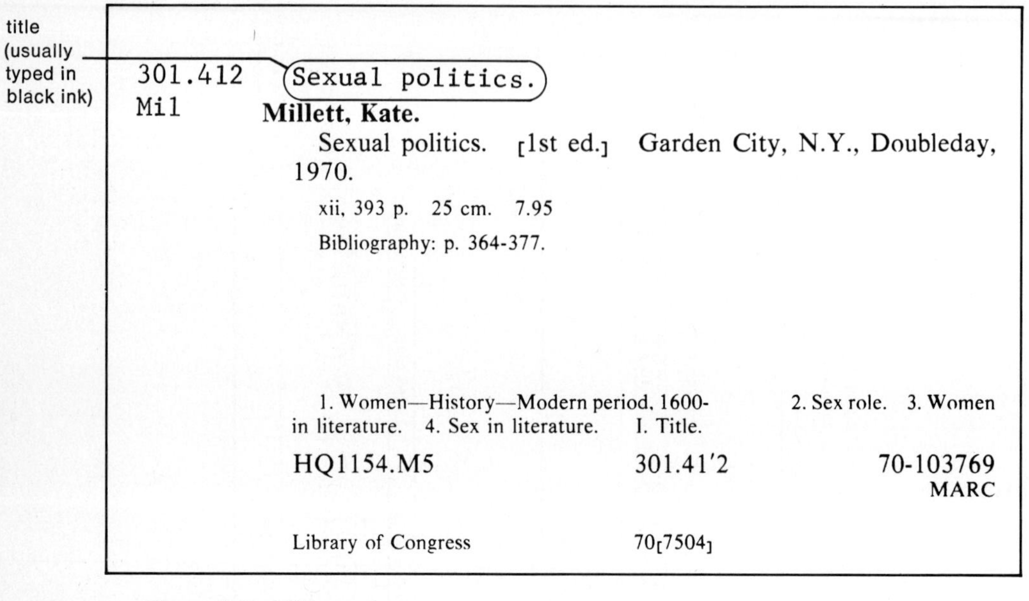

301.412 Sexual politics.
Mil

Millett, Kate.

Sexual politics. [1st ed.] Garden City, N.Y., Doubleday, 1970.

xii, 393 p. 25 cm. 7.95

Bibliography: p. 364-377.

1. Women—History—Modern period, 1600- 2. Sex role. 3. Women in literature. 4. Sex in literature. I. Title.

HQ1154.M5 301.41'2 70-103769
MARC

Library of Congress 70[7504]

Figure 3-2 Title card

Figure 3-3 Subject card

subject heading (usually typed in red ink)

301.412 WOMEN--HISTORY
Mil

Millett, Kate.

Sexual politics. [1st ed.] Garden City, N.Y., Doubleday, 1970.

xii, 393 p. 25 cm. 7.95

Bibliography: p. 364-377.

1. Women—History—Modern period, 1600- 2. Sex role. 3. Women in literature. 4. Sex in literature. I. Title.

HQ1154.M5 301.41'2 70-103769
MARC

Library of Congress 70[7504]

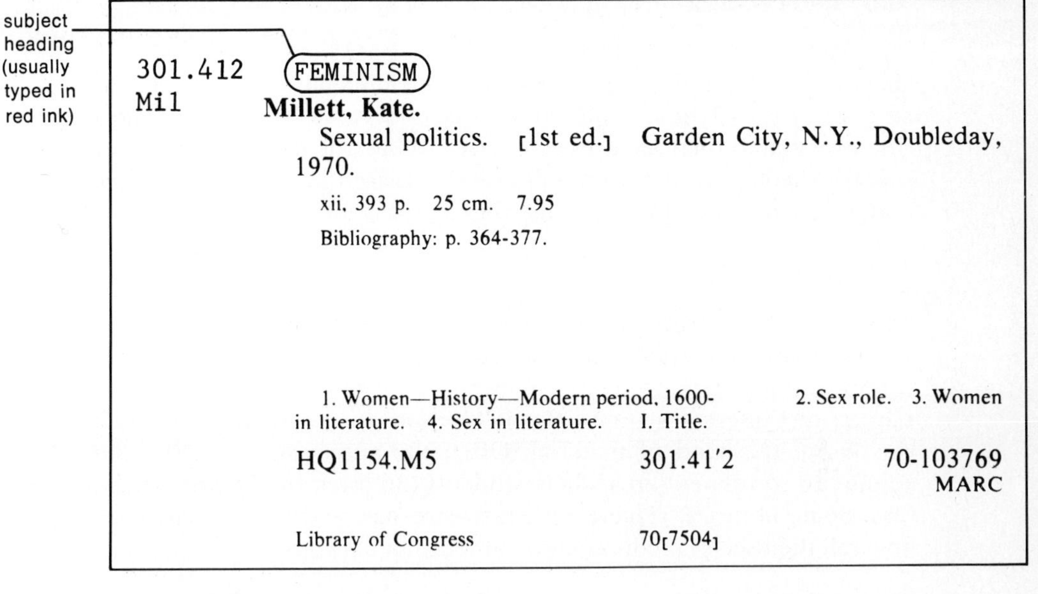

301.412 FEMINISM
Mil
Millett, Kate.
Sexual politics. [1st ed.] Garden City, N.Y., Doubleday, 1970.
xii, 393 p. 25 cm. 7.95
Bibliography: p. 364-377.

1. Women—History—Modern period, 1600- 2. Sex role. 3. Women in literature. 4. Sex in literature. I. Title.
HQ1154.M5 301.41'2 70-103769
MARC
Library of Congress 70[7504]

Figure 3-4 Cross-reference card

closed. If the stacks are open, readers may roam at will among the shelves and handle the books; if the stacks are closed, readers are denied direct access to the shelves, and must obtain books from clerks by listing the title of the book, its author, and its call number on a request slip. Closed stacks are more common at larger libraries; in smaller libraries the stacks are usually open. While inconvenient to a reader, closed stacks reduce the chance of pilferage, misfiling, and defacement of books. Open stacks, on the other hand, allow a reader to browse at leisure.

3a-4 Reference room

Encyclopedias, indexes, gazetteers, and other works that are ordinarily consulted for information, rather than read from cover to cover, are stored in a reference room. Usually large and unwieldy, these volumes are generally confined to use within the reference room; they cannot be checked out and taken home.

3a-5 Main desk

The main desk functions as an information center as well as a checkout counter for books. Librarians and clerks stationed here are trained to help the researcher find material or track down difficult sources. Library personnel can be of invaluable assistance; if you are confused and lost, don't be afraid to ask them for help.

3a-6 Reserve desk

Reserve books are kept at the reserve desk. Books on reserve are available for use only in the library and only for a limited time—generally for an hour or two. Teachers will often place on reserve any book or magazine essential to their lectures or courses. When the demand for a book exceeds the supply, the book will often be placed in the reserve collection, which in many libraries is listed in a separate reserve catalog.

3a-7 Audiovisual room

Cassettes, tapes, picture slides, filmstrips, and other nonbook media are stored in an audiovisual room and generally indexed by whatever conventional filing system the library uses (see Dewey Decimal System and Library of Congress System below). The audiovisual librarian will help you locate this kind of material. Often the audiovisual supply room adjoins an equipment area where students can listen to tapes or watch a film. Some libraries, replete with extensive new audiovisual hardware, now call themselves media centers rather than libraries.

3a-8 Microform room

Microfilm and microfiche are stored in a microform room. Microfilm is material photographically stored on filmstrips; microfiche is material photographically mounted on frames. For centuries, back issues of journals, magazines, and newspapers were piled up in dusty heaps in the dark, cobwebbed stock rooms of libraries. But with the advent of cameras that can reduce entire pages to a tiny filmstrip, periodical material is now economically stored in this microscopic form and read with magnifying equipment.

3a-9 Newspaper racks

Many libraries subscribe to major national and foreign newspapers. Current issues are generally displayed on long wooden clamps, known as newspaper racks, that hold and store the newspapers. Often the newspaper racks are surrounded by comfortable chairs in which a reader can sit for a leisurely assessment of world events. Typical newspapers found in these racks include the *New York Times*, the *Washington Post*, the *Los Angeles Times*, the *Christian Science Monitor*, the *Wall Street Journal*, the *London Times*, the *Manchester Guardian*, the *Hindustan Times*, and *Die Zeit*.

3a-10 Copy room

Duplicating machines are available in most libraries for photocopying. The charge for this service ranges anywhere from a nickel to a quarter.

3a-11 Typing room

Typewriters are available in many libraries, either at a reasonable rental rate or without charge. The machines are usually kept in a designated typing room, which is often soundproof.

3a-12 Carrels

Carrels are small enclosed desks equipped with bookshelves, and are especially designed to provide students with a quiet, insulated enclosure for reading or research. The carrel section of a library is set aside for students intent on serious scholarship. Some libraries even impose fines on students caught capering in this area. Carrels can generally be reserved by advanced students for either a semester or an entire school year; the remaining carrels are distributed among lower-division students on a first-come, first-served basis.

3a-13 The computer

The computer is fast becoming an invaluable research tool in the library. Information is stored in databases and accessed through a terminal. Section 4c discusses the use of a computer to search for sources and information.

3a-14 Interlibrary loan

Most libraries are part of an interlibrary loan (ILL) system that makes sources from other libraries available on a loan basis. More and more students are finding ILL to be essential to their research.

3b

Organization of the library

Even the great libraries of antiquity, such as the one in Nineveh in the sixth century B.C., or in Alexandria in the third century B.C., searched constantly for more efficient systems of organizing their collections. Clay tablets were grouped by subject and stored on shelves; papyrus rolls were stacked in labeled jars. The Chinese, whose library tradition dates back to the sixth century B.C., grouped their writings under four primary headings: classics, history, philosophy, and belles lettres. And by 1605 the English philosopher Sir Francis Bacon had independently devised a system of classifying all knowledge into three similar categories of history, poetry, and philosophy, which were then further subdivided to yield specific subjects.

Knowledge has grown so enormously, and classification systems have become so complex, that today librarians are trained extensively in classifying books. The two major classification systems now used by libraries are the Dewey Decimal System and the Library of Congress System.

3b-1 The Dewey Decimal System

Devised in 1873 by Melvil Dewey and first put to use in the library of Amherst College, the Dewey Decimal System divides all knowledge (fiction and biography excepted) into ten general categories:

000–099	General Works
100–199	Philosophy and Psychology
200–299	Religion
300–399	Social Sciences
400–499	Language
500–599	Pure Science
600–699	Technology (Applied Sciences)
700–799	The Arts
800–899	Literature
900–999	History

Each of these ten general categories is subdivided into ten smaller divisions. For example, the category of Literature (800–899) is further divided into:

800–809	General Works (about Literature)
810–819	American Literature
820–829	English Literature
830–839	German Literature
840–849	French Literature
850–859	Italian Literature
860–869	Spanish Literature
870–879	Latin Literature
880–889	Greek and Classical Literature
890–899	Literature of Other Languages

The specific category of English Literature is further divided into narrower groups:

820	English Literature (General)
821	Poetry
822	Drama
823	Fiction
824	Essays
825	Speeches
826	Letters
827	Satire and Humor
828	Miscellany
829	Minor Related Literature

An endless number of more specific headings is easily created through the addition of decimal places. For instance, from the category of English Literature—820—the more specific heading of Elizabethan Literature is devised: 822.3. The addition of another decimal place creates an even more specific category for the works of Shakespeare: 822.33.

The obvious advantage of the Dewey Decimal System is the ease with which it yields specific categories to accommodate the rapid proliferation of books. Probably for this reason, the system is currently used in more libraries throughout the world than all other systems combined.

3b-2 The Cutter/Sanborn Author Marks

The Dewey Decimal System is generally used in conjunction with the Cutter/Sanborn Author Marks, devised originally by Charles Ammi Cutter and later merged with a similar system independently invented by Kate Sanborn. The Cutter/Sanborn Author Marks distinguish between books filed under an identical Dewey number. In the early days of the Dewey system, books with the same Dewey number were simply shelved alphabetically by author. But as more and more books were published, alphabetical shelving became impossibly difficult, leading eventually to the invention of the Author Marks.

The Author Marks eliminate alphabetical shelving by assigning a number to every conceivable consonant/vowel or vowel/consonant combination that can be used to spell the beginning of an author's surname. These numbers are published in a table that alphabetically lists the various combinations and assigns each a number. For instance, the "G" section of the Cutter/Sanborn Table lists the following combinations and numbers:

Garf	231	Garn	234
Gari	232	Garnet	235
Garl	233	Garni	236

To assign, for example, an Author Mark to the book, *Double Taxation: A Treatise on the Subject of Double Taxation Relief*, by Charles Edward Garland, a librarian (1) looks up the combination of letters in the Cutter/Sanborn Table closest to the spelling of the author's surname—in this case, "Garl," with the number 233; (2) places the first letter of the author's surname before the number; and (3) places after the number the first letter or letters of the first important word in the title, giving an Author Mark of G233d. The call number of the book is its Dewey Decimal number plus its Author Mark:

336.294
G233d

Similarly, the book *Religion and the Moral Life*, by Arthur Campbell Garnett, has a Dewey Decimal number of 170 and an Author Mark of G235r, giving the following call number:

170
G235r

Under this dual system, a book is shelved first by sequence of its Dewey Decimal number, and then by sequence of its Author Mark. To find any title, a student must therefore first locate the Dewey Decimal category on the shelf, and then identify an individual book by its Author Mark.

Fiction and biography are classified in a special way under the Dewey Decimal System. Fiction is marked with the letter "F" and biography with the letter "B." Fiction is alphabetized by author, biography by subject. For example, F-Pas is the classification of a novel by Boris Pasternak; B-C56 is one of the several biographies about Sir Winston Churchill. If the library has an especially large fiction or biography collection, these books might also be given Author Marks.

3b-3 The Library of Congress System

The Library of Congress System is named for the library that invented it. Founded in 1800, the Library of Congress at first simply shelved its books by size. Its earliest catalog, issued in 1802, showed the United States as the owner of 964 books and 9 maps. By 1812 the nation's collection had increased to 3,076 books and 53 maps. By 1897, when the library finally acquired a building of its own, the collection had grown to half a million items and was increasing at the staggering rate of 100,000 per year. The library had acquired such a vast and expansive collection that a new system was necessary for classifying it. Published in 1904, the Library of Congress Classification System has since grown immensely in popularity and is now widely used, especially by larger libraries.

The system represents the main branches of knowledge with twenty-one letters of the alphabet. These branches are further divided by the addition of letters and Arabic numerals up to 9999, allowing for a nearly infinite number of combinations. The system is therefore especially useful for libraries possessing enormous collections. Here is a list of the general categories:

A	General Works—Polygraphy
B	Philosophy—Religion
C	History—Auxiliary Sciences
D	History and Topography (except America)
E–F	America
G	Geography—Anthropology
H	Social Sciences
J	Political Science
K	Law
L	Education
M	Music
N	Fine Arts
P	Language and Literature
Q	Science
R	Medicine
S	Agriculture—Plant and Animal Industry
T	Technology
U	Military Science

V	Naval Science
Z	Bibliography and Library Science

These general categories are narrowed by the addition of letters. Numerous minute subdivisions are possible. The Language and Literature category, designated by "P," is further subdivided thus:

P	Philology and Linguistics: General
PA	Greek and Latin Philology and Literature
PB	Celtic Languages and Literature
PC	Romance Languages (Italian, French, Spanish, and Portuguese)
PD	Germanic (Teutonic) Languages

The addition of numerals makes possible even more minute subdivisions within each letter category. From the general category "P"—Language and Literature—is derived the more specific category of Literary History and Collections, designated by "PN." The call number PN 6511 indicates works dealing with Oriental Proverbs; PN 1993.5 U65, on the other hand, is the call number for a book about the history of motion pictures in Hollywood.

The classification under this system proceeds from the general to the specific, with the longer numbers being assigned to the more specialized books. Like the Dewey Decimal System, the Library of Congress System also uses an author number to differentiate books shelved within a specific category. To locate a book with a Library of Congress classification, the student must first find the subject category on the shelf, and then track down the individual title by its author number. Two printed volumes entitled *Library of Congress Subject Headings* (LCSH) are available in most libraries. These books use subject headings to group materials on the same or a similar topic under one term. You may find it helpful to look up your topic in LCSH.

3b-4 Classification of periodicals

Periodicals and newspapers are classified differently from books. Current issues are usually shelved alphabetically by title and are accessible to the public (some libraries shelve current issues by call number). Back issues either bound in book form or reproduced on microfilm, are stored elsewhere—usually in a special section of the library to which the public may or may not be admitted, depending on whether the stacks are open or closed.

3b-5 Classification of nonbooks

Nonbook materials—films, microfilms, recordings, news clippings, sheet music, reproductions of masterpieces, transparencies, slides, programmed books, and other audiovisual material—may be listed either in the general catalog or as a special collection. No hard-and-fast rule exists for classifying this kind of material; ask your librarian how it is cataloged. (See Figure 3-5, p. 26.)

Figure 3-5 Cross-reference sample catalog cards for nonbook materials

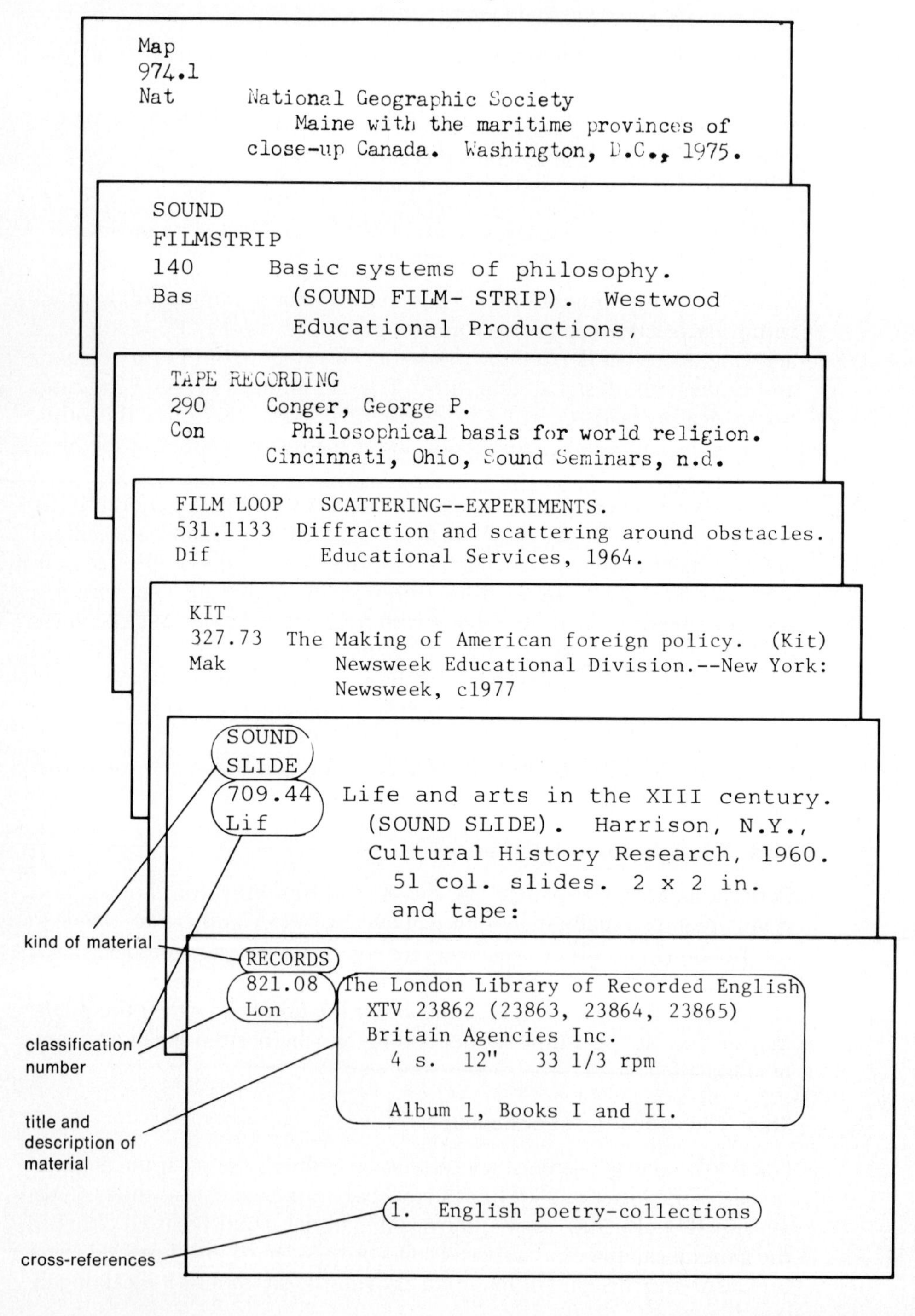

4

Doing the Research

4a What information to look for

4b Where to look for information

4c Using the computer in your search

4d Assembling a working bibliography

4e Selecting your sources

4f Note-taking

4g Plagiarism: what it is and how to avoid it

4a

What information to look for

Library materials—the sources you will actually cite as supporting references in your paper—typically consist of book chapters or essays, magazine articles, journal articles, treatises, pamphlets, newspaper articles, and tape or disc transcriptions. These materials may be in printed form or on microfilm, microfiche, computer disk, or tape. Exactly what kind of material you will need to look for will largely depend on your topic, thesis, and even the point of view you will use in the paper. Generally speaking, however, all library materials may be usefully grouped into three broad categories: single-fact information, general information, and in-depth information.

4a-1 Single-fact information

Single-fact information answers such specific and factual questions as: In what year was Julius Caesar born? What percentage of students admitted into Harvard medical school in 1988 were Hispanic? How many cantons does Switzerland have? What was the first bank established in the United States? What museum has da Vinci's *Mona Lisa*? What is the literary definition of *pastoral*? Answers to these and similar single-fact questions can be found in dictionaries, almanacs, encyclopedias, novels, reports, magazines, or even telephone books. To get the answers to such questions you can always ask for the help of the reference librarian, who is specially trained in information management, storage, and retrieval. Some libraries even have a reference librarian available to answer readers' queries over the telephone.

4a-2 General information

General information sources are those that provide an overview of a subject or a particular topic. They can also steer you to important in-depth sources. For example, if you were writing a paper on Zionism, the movement to create a Jewish national state in Palestine, the *Columbia Encyclopedia* would be a good general information source for a summary history. A brief article will answer such general questions as: When did the movement start? What brought it about? Who were its leaders? Where does the movement stand today? Encyclopedias and other general information sources are usually found in a reference room or reference section in most college libraries. (For further guidelines about general information sources, see Section 4c.)

4a-3 In-depth information

In-depth information is derived from sources that provide detailed coverage of a specific topic. For example, *Admiral of the Ocean Sea*, by naval historian Samuel Eliot Morrison, provides in-depth information about the voyages and life and times of Christopher Columbus. *The Soul of a New Machine* by Tracy Kidder gives an in-depth look at the process of building a new computer system. In-depth information is usually found in books, since many topics are too complex to be detailed in any other form. But essays and articles can also be useful sources of in-depth information, especially about new or particularly focused topics. For example, an article on computer viruses in the September 26th issue of *Time* magazine provides an in-depth look at this latest variation in technological vandalism.

Research papers will typically blend all three kinds of information—single-fact, general, and in-depth—the proportion between them varying with the nature and complexity of the particular topic.

4a-4 Retrospective and contemporary sources

Library materials may also be classified as retrospective or contemporary. *Retrospective* materials are those written long after the fact, event, or idea; *contemporary* materials are those written close to or at the occurrence of the fact, event, or idea. Because the backward look is generally more analytical and detached than the one penned during the heat and ferment of events, retrospective materials tend to have the edge in objectivity over contemporary ones.

For example, a paper on Stalin's rise to power in the Soviet Union would do well to rely on retrospective materials, especially if Soviet sources are consulted. Since Stalin did not take kindly to criticism, accounts of his rule written during his lifetime are inevitably tainted by partisanship. On the other hand, if you were writing a paper on the media's treatment of President Reagan during his final month in office, the latest advances in artificial intelligence, or on recent federal legislation to curb ocean pollutants, you would need to consult contemporary materials—usually articles in magazines, journals, and newspapers. Other topics may force you to draw on a combination of the two types of sources. For example, a paper comparing the Gregorian chant to rock music, or one tracing the influence of the Indian shaman from earliest recorded history to the present day, will no doubt have to cite both retrospective and contemporary materials.

4b

Where to look for information

Libraries differ markedly in their cataloging and indexing of available material. Some offer sophisticated computer cataloging of all available sources. The majority, however, rely heavily on printed lists and card catalogs. We shall have more to say about computer searches in Section 4c. But for those of you who must use a traditional library, we suggest the following steps:

- To find the subheadings related to your subject, scanning an encyclopedia article on it is usually a helpful first step. For example, if you were researching ancient Egyptian art, the encyclopedia entry "Egypt" would list "Mesopotamia," "Predynastic Egypt," and "ceramic art" as related subheadings. "Fascism," "Italy," "dictatorship," and "totalitarianism" are related subheadings on the topic of Benito Mussolini. "Abigail Adams," "Mercy Warren," "Elizabeth Stanton," and "Susan B. Anthony" are possible subheadings on the early feminist movement in the United States. In searching the card catalog for sources, look under both the main headings as well as the related subheadings. If your library uses the Library of Congress System, consult the two-volume *Library of Congress Subject Headings* (LCSH) for a list of subject headings.
- Consult the appendix of this book for an annotated listing of useful reference sources.
- Check the bibliography at the end of encyclopedia articles.
- For definitions of technical or controversial terms, check the various standard dictionaries.
- Check the card catalog under the subject heading as well as under any cross-listings noted on the cards.
- Check the various periodical indexes for magazine articles on your subject. For general subjects, check the *Readers' Guide to Periodical Literature*. For a subject in the social sciences, check the *Social Science Index*; for one in humanities or education, search the *Humanities Index* or the *Education Index*.
- Check the *Book Review Digest* for summaries of the contents of reviewed books.
- Check the various *Who's Who* volumes for information about noteworthy people.
- For information about places and countries, consult gazetteers and atlases.

The search for sources is governed by a kind of domino theory, with one source leading to another. A book will suggest an essay; an essay will steer you to a pamphlet or treatise. This is the time you will discover whether your topic is too narrow or broad. If it is too narrow, you will hunt and peck for pitifully few sources; if it is too broad, you will be engulfed by a tidal wave of references. In either case, it is not too late to change your focus, your direction, or even your topic. Check with your instructor.

Remember also to make liberal use of the researcher's most powerful tool: the mouth. Ask library personnel for help. They are trained in the intricate layout and organization of libraries and will prove invaluable in helping you uncover material on your topic.

4c

Using the computer in your search

Library computers are designed to manage vast amounts of cataloged materials and can perform numerous helpful functions for a researcher. The computer terminal, consisting of a video screen and typewriter keyboard, is the focal point for researchers working in a computerized library. Generally "user-friendly," terminals typically allow you to call up a subject heading list, bibliographic information connected with written works, or, in a sophisticated library with on-line databases, the actual works themselves. To find all subheadings of a given subject, say *apartheid*, you typically type in the library's own access number, "APARTHEID," and then press DISPLAY/RECORD, followed by SEND. A list of all subheadings related to your subject will appear on the screen. Type in the title of a book and its card catalog information will be displayed: call number, author, publisher, publication date, number of pages, as well as related subject headings. A note on the screen will also tell you if the library owns a copy of the book. For a display of all the works written by a certain author, simply type in the author's name.

Computerized libraries can also retrieve vast quantities of information stores in a database. Basically, a *database* is a complex program for the computerized storage and management of information. Databases make entire books, magazine articles, or abstracts available to a researcher via a keyboard and terminal. Most databases are menu-driven—that is, the user is prompted by a variety of choices on the screen and gradually led through a series of narrowing options. Among the many databases that are available on-line to libraries, the following are the most common:

DIALOG:	DIALOG consists of over 100 databases cataloging information in a wide range of subjects, including government, health, education, social and physical sciences, humanities, and business. It is operated by Lockheed Information Systems.
BRS:	Bibliographic Retrieval Services offers access to over 30 databases.
Mead Data Control:	Mead distributes and produces LEXIS and NEXIS. The first is an enormous library of legal information, including millions of court opinions and federal and state statutes. NEXIS is a news retrieval service.

New York Times Information Service:	Abstracts over 20 news services along with many special and general interest publications.
ERIC:	ERIC is an acronym for the Educational Research Information Center, a network of clearinghouses that gather and produce unpublished materials such as project reports, dissertations, and research findings. The 16 ERIC clearinghouses specialize in one of these subjects: career education; counseling and personnel services; early childhood education; educational management; handicapped and gifted children; higher education; information resources; junior colleges; languages and linguistics; reading and communication skills; rural education and small schools; science, mathematics, and environmental education; social studies and social science education; teacher education; tests, measurement, and evaluation; and urban education.
OCLC:	Online Computer Library Center, based in Columbus, Ohio, is a database listing the collections of over 1,000 member libraries. OCLC also includes an on-line listing of all Library of Congress materials in English catalogued since 1968. Many member libraries have interlibrary loan arrangements that permit a student to obtain a needed book from the collection of another school.

This list gives you an idea of the kinds of databases available to many libraries. Ask your librarian about the facilities of your own library.

There are two general points you should remember in using your library's computer. First, since some libraries charge a fee for database searches, you should be fairly certain that a source is likely to be useful before you begin the search and incur the expense. Second, library computers will typically not accept the full title of a book or the full name of an author, but only a few letters of each word. For instance, the pattern for a title might be 3.2.2.1—meaning that you must type in only the first three letters of the first word of the title, the first two letters of the second word, the first two letters of the third word, and the first letter of the fourth word. Commas must be typed in to separate groups of letters. For example, to type in the title for Dunn and Dobzhansky's *Heredity, Race and Society*, you would enter: HER,RA,AN S. In sum, to use the specific computer in your library, you need to become familiar with its particular system.

While the actual response to a database search request will naturally vary from one library to another, the following are fairly typical:

4c-1 Sample subject display

You have asked the computer for a list of subject headings on "Chinese literature." Here is the result:

```
T S CHINESE LITERATURE
                                      SUMMARY DISPLAY
RESULT:     57 headings.
```

The computer indicates that there are 57 subject headings on Chinese literature. You can ask the computer to display these subjects ten headings at a time:

```
S 1-10
                                    AUTHORITY DISPLAY
     2. Chinese literature
     3.     --To 221 B.C.
     4.     --Chin and Han dynasties, 221 B.C.-220 A.D.
     5.     --Three kingdoms, 220-265
     6.     --220-589
     7.     --Chin dynasty, 265-419
     8.     --Northern Sung dynasty, 420-479
     9.     --Sui dynasty, 581-618
    10.     --Tang dynasty, 618-907
```

4c-2 Sample bibliographic display

You can also ask the computer to tell you what books are available on the subject heading you identified:

```
F S CHINESE LITERATURE
                                      SUMMARY DISPLAY
RESULT:     95 bibliographic items.
```

The computer indicates that 95 items are listed under that heading in the bibliographic file. You can now ask the computer to display the full bibliographic record of any of these items. Here is an example:

```
S 1
                                 BIBLIOGRAPHIC DISPLAY

     Mao's harvest : voices from China's new
generation / edited by Helen F. Siu and Zelda Stern. New
York : Oxford University Press, 1983.
     lvi, 231 p. : ill. ; 24 cm.
     ISBN 0195032748 : $$17.95
       1. Chinese literature--20th century
2. China--Politics and government--1949-1976--
Addresses, essays, lectures.  3. China--History--
1949-1976--Literary collections.  I. Siu, Helen
F.  II. Stern, Zelda.
     ocm08-763349
```

Notice that the computerized entries are similar to those of the card catalog.

4c-3 Sample database source display

You have initiated a database search on the subject of "education and nuclear war." Here is one printout:

```
DIALOG File 11: PSYCINFO - 67-85/NOV (Copr. Am. Psych.
Assn.)

72-23763
  A decisionmaking approach to nuclear education.
Special Issue, Education and the threat of nuclear war.
  Snow, Roberta; Goodman, Lisa
  Harvard Medical School, Boston
  Harvard Educational Review, 1984 Aug Vol 54(3)
321-328 CODEN: HVERAP ISSN: 00178055
  Journal Announcement, 7209
  Language: ENGLISH Document Type: JOURNAL ARTICLE
  Describes a US senior high school curriculum that
addresses 4 areas: personal values as a basis for
political views, technological aspects of the nuclear
arms race, the history of the nuclear arms race, and
action for social change. The program's content, focus,
and structure are detailed, and its effects on student
attitudes are discussed. Excerpts from student essays
are presented, and examples of appropriate class
projects are suggested.
  Descriptors: NUCLEAR WAR .(34567); STUDENT
ATTITUDES .(50300); EDUCATION .(16000); CURRICULUM
.(12810); HIGH SCHOOL STUDENTS .(22930); ADOLESCENCE
.(00920)
  Identifiers: high school curriculum, decision-
making approach to nuclear education, high school
students
  Section Headings, 3530 .(CURRICULUM PROGRAMS
TEACHING METHODS)
```

The computer has given you a summary of the source. Sometimes full articles can be displayed.

4d

Assembling a working bibliography

The bibliography is a list of sources on the research topic. The *working bibliography* is made up of those sources consulted for information; the *final bibliography* is an alphabetical list of those sources actually used in the paper.

The working bibliography is assembled as the researcher scans the references and card catalog for information on the subject. Promising sources are noted down on 3 × 5 bibliography cards (to be distinguished from the 4 × 6 note cards). The bibliography card should contain information about the sources to be consulted, along with a brief note on why it is likely to be useful. (See examples on pp. 35–37.)

Some instructors do not require that students use cards for a working bibliography, merely that they have one, however compiled. Others insist that the cards be used in the form described here.

If you have a choice, use the bibliography cards. Because they are portable and can be easily arranged in alphabetical order, they are generally more useful than a notebook or scraps of paper. Each source actually *used* will be recorded on two kinds of cards: the title will appear on the smaller bibliography card; notes on the source will appear on the larger note card. If the source is merely checked but not used, it will appear only on the working bibliography card. Once the source is eliminated from contention, its card can be placed in an inactive pack.

- Record each source in ink on a separate 3 × 5 card.
- Use the same form on the bibliography cards as will be used later in the final bibliography. This makes it possible to prepare the final bibliography by simply transcribing from the cards those titles actually used in writing the paper. The following basic information must be listed on the cards:

  Name of author(s)
  Title of work
  Facts of publication
  Page(s) of information

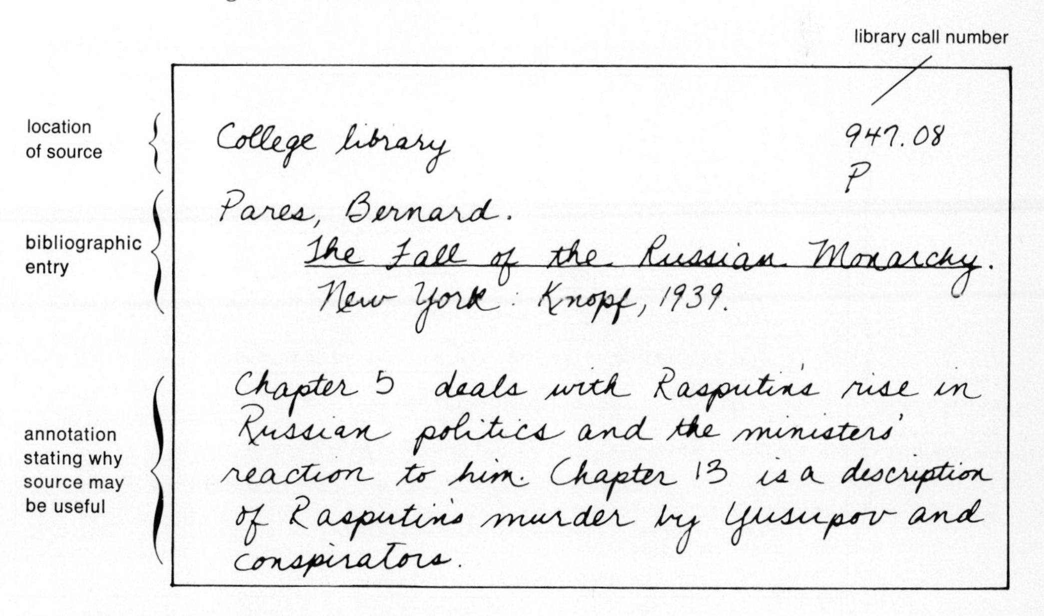

Figure 4-1 Bibliography card for a book

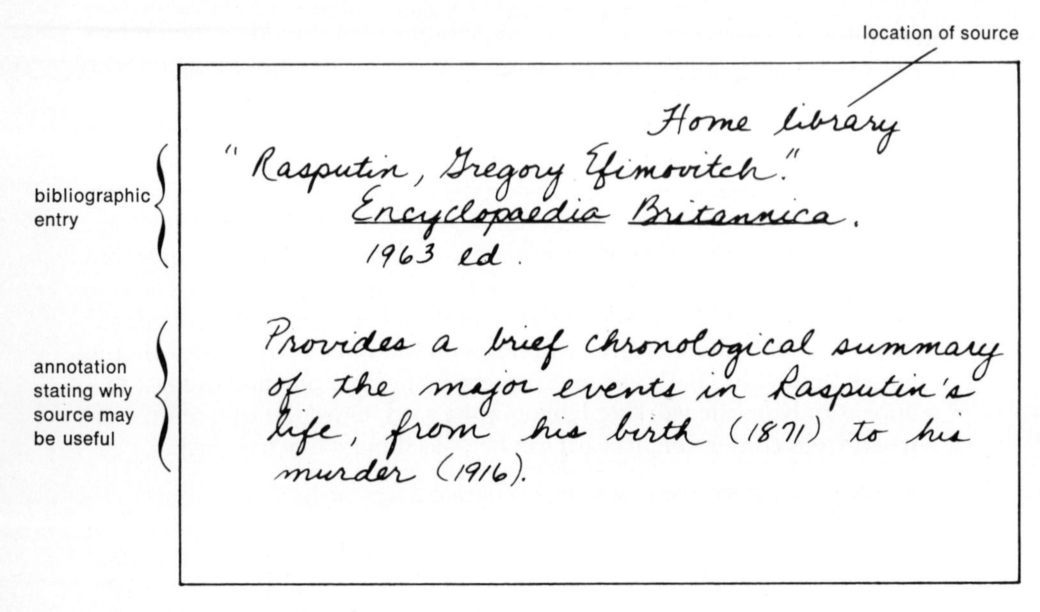

Figure 4-2 Bibliography card for an encyclopedia article

Figure 4-3 Bibliography card for a periodical

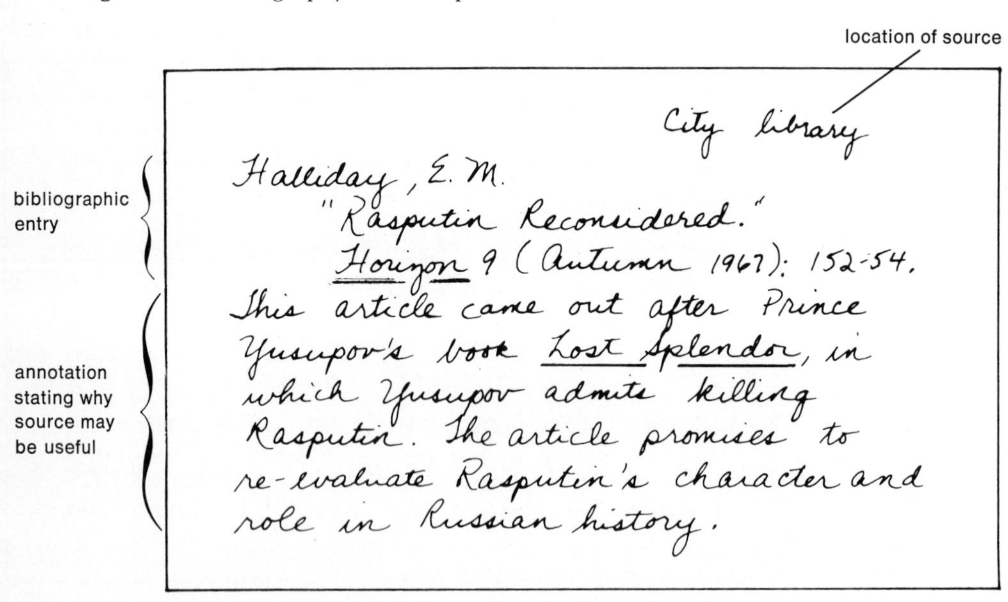

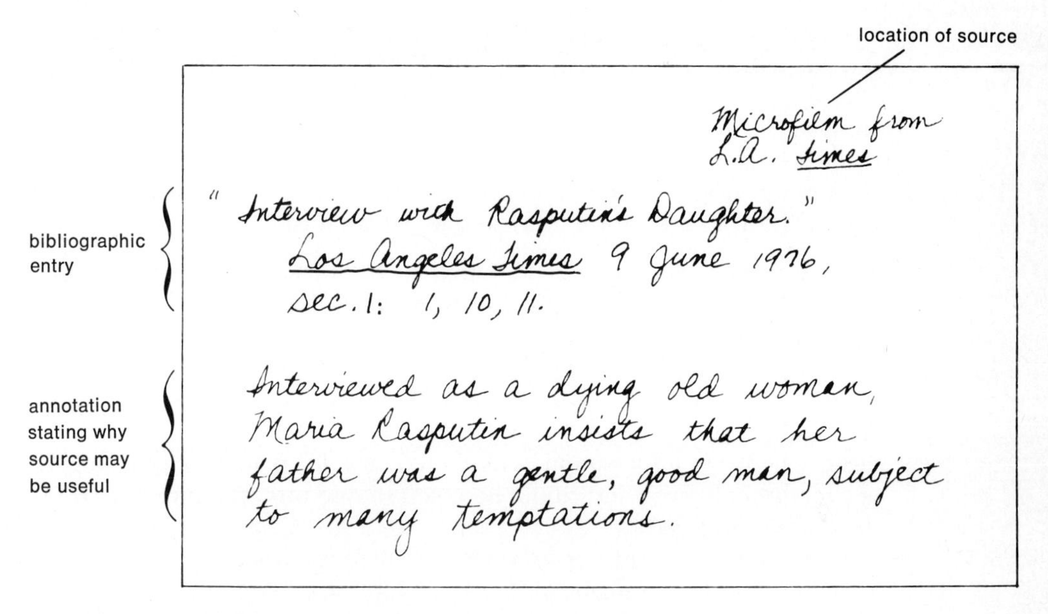

Figure 4-4 Bibliography card for a newspaper article

- In the upper right-hand corner of the card, name the library or place where the source was found, as for example, "Main City Library."
- In the upper left-hand corner of the card, cite the library call number of the source, so that it can be easily found even if reshelved (see Fig. 4-1).

Generally you will end up with many more sources in the working bibliography than are listed in the final bibliography. This is as it should be. Many sources will be consulted, but few chosen. False starts and dead-end trails are to be expected. Books will lure one on with a promising table of contents and title, but once skimmed, will prove to be excessively technical, dated, or simply beside the point. The researcher must ignore the irrelevant and worthless sources, while tracking down those articles, essays, and books that promise to be worthwhile and useful.

4e

Selecting your sources

Researchers seldom have time to faithfully read every book or article written about their subject. Instead, the experienced researcher will initially skim a source to determine its usefulness. In skimming, one searches for major ideas in a piece of writing merely to confirm its appropriateness as a research source. If an initial skimming indicates the source is helpful and to the point, it can be read carefully later. However, if the source appears to be farfetched, ponderous, dated, irrelevant, or otherwise useless, then it should be set aside and more promising leads pursued. Do not, however, destroy the bibliography card of the discarded source, since you may wish to return to it later.

Skimming, like most skills, improves with practice. Here are some hints on how to skim a piece of writing for major ideas:

- Glance at the preface of a book. Often an author will state there what the book is about. Likewise, an afterword will often recount the major ideas of a book.
- Look up the subject in the index of the book. Frequently one can tell from the number of pages devoted to the subject whether or not the book is likely to be useful. For instance, if you are looking in a Russian history book for information on Rasputin, and see from its index that it contains only two pages about him, you should probably move on to some other source.
- Read the chapter headings. Often these will reveal what the chapter is about. Similarly, the major ideas in a chapter are sometimes summarized in headnotes to its various sections.
- Read the first and last two sentences in a paragraph to find out what information it contains. Generally, the main idea of a paragraph is stated in its initial sentences, and summed up in its final sentences.
- Glance at the opening paragraph of an article, essay, or book chapter. Often the author's thesis will be stated in the first paragraph or two of an article or essay. Similarly, the thesis of a chapter may be given in its initial paragraph.
- Glance at concluding paragraphs in an article, essay, or book chapter. Often these final paragraphs will sum up the discussion and restate major ideas.
- Run your eye down the page, reading randomly every fourth or fifth sentence. Most readers who do this can get a fair inkling of what the material is about.

4e-1 Primary and secondary sources of evidence

The judgments or conclusions in your paper must be based on evidence. *Primary* sources of evidence are original writings by an author, documents, artifacts, laboratory experiments, or other data providing firsthand information. A literary paper about an author might quote letters, memoirs, an autobiography, novels, short stories, plays, personal notes by the author and the like as primary sources of evidence.

Secondary sources of evidence are writings, speeches, and other documents *about* a primary source. The opinions of critics are important and widely used secondary sources. An experiment may be a primary source; commentary on it by others is a secondary source. Making a legalistic distinction between these two is not necessary. It is merely necessary to know that your papers will consist of both kinds of evidence. You should also know that for some kinds of papers—especially those on literary topics—primary sources are best. But primary sources require that you expend the effort to interpret them.

4e-2 Evaluating sources of evidence

All sources are not created equal. They vary in quality of scholarship, force of argument, and acuracy of detail. Some sources are useful, scholarly, and accurate; others are worthless, silly, and misleading. For example, a student writing a paper on human evolution would be grievously mistaken in taking the fossil remains of the Piltdown Man to be the "missing link"—no matter how many library sources said so. In a brief burst of glory the Piltdown Man was hailed as the "missing link" in human evolution. Many articles and books in the library still make this claim, though their authors would now dearly love to retract, since the Piltdown Man has been exposed as an elaborate hoax. Anthropologists know all about the Piltdown Man's checkered career, though a student researcher might not. All fields are similarly littered with past errors preserved in the collections of libraries. Yet, the researcher, who is often a novice in the subject, must nevertheless dicriminate between error and truth in the writings of experts—a tricky thing to do.

Fortunately, there are some common-sense ways of evaluating sources of evidence:

- Verify one opinion against another. No one who has conscientiously researched the literature on human fossils would be duped by the early claims on behalf of Piltdown Man, for these have been thoroughly discredited in later writings. In any given field authors often comment on the work of their peers. The diligent researcher soon perceives a consensus of opinion among the experts that can be used to judge the reputation of an author or source.
- Note the date of the evidence. In researching any topic you should attach greatest importance to the most recent data. If two sources are identical except in date, cite the later one as your authority.
- Use common sense. Try to evaluate the logic and probable authenticity of any source you intend to use. For example, if you are doing a paper on the possible existence of UFOs, you can and should carefully analyze the testimony of alleged eyewitnesses. Common sense and keen attention to detail are the chief requirements for evaluating this kind, as well as many other kinds, of evidence.

- Check your evaluations against those of professionals. For example, the opinions of critics can give you an inkling of how experienced readers have viewed a certain novel. The *Book Review Digest* is a good source for critical opinions on books. You can also check the credentials of an author or expert in any of the various biographical dictionaries or *Who's Who* volumes to judge how much weight an expert evaluation should be given.
- Beware of statistics. Because we tend to believe that figures are more accurate than words, we can easily be duped by statistics. A student reading, "At present 35% of children 12 to 18 use alcohol, compared with only 1% in 1940" needs to note carefully that the statistic does not apply to *all* children. The accuracy and inclusiveness of the study that produced the statistics should also be determined. You should question the credibility of a source that uses general and exaggerated numbers such as, "Millions of black youths walk the streets of Atlanta, unemployed." The attentive reader will recognize this assertion as figurative language and strive for impartiality. Admittedly this is hard to do, especially if your position is already biased. Nevertheless, you should try to evaluate all data and statistics with an open mind.

4f Note-taking

The information uncovered on your topic through research should be transcribed onto 4 × 6 note cards and eventually incorporated into the body of the paper. Bear in mind, as you read and take notes, that a research paper should contain a variety of material taken from different sources. It is not enough to simply write down your own ideas and speculations, while ignoring everyone else's opinion on the subject. Your own ideas should be derived from evidence and information uncovered on the subject through research, and the reader should be made aware not only of your conclusions, but also of the substance and reasoning that led you to them.

Students are often puzzled about how much of the paper should consist of their original writing, and how much of material drawn from researched sources. No exact rule exists. You should not write a paper consisting of a string of quotations and paraphrases but containing nothing of your own. Nor should you glut the paper entirely with your own notions, with only a token quotation or paraphrase added here and there to give the illusion of research. Ideally, the paper should consist of information from sources blended judiciously with your own commentary and interpretation. Certainly you should say what you think, but you should also say why you think it—what evidence exists to support your opinions; which authorities on the subject agree with you; and why those of a different opinion are probably in error. In sum, the paper demands not merely opinionated conclusions, but conclusions supported by other opinions.

4f-1 Format of the note cards

- Use 4 × 6 cards for note-taking. Large enough to accommodate fairly long notes, 4 × 6 cards are also unlikely to be confused with the smaller 3 × 5 bibliography cards.
- Write in ink rather than pencil so that the cards can be shuffled without blurring the notes.
- Write down only one idea or quotation on each card. Cards with only a single note can be put in any sequence simply by shuffling. If the note is so long that two cards have to be used, staple them together.
- Identify the source of the note in the upper left-hand corner of the card. Since the bibliography card already lists complete information on the source, use only the author's last name or key words from the title followed by a page number. For example, use "Fülöp-Miller 10," or "Holy Devil 10," to identify a note taken from page 10 of *Rasputin, the Holy Devil*, by René Fülöp-Miller.
- Jot down in the upper right-hand corner of the card a general heading for the information the card contains. These headings make it easy to organize the notes by shuffling the cards. (Write in pencil so that the heading can be changed.)

4f-2 Kinds of note cards

The notes gathered from your research must be blended into the body of the paper to provide documentation, proof, and evidence in support of the thesis. These notes are of four kinds: the *summary*, the *paraphrase*, the *quotation*, and the *personal comment*.

a. The summary

A summary is a condensation of significant facts from an original piece of writing. A chapter is condensed into a page, a page into a paragraph, or a paragraph into a sentence, with the condensation in each case retaining the essential facts of the original. Consider the following summary of an eight-page description of Rasputin:

Fülöp-Miller 3-10. Rasputin's appearance

Rasputin's appearance was a combination of coarse, unkempt peasant burliness and mystical, poetic religiosity. He was at once repulsive and attractive. Strangers who met him were first disgusted by such details as his pock-marked skin and his dirty fingernails, but inevitably they came under the spell of his urgent, probing blue eyes.

Figure 4-5 Sample note card containing a summary

Common sense should govern your use of the summary. Some facts need to be quoted in detail, but others do not, and can be just as effectively summarized. For instance, the note card shown was for a paper on Rasputin that dealt mainly with the historical truth about the man, not with his physical appearance. It was therefore enough for the student to summarize certain features of Rasputin that made him simultaneously repulsive and attractive. In another context, say in a paper on the physical disfigurement of famous people, it might have been necessary for the student to quote generously from the eight-page description which, in this instance, she needed only to summarize.

b. The paraphrase

To paraphrase means to say in one's own words what someone else has said. The paraphrase—unlike the summary—does not condense, but restates a passage in approximately the same number of words as the original, using the syntax and vocabulary of the paraphraser. Ordinarily, the paraphrase is the most frequently used note in the preparation of a research paper.

Paraphrasing achieves two purposes: first, it shows that the student has mastered and assimilated the material to the extent of being able to state it in his or her own words. Second, it gives the paper an even, consistent style, since both original and source material are cast in the words of the student writer. Below is a short passage from *The Fall of the Russian Monarchy* by Bernard Pares. An appropriate student paraphrase is given in Figure 4-6.

> Meanwhile Rasputin, as he appears to have done earlier, disappeared into the wilds of Russia. Here too he was true to an historical type. Always, throughout Russian history, there had been *stranniki* or wanderers who, without any ecclesiastical commission, lived in asceticism, depriving themselves of the most elementary of human needs, but gladly entertained by the poor wherever they passed. Some of them went barefoot even throughout the winter and wore chains on their legs. This self-denial gave them a freedom to address as peasant equals even the Tsars themselves, and there are many instances of their bold rebuke scattered over Russian history.

c. *The quotation*

The quotation reproduces an author's words exactly as they were spoken or written, preserving even peculiarities of spelling, grammar, or punc-

Pares 134-35. Rasputin as nomad, ca. 1902

For some time Rasputin became like the well-known <u>stranniki</u>, those wandering ascetics who, without official priestly license, wandered all over Russia depending, wherever they passed, on the poor for food and shelter. Some of the nomads even walked barefoot in the freezing Russian winter with chains clinking around their legs. This kind of self-denial bestowed on them the peculiar right to address even a Tsar as their peasant equal. In this role of half priest half beggar, Rasputin roamed the wilds of Russia.

Figure 4-6 Sample note card containing a paraphrase

tuation. Use of an occasional quotation is justified only where the authority of the writer is being evoked, or where the original material is so splendidly expressed as to be altogether ruined by any attempt at either summary or paraphrase.

Student papers are commonly flawed by the overuse of quoted material. Moreover, many teachers regard the excessive inclusion of quotations as a sign of padding. A good rule of thumb is therefore to limit quoted material to no more than ten percent of the total paper. Another good rule is to quote only when the authority of the writer is needed, or when the material simply cannot be either paraphrased or summarized.

The rules for placing quotations on note cards are:

- Place quotation marks around the quotation.
- Introduce the quotation or place it in proper context.
- Copy quotations exactly as they are written. (See pp. 73–81 for how to introduce quotations, and pp. 81–85 for how to use ellipses.)

Occasionally, a summary or paraphrase is combined with a quotation on a note card, the key phrases or words from the original source being used to add literary flavor or authenticity to the note. Below is an original passage from *The Fall of the Russian Monarchy* by Bernard Pares, followed by a note card that combines a paraphrase with a quotation from this source.

> Nothing is more untrue than the easy explanation that was so often given, that he became the tool of others. He was far too clever to sell himself to anyone. He did not ask for presents and had no need; he had only to accept all that was showered upon him, and that he did briefly and almost casually, in many cases at once passing on the largess to the poor; his position was that of one who plundered the rich for the poor and was glad to do it.

d. The personal comment

Personal-comment notes can be used to record any ideas, conjectures, or conclusions that occur to you during the research. These notes are generally used to explicate a fuzzy statement, stress a particular point, draw a conclusion, clarify an issue, identify an inconsistency, or introduce a new idea. Jot down these ideas as they dawn on you. If the personal-comment note deals with material contained on another card, staple the two cards together. An example of a personal-comment note card is given in Figure 4-9 (p. 46).

Fülöp-Miller 366. The murder of Rasputin

Farewell letter from Empress Alexandra to the murdered Rasputin:

"My dear martyr, grant me your blessing to accompany me on the sorrowful road I have still to tread here below. Remember us in Heaven in your holy prayers. Alexandra."

Figure 4-7 Sample note card containing a quotation

Pares 140, 141. Rasputin's generosity to the poor

Some critics have accused Rasputin of becoming "the tool of others" in order to acquire expensive personal gifts or other material advantage. Nothing could be further from the truth. Rasputin was too clever "to sell himself to anyone." He did not need to. All he had to do was sit back and accept all the luxuries offered to him by high society. And, in fact, one of his favorite roles was that of a Russian Robin Hood who "plundered the rich for the poor" by taking gifts offered and immediately passing them on to people in need.

Figure 4-8 Sample note card combining paraphrase and quotation

Personal Comment The Czarina's initial attraction to Rasputin

It becomes clear, from all accounts describing the first meeting between Alexandra and Rasputin, that initially this peasant monk gained entrance to the Czarina's confidence by offering hope for the health of her hemophiliac son, at a time when she was utterly sunk in grief and despair. In the grip of maternal terror, she wanted to believe that God had sent a simple peasant to perform miracles.

Figure 4-9 Sample note card containing a personal comment

4g

Plagiarism: what it is and how to avoid it

Plagiarism is the act of passing off another's words and ideas as one's own. The question of when one has plagiarized and when one has simply asserted a general truth from an unknown source, can be sometimes puzzling. In a cosmic sense, the process of learning is made up of countless tiny crimes of plagiarism, since we all borrow freely from one another. No generation speaks a language of its own invention; few people are creators of the proverbs and sayings that they utter daily. The mother who tells her child, "A thing of beauty is a joy forever," is plagiarizing from the poet John Keats; the father who warns his son, "Hell hath no fury like a woman scorned," has plagiarized from the playwright William Congreve. Innumerable other examples can be given to show how we freely and wantonly borrow ideas and expressions from one another.

Blatant plagiarism, however, involves the conscious and deliberate stealing of another's words and ideas, generally with the motive of earning undeserved rewards. The student who copies the paper of a friend is guilty of blatant plagiarism. Likewise, the student who steals an idea from a book, expresses it in his or her own words, and then passes it off as original, has committed an act of plagiarism.

The conventions of writing research papers dictate that students must acknowledge the source of any idea or statement not truly their own. This acknowledgment is made in a note specifying the source and author of the borrowed material. All summaries, paraphrases, or quotations must be documented; only personal comments may remain undocumented. In sum, to avoid plagiarism students must:

- Provide a note for any idea borrowed from another.
- Place quoted material within quotation marks.
- Provide a bibliography entry at the end of the book for every source used in the text or in a note.

Not every assertion is documentable, nor is it necessary for students to document matters of general and common knowledge. For instance, it is commonly known that the early settlers of America fought wars with the Indians—an assertion a student could safely make without documentation. Similarly, a student could write, "Russia was in turmoil during the years preceding the Bolshevik Revolution," without documenting this statement, since the turmoil of prerevolutionary Russia is common knowledge. As a rule of thumb, a piece of information that occurs in five or more sources may be considered general knowledge. Proverbs, and sayings of unknown origins, are also considered general knowledge and do not have to be documented.

The following, however, must be accompanied by a citation specifying author and source:

- Any idea derived from any known source.
- Any fact or data borrowed from the work of another.
- Any especially clever or apt expression, whether or not it says something new, that is taken from someone else.
- Any material lifted verbatim from the work of another.
- Any information that is paraphrased or summarized and used in the paper.

In writing research papers, students are expected to borrow heavily from the works of experts and authorities—indeed, this is partly the purpose of the research; but they are also expected to acknowledge the sources of this borrowed material.

To illustrate plagiarism in different degrees, we have reproduced a passage from a book, followed by three student samples, two of which are plagiarisms.

Original passage

Alexander III died on 20 October, 1894, and was succeeded by his son Nicholas. The new emperor was more intelligent and more sensitive than his father. Both those who knew him well, and those who had brief and superficial contact with him, testify to his exceptional personal charm. The charm was, however, apparently associated with weakness and irresolution. Nicholas appeared to agree with the last person he had talked to, and no one could tell what he would do next.

Student Version A (plagiarized)

When Alexander III died on October 20, 1894, he was followed by his son Nicholas, who was more intelligent and more sensitive than his father. People who knew him well and also some who knew him only superficially testify that he was exceptionally charming as a person. This charm, however, was associated with weakness and an inability to make decisions. Nicholas always seemed to agree with the last person he had talked to, and no one could predict what he would do next.

This is an example of outright plagiarism. No documentation of any sort is given. The student simply repeats the passage almost verbatim, as though he or she had written it.

Student Version B (plagiarized)

When Alexander III died on October 20, 1894, he was followed by his son Nicholas, who was more intelligent and more sensitive than his father. People who knew him well, and also some who knew him only superficially, testify that he was exceptionally charming as a person. This charm, however, was associated with weakness and an inability to make decisions. Nicholas always seemed to agree with the last person he had talked to, and no one could predict what he would do next.[3]

[3] Hugh Seton-Watson, The Russian Empire, 1801-1917, vol. 3 of The Oxford History of Modern Europe (Oxford: Oxford UP, 1967) 547.

Though documented with a footnote, the passage is still a plagiarism because the student has merely changed a word or two of the original, without doing a proper paraphrase.

Student Version C (acceptable)

Emperor Nicholas II, who came to the throne of Russia following the death of his father, Alexander III, was apparently a man of exceptional personal charm and deep sensitivity. Ample testimony has come to us from both intimate as well as casual acquaintances, indicating that indeed he possessed a magnetic personality. However, the general consensus is also that he was a man who lacked the ability to make hard decisions, preferring to agree with the last person he had seen, and thus making it impossible to predict what he would do next.[3]

[3] Hugh Seton-Watson, The Russian Empire, 1801-1917, vol. 3 of The Oxford History of Modern Europe (Oxford: Oxford UP, 1967) 547.

This is an acceptable use of the material. The original is properly paraphrased and its source documented with a footnote.

5

The Thesis and the Outline

5a The thesis: definition and function

5b The outline

5a

The thesis: definition and function

The thesis is a statement that summarizes the central idea of the paper. By convenience and custom, this statement is usually the final sentence of the opening paragraph, as in the following example.

The Bilingually Handicapped Child

There are approximately five million children in the United States who attend public schools and speak a language other than English in their homes and neighborhoods. Many of these children are handicapped in communication and thought processes, and have to repeat the first grades in school several times. The bilingual child is usually unable to conceptualize in the English language taught at school, since he is from a different cultural and language background. Early compensatory educational programs would give the bilingual child a head start and he would be better prepared for handling school work.

The underlined sentence is the thesis—the central idea for which the writer intends to argue. Once readers have gotten through this first paragraph, the aim of the paper is abundantly clear to them; they know what to anticipate.

The thesis serves at least three functions. First, it establishes a boundary around the subject that discourages the writer from wandering aimlessly. Most of us are often tempted to stray from the point when we write. We begin by intending to write a paper about Rasputin's place in history, then stumble onto some fascinating fact about Russian monasteries and become eager to somehow work it in. With a clear thesis before us, however, we are less likely to be seduced by a digression. Formulated before the actual writing of the paper begins, the thesis commits us to argue one point, discuss one subject, clarify one issue. Writers so committed will not leapfrog from topic to topic, nor free-associate erratically from one minor point to another.

Second, the thesis—if worded properly—can chart an orderly course for the paper, making it easier to write. Consider for instance this thesis:

> Two defects in the design of the Titanic contributed to her sinking: her steering was sluggish and unresponsive, even for a ship of her immense size; her traverse bulkheads, which should have made her virtually unsinkable, did not extend all the way up to her deck.

The course before the writer is as plain as day: first, the sluggish steering of the *Titanic* must be discussed and clarified with appropriate facts and details; second, the design of her traverse bulkheads must be dealt with, and the defect thoroughly explained. The writer's job is easier because the thesis has conveniently divided the paper into two parts, establishing not only the topics to be discussed, but also their sequence. It is better and easier by far to write about such a thesis than to write randomly about the sinking of the *Titanic*.

Third, the thesis gives the reader an idea of what to expect, making the paper consequently easier to read. Textbooks have elaborate chapter headings and section headnotes just for this purpose. Newspaper stories are captioned and headlined for a similar reason. It is easier to read virtually anything if we have an idea of what to anticipate since the anticipation narrows and focuses our attention. A paper without a thesis creates no such anticipation in a reader and is therefore more difficult to follow.

5a-1 Formulating the thesis

There is no chicken-and-egg mystery about which comes first—the notes or the thesis. One cannot formulate a thesis about a subject unless one first knows a great deal about it. Ordinarily, students will therefore be well into the research and notes before they can formulate the thesis.

Basically, you are looking for a central idea that summarizes the information you have gathered on the subject. Consider for instance the paper on Rasputin, which we have been using as our prime example. The student, after much reading and note-taking, discovered that despite his diabolic reputation, Rasputin did do some good. Specifically, she discovered that: (1) Rasputin had intense religious feelings; (2) he had a passionate desire for peace in Russia; (3) he was deeply devoted to his family and friends. She therefore summarized her findings about Rasputin in the following thesis:

Thesis: After six decades of being judged a demoniacal libertine, Rasputin now deserves to be viewed from another point of view—as a man who was intensely religious, who passionately desired peace, and who was deeply devoted to his family and friends.

Notice that the thesis, as worded, specifies exactly what the writer has to do, and what information she will need to do it. To begin with, she will have to document Rasputin's reputation as a demoniacal libertine. Having done that, she will have to support her three contrary assertions: that Rasputin was intensely religious, that he passionately desired peace, and that he was deeply devoted to his family and friends. The thesis, moreover, suggests exactly the kind of information that the student will need to write the paper. First, she must cite historical opinion that portrays Rasputin as a demoniacal libertine. Second, she will need to produce anecdotal material, eyewitness accounts, biographical opinions, and similar evidence that support her contrary assertions about Rasputin.

5a-2 Rules for wording the thesis

To be useful, the thesis must be properly worded. A vague, confused, or lopsided thesis will either inflict similar miseries on the paper, or cause the writer to flounder helplessly among a disarray of note cards. Properly worded, the thesis should: (1) be clear, comprehensible, and direct; (2) predict major divisions in the structure of the paper; (3) commit the writer to an unmistakable course, argument, or point of view. The thesis on Rasputin is clear, implies a four-part division in the structure of the paper, and obligates the writer to argue a single proposition: that Rasputin was harshly judged by history. Likewise, the thesis on the *Titanic* disaster is clear and direct, divides the paper into two principal parts, and commits the writer to a single argument: that the ocean liner sank because of defects in her steering and bulkheads. Listed below is a series of rules to guide you in properly wording your thesis.

- *The thesis should commit the writer to a single line of argument.* Consider this example:

Poor The Roman theater was inspired by the Greek theater, which it imitated, and eventually the Romans produced great plays in their theatrons, such as those by Plautus, who was the best Roman comic writer because of his robustness and inventiveness.

A single topic is difficult enough to research and write about; with two topics in a single paper, the writer's task becomes almost impossible. The thesis just given threatens to wrench the paper in two contrary directions: it commits the student to cover both the origins of Roman theater and the theatrical career of Plautus, one of Rome's greatest comic playwrights. This dual thesis came about because the student had laboriously accumulated two sets of notes—one on the origins of Roman theater and another on the career of Plautus—and was determined to devise a thesis that would allow the use of both. The result is this curiously dual thesis that skews the paper in two contrary directions. Persuaded to relinquish the notes on the origins of the Roman theater and to focus the paper entirely on the career of Plautus, the student drafted the following improved thesis:

Better Because of his robust language and novel comic plots, Titus Maccicus Plautus can be considered the best Roman comic playwright; his plays are still successfully staged today.

The paper is now committed to a single line of argument, and its focus is therefore vastly improved.

- *The thesis should not be worded in figurative language.* The reasoning behind this rule is obvious: figurative language is too indefinite and oblique to constitute the central idea of a paper. Consider this thesis:

Poor Henry James is the Frank Lloyd Wright of the American novel.

No doubt the writer knew exactly what was meant by this allusion, but its significance is murky to a reader. If one cannot understand the central idea of a paper, what hope does one have of understanding the paper? The following plainly expressed thesis is vastly better:

Better The novels of Henry James have internal consistency because of the way he unifies his themes, patterns his episodes, and orders his images.

- *The thesis should not be vaguely worded.* Vagueness may tantalize, but it does not inform. Moreover, a paper with a vague thesis is a paper without direction, and all the more difficult to write. Consider this example of a vague thesis:

Poor Cigarette smoking wreaks havoc on the body.

Doing a paper on such a thesis will truly put a writer to the test. The thesis suggests no direction, provides no structure, proposes no arguments. Contrast it with this improved version:

Better Cigarette smoking harms the body by constricting the blood vessels, accelerating the heartbeat, paralyzing the cilia in the bronchial tubes, and activating excessive gastric secretions in the stomach.

The writer knows exactly what points to argue and in what order.

- *The thesis should not be worded as a question.* The thesis worded as a question does not provide the writer with the kind of obligatory direction given by the one phrased as a statement. Here is an example:

Poor Who makes the key decisions in U.S. cities?

This is the sort of question that makes a good starting point for research. Indeed, most research will begin with an unanswered question in the mind of the researcher. But the eventual thesis should not be your original question; it should be the answer uncovered in your research.

Better Key decisions in large U.S. cities are made by a handful of individuals, drawn largely from business, industrial, and municipal circles, who occupy the top of the power hierarchy.

- *The thesis should be as concise as possible.* If ever a writer should try for conciseness, it is in the drafting of the thesis. A long, cumbersome thesis is likely to muddle the writer and send the paper flying off in different directions. The reader who cannot fathom the thesis of a paper is even less likely to make sense of its contents. Here is a muddled thesis:

Poor Despite the fact that extensive time consumed by television detracts from homework, competes with schooling more generally, and has contributed to the decline in the Scholastic Aptitude Test score averages, television and related forms of communication give the future of learning its largest promise, the most constructive approach being less dependent on limiting the uses of these processes than on the willingness of the community and the family to exercise the same responsibility for what is taught and learned this way as they have exercised with respect to older forms of education.

This passage is difficult to unravel. A whole paper based on this thesis would be equally unclear. Here is an improved version:

Better While numerous studies acknowledge that the extensive time spent by students watching television has contributed to the decline in the Scholastic Aptitude Test scores, leading educators are convinced that television holds immense promise for the future of learning, provided that the family and the community will prudently monitor its use.

To paraphrase an old saying, "Like thesis, like paper." A muddled, incoherent thesis will generate an equally muddled and incoherent paper.

5a-3 Placing the thesis

The thesis is usually introduced in the final sentence of the first paragraph—a position that gives the writer a chance to establish an opening context yet is still emphatic enough to draw attention to the thesis. Some variation in placement of the thesis does exist, but most teachers distinctly prefer it to be stated as the final sentence of the initial paragraph. Here are three examples of theses introduced in this customary place:

He is a vagabond in aristocratic clothing––shabby but grand. As he scurries along in his cutaway and derby hat, aided by a cane, he is obviously a tramp, but a tramp with the impeccable manners of a dandy. He is willing to tackle any job, but seldom does it properly. He often falls in love, but usually the affair sours in the end. His only enemies are pompous people in places of authority. The general public adores him because he is everyman of all times. *Thesis* Charlie Chaplin's ''Tramp'' has remained a favorite international character because he is a character with whom the average person can empathize.

A quarter of a million babies are born each year with birth defects. Of these defects, only 20 percent are hereditary. Most of them could have been prevented because they are the tragic results of poor prenatal care. *Thesis* An unfavorable fetal environment, such as can be caused by malnutrition in the mother or her use of drugs, is a primary cause of many kinds of birth defects.

```
Theodor Seuss Geisel writes and illustrates zany
children's books, usually in verse, under the
pseudonym of ''Dr. Seuss.''  He has written twenty-six
best sellers over a period of thirty years, and they
are all still in print.  In story after story, this
author creates a topsy-turvy world where the normal
becomes aberrant and the aberrant becomes normal.
```

Thesis The simple vocabulary and rhyming lines of Dr. Seuss's books make them easy for children to read, but the author's illustrations are primarily responsible for the imaginative flair in his work.

5a-4 Title of the research paper

No magic formula exists to tell you when to decide on the final wording of your title. Some writers like to work from a title whereas others prefer to word the title after the paper is written. Regardless of when you decide on your title, be sure to make it informative, clear, and specific. For instance, the title "Downward Spiral" gives no clue to the subject of the research. The title "Drugs" is not much better since it is too general. A better title is "Why Women Should Not Take Narcotic Drugs During Their Pregnancies." Usually your thesis statement will provide an excellent springboard for your title.

5b
The outline

The outline is an ordered listing of the topics covered in the paper. Varying in complexity and style, outlines are nevertheless useful to both the writer and the reader. The writer who writes from an outline is less likely to stray from the point, or to commit a structural error such as overdeveloping one topic while skimping on another. The reader, on the other hand, benefits from the outline as a complete and detailed table of contents.

5b-1 Visual conventions of the outline

The conventions of formal outlining require that main ideas be designated by Roman numerals such as I, II, III, IV, V. Subideas branching off from the main ideas are designated by capital letters A, B, C, D, and so on. Subdivisions of these subideas are designated by Arabic numerals 1, 2, 3, 4, and so forth. Minor ideas are designated by lower-case letters a, b, c, d, etc. Here is an example of the proper form of an outline:

```
 I.  Main idea

     A.  Subidea

     B.  Subidea

         1.  Division of a subidea

         2.  Division of a subidea

             a.  Minor idea

             b.  Minor idea

II.  Main idea
```

The presumption behind this sort of arrangement is obvious: namely, that students will not merely generalize, but will support their contentions and propositions with examples and details. Indeed, that is exactly what the writer of a research paper is expected to do—to make assertions that are supported by concrete examples and specific details. If you have done your research badly and have not been diligent in gathering specific facts about the topic, this deficiency will now become painfully obvious.

Notice that every category must be subdivided at least once, since it is impossible to divide anything into fewer than two parts. An outline dividing the subject into three or four levels—that is, down to examples or details—is generally adequate for most college-level research papers. If further subdivisions are necessary, the format is as follows:

```
I.
    A.
        1.
            a.
                (1)
                    (a)
```

The basic principle remains the same: larger ideas or elements are stacked to the left, with smaller ideas and elements to the right.

5b-2 Equal ranking in outline entries

The logic of an outline requires that each entry be based on the same organizing principle as another entry of equal rank. All capital-letter entries must consequently be equivalent in importance and derived from the same organizing principle. Notice the lack of equal ranking in the following example:

```
I.  Rousseau gave the people a new government to work toward.

    A.  It would be a government based on the general will.

    B.  The new government would serve the people instead of the
        people serving the government.

    C.  The people tore down the Bastille.
```

The C entry is out of place because it is not of equal rank with entries A and B. A and B are subideas that characterize the new government proposed by Rousseau; C is a statement that describes the revolt of the French people against the old government.

5b-3 Parallelism in outline entries

The clarity and readability of an outline are immeasurably improved if its entries are worded in similar grammatical form. Notice the lack of parallelism in the following outline:

```
I.  The uses of the laser in the military

    A.  For range-finding

    B.  For surveillance

    C.  To illuminate the enemy's position
```

Entries A and B consist of a preposition followed by a noun, while entry C is worded as an infinitive phrase. C should therefore be reworded to make it grammatically similar to entries A and B:

```
I.  The uses of the laser in the military

    A.  For range-finding

    B.  For surveillance

    C.  For illuminating an enemy's position
```

The outline is now easier to read because its entries are grammatically parallel.

5b-4 Types of outlines

The three main types of outlines are the topic outline, the sentence outline, and the paragraph outline. The formats of these different outlines cannot be mixed or combined; one type of outline must be used exclusively.

a. The topic outline

The topic outline words each entry as a phrase, breaking down the subject into major subheadings. Topic outlines are particularly useful for outlining relatively simple subjects. Here is a topic outline of the paper on Rasputin:

```
                    Rasputin's Other Side

Thesis: After six decades of being judged a demoniacal libertine,
        Rasputin how deserves to be viewed from another point of
        view--as a man who was intensely religious, who passion-
        ately desired peace, and who was deeply devoted to his
        family and friends.
  I.  The ambiguity of the real Rasputin
      A.  His birth
      B.  Popular historical view
          1.  His supporters
          2.  His detractors
 II.  Rasputin's religious feelings
      A.  His rich nature and exuberant vitality
      B.  His simple peasant faith
```

III. Rasputin's desire for peace in Russia

A. His concern for the Russian underdog

1. His loyalty to the peasantry

2. His opposition to anti-Semitism

B. His opposition to all wars

IV. Rasputin's gentle, compassionate side

A. His kindness to the Romanovs

B. His love for family

Notice that the thesis of the paper is placed as a separate entry immediately after the title. It is also customary to omit "introduction" and "conclusion" entries.

b. The sentence outline

The sentence outline uses a complete grammatical sentence for each entry. (Some instructors allow the entries to be worded as questions, but most prefer declarative sentences.) Sentence outlines are especially well-suited for complex subjects, the detailed entries giving the writer an excellent overview of the paper. Here is a sentence outline of the paper on Rasputin:

Rasputin's Other Side

Thesis: After six decades of being judged a demoniacal libertine, Rasputin now deserves to be viewed from another point of view--as a man who was intensely religious, who passionately desired peace, and who was deeply devoted to his family and friends.

I. The real Rasputin is difficult to discover.

A. The birth of Rasputin coincided with a ''shooting star.''

- B. The popular historical view of Rasputin portrays him as primarily evil.
    1. Supporters called him a spiritual leader.
    2. Detractors called him a satyr and charged that his depraved faithful were merely in awe of his sexual endowments.

II. Rasputin had intense religious feelings.

- A. He had a rich nature and exuberant vitality.
- B. He had a simple peasant faith in God.

III. Rasputin's passionate desire for peace in Russia revealed itself in several ways.

- A. He was concerned for the Russian underdog.
    1. He wanted a Tsar who would stand mainly for the peasantry.
    2. He spoke out boldly against anti-Semitism.
- B. Because of his humanitarian spirit, he was opposed to all wars.

IV. Rasputin had a gentle, compassionate side.

- A. He showed great kindness to the Romanovs.
- B. Maria Rasputin tells of her father's love for his family.

c. The paragraph outline

The paragraph outline records each entry as a complete paragraph, thus providing a condensed version of the paper. This form is useful mainly for long papers whose individual sections can be summarized in whole paragraphs, but is seldom recommended by instructors for ordinary college papers. Here is the Rasputin paper in the form of a paragraph outline:

Rasputin's Other Side

Thesis: After six decades of being judged a demoniacal libertine, Rasputin now deserves to be viewed from another point of view——as a man who was intensely religious, who passionately desired peace, and who was deeply devoted to his family and friends.

I. Rasputin himself always attached great significance to the fact that at the time of his birth, a shooting star was seen streaking across the horizon. He saw this phenomenon as an omen that he was fated to have influence and special powers. The popular historical view of Rasputin paints him primarily as evil. In his day, however, he attracted numerous supporters who viewed him as their spiritual leader. But he also had many detractors who called him a satyr and accused his followers of sexual depravity.

II. Rasputin had intense religious feelings. He was so filled with exuberance and vitality that he could stay awake until the early hours of the morning, dancing and drinking in frenzied religious fervor. He did not have the theology of a sophisticated church cleric, but rather he expressed his religion in the simple terms of a Russian peasant.

III. Rasputin's passionate desire for peace in Russia revealed itself in several ways. For instance, he was concerned for such Russian underdogs as the peasants and the Jews, always encouraging the Tsar to protect these unfortunate groups.

Also, his humanitarian and pacifist nature made him a determined opponent of all wars.

IV. Rasputin had a gentle, compassionate side. He was completely devoted to the Tsar's family and was known to have had a calming influence on the hemophiliac son of the Tsar. Maria Rasputin gives a glowing report of her father's kindness and love.

5b-5 The decimal notation of an outline

Other outline forms exist that use various methods of indenting, labeling, and spacing. One form that has been gaining favor in business and science is the decimal outline. Based on the decimal accounting system, this outline form permits an infinite number of possible subdivisions through the simple addition of another decimal place. Here is the body of the Rasputin paper notated in the decimal outline form:

Rasputin's Other Side

```
1.  The ambiguity of the real Rasputin
    1.1.  His birth
    1.2.  Popular historical view
          1.2.1.  His supporters
          1.2.2.  His detractors

2.  Rasputin's religious feelings
    2.1.  His rich nature and exuberant vitality
    2.2.  His simple peasant faith

3.  Rasputin's desire for peace in Russia
    3.1.  His concern for the Russian underdog
          3.1.1.  His loyalty to the peasantry
          3.1.2.  His opposition to anti-Semitism
    3.2.  His opposition to all wars

4.  Rasputin's gentle, compassionate side
    4.1.  His kindness to the Romanovs
    4.2.  His love for family
```

Notice that though a decimal notation is used, this outline arranges its entries on the same indentation principle used in other outlines, with larger ideas stacked to the left, and smaller ideas to the right.

5b-6 Which kind of outline should you use?

If you have a choice, if you are a beginning writer, and if your research has uncovered much detail on your subject, don't hesitate a minute: use a detailed sentence outline. Develop it at least down to the third level—the level of Arabic numerals. In doing so you actually erect a kind of scaffolding for the essay. To write the rough draft, you merely transcribe from the outline, fill in the blanks, insert transitions and connectives, and you have an essay.

The main entries of this outline should be the topic sentences of various paragraphs. Its details should be exactly the kind you intend to use to support the topic sentence. Here, as an example, is an outlined paragraph from a sentence outline of a paper on Agatha Christie's fictional sleuth, Hercule Poirot:

I. Hercule's unique personality and character set him apart from other fictional detectives.

    A. His physical appearance was unique.

        1. He was 5′4″, had a black handlebar mustache, an egg-shaped head, and catlike eyes that grew greener as the solution to a crime drew near.

        2. He wore a black coat, pin-striped pants, a bow tie, shiny black boots, and, usually, a coat and muffler.

Here is the paragraph as it appeared in the essay:

Hercule's unique personality and character set him apart from other fictional detectives. One of the memorable features of his personality and character was his physical appearance. He was "a diminutive five foot four inches tall and slender."[7] His hair was an "unrepentant" black, neatly groomed with hair tonic. His upper lip displayed his pride and joy and his more distinctive feature, a small black handlebar mustache.[8] He had catlike eyes that grew greener as the solution to a crime drew near and a head the

```
shape of an egg.  Thus Poirot has been referred to as a ''mus-
tachioed Humpty Dumpty.''[9]  This ''extraordinary looking little
man, who carried himself with immense dignity,'' almost always
wore the same outfit, consisting of a black jacket, striped pants,
a bow tie, and, in all but the hottest weather, an overcoat and
muffler.  He also wore patent leather boots that almost always
displayed a dazzling shine.[10]
```

Notice the close correspondence between the outline and the final paragraph. First, the main entry of the outline is exactly the same as the topic sentence of the paragraph. Second, subidea A is fleshed out and used in the paragraph to introduce the details that follow. Third, the details in the outline are used nearly word-for-word in the paragraph. Naturally, there is more material in the paragraph than in the outline, which is not surprising, since the second is a short-hand version of the first.

If you are going to be following an outline as you write, this is the kind that is especially useful. Once drafted, it becomes a condensed version of the essay. Any paragraph is easy to write when you know exactly what its main point must be and what details it should contain. That and more is provided by the detailed sentence outline.

6

Transforming the Notes into a Rough Draft

6a Preparing to write the rough draft: a checklist

6b Incorporating note-taking into the flow of the paper

6c Writing the paper with unity, coherence, and emphasis

6d Using the proper tense

6e Aiming for a readable style

6f Writing the abstract

6a

Preparing to write the rough draft: a checklist

The following is a practical checklist of things you should do before beginning to write the rough draft:

- You should formulate a thesis. The research paper is the sort of writing that requires considerable premeditation from a writer. Information sifted from the sources and assembled on the note cards has to be carefully grafted into the main body of the paper. Arguments have to be thought out in advance and checked against the opinions of experts. In sum, no matter how spontaneous a writer you may be, you should nevertheless have a definite thesis in mind before you begin to write the rough draft.

- You should go over the note cards, picking out those cards relevant to the thesis, and setting aside all others. Bear in mind, moreover, that you are very likely to have more notes than you can use. To attempt to cram every single note into the paper is to be misled by an impulse that has ruined thousands of papers. You must exercise selectivity over the note cards, based upon the wording of the thesis, or the paper will end up an incoherent muddle of unrelated notes.

- You should arrange and rearrange the cards until they are organized in the order in which they will be used. This order should be dictated by the wording of the thesis, and the nature of the information entered on the individual cards.

- You should sketch an outline or abstract of the paper, breaking down the thesis into an ordered listing of topics. This is the stage at which you should experiment with different approaches to your research subject. Juggle the topics until they are arranged in the most logical and emphatic order. If necessary, rephrase the thesis until it generates a more definite structure for the paper.

Once you have formulated the thesis, sorted the cards in their proper sequence, and drafted the outline or abstract, you are ready to begin writing the rough draft. Word from the outline and note cards. Triple space the rough draft to allow room for penciling in afterthoughts or corrections. Use a separate sheet for each paragraph so that additional ideas, words, or phrases that occur to you can be tacked on to the paragraphs without creating an unreadable jumble. Keep a dictionary and thesaurus handy, using the first to avoid misspelled or incorrect words, and the second to insure word precision and variety, even in your first draft.

6b

Incorporating note-taking into the flow of the paper

The notes you have taken must be blended smoothly into the natural flow of the paper—this is the prime rule for writing the rough draft. Documentation should add clarity, not clutter. Paraphrases, summaries, indirect quotations, and allusions must be edited for smoothness. Quotations, of course, have to be used verbatim, and must not be tampered with. Transitions between ideas should be made logically and smoothly. The paper should not seem a cut-and-paste hodgepodge bristling with numerous unrelated quotations. In sum, you must observe the rhetorical principles of unity, coherence, and emphasis (see Section 6c).

6b-1 Using summaries and paraphrases

The sources of summaries and paraphrases must be given within the text or in parentheses. Below is an example of a paraphrase used without mention of its source in the text:

> When the court life of Russia died out at the imperial palace of Tsarskoe Selo, all kinds of political salons suddenly made their appearance in various sections of St. Petersburg. While these new salons became the breeding ground for the same kinds of intrigues, plots, counterplots, and rivalries that had taken place at the imperial palace, somehow their activities seemed dwarfed and their politics lacked the grandeur and dazzle that had accompanied the political style at the palace (Fülöp-Miller 101).

In this case, parenthetical documentation of the paraphrase is sufficient. However, the writer who wishes to state a paraphrase more emphatically, or to throw the weight of an expert or authority behind the summary, should mention the source in the text, as in the following example:

> As Hugh Seton-Watson points out in the preface to his book on the Russian empire, most people tend to forget that the Russian empire was multinational and therefore peopled with many non-Russian citizens, most important of which were the Polish (ix).

The summary here is more emphatic because it is coupled with the name of the authority whose work is being summarized.

Sometimes students are so dazzled by the writing style of a source that they unwittingly adopt its flavor and language in their summaries; the result is a discordant mixture of styles within a single paragraph. Here is an example:

> The hull of the Titanic was traversed by watertight bulkheads, capable of withstanding enormous pressure. The engineering notion was that if the ship sprang a leak, water would seep into individual compartments and be harmlessly trapped. At worse, the liner would list, and her passengers be slightly uncomfortable as she limped her way back to port. Metallurgical fabrication techniques employed in the construction and deployment of each bulkhead were consonant with the best engineering and metallurgical knowledge extant at the time of the Titanic's construction. In short, the Titanic, though considered "unsinkable," was neither better nor worse built than any of her other sisters then at sea.

The underscored sentence is a summary of information found in a book on marine engineering. Notice how stylistically different the summary seems from the rest of the paragraph. Having pored over the book, the student then unconsciously mimicked its wooden flavor when writing the summary. Before using it, she should have edited the summary to blend it in with the style of the paragraph. Here is an improved version:

> The hull of the Titanic was traversed by watertight bulkheads, capable of withstanding enormous pressure. The engineering notion was that if the ship sprang a leak, water would seep into individual compartments and be harmlessly trapped. At worse, the liner would list, and her passengers be slightly uncomfortable as she limped her way back to port. These bulkheads were built according to the best metallurgical techniques known at the time of

> the Titanic's construction. In short, the Titanic, though considered ''unsinkable,'' was neither better nor worse built than any of her other sisters then at sea.

6b-2 Using direct quotations

Quotations must be reproduced in the exact phrasing, spelling, capitalization, and punctuation of the original. Staple or paste the quotation note card to the rough draft rather than copy the quotation. Later, when you write the final draft, you will have to transcribe the quotation from the note card onto the paper. By stapling the note card to the rough draft, you avoid having to transcribe quotations twice, thus reducing the chance of error.

Any modification made in a quotation—no matter how minor—must be indicated either in a note placed in square brackets within the quotation, or in parentheses at the end of the quotation.

> Milton was advocating freedom of speech when he said, ''Give me the liberty to know, to think, to believe, and to utter freely [emphasis added] according to conscience, above all other liberties'' (120).

Quotations must fit logically into the syntax of surrounding sentences, so as not to produce an illogical or mixed construction. The following quotation is poorly integrated:

> Chung-Tzu describes a sage as ''suppose there is one who insists on morality in all things, and who places love of truth above all other values'' (58).

Here is the same quotation properly integrated into the sentence:

> Chung-Tzu describes a sage as ''one who insists on morality in all things, and who places love of truth above all other values'' (58).

Here is another example of a badly integrated quotation:

> The poet showed his belief in self-criticism by writing that ''I am a man driven to scold myself over every trivial error'' (15).

Here is the quotation properly handled:

> The poet showed his belief in self-criticism when he wrote this about himself: ''I am a man driven to scold myself over every trivial error'' (15).

a. Overuse of quotations

No passage in the paper should consist of an interminable string of quotations. A mixture of summaries, paraphrases, and quotations is smoother and easier to read; moreover, such a mixture gives the impression that students have done more than patch together bits and pieces from books and articles they have read. Here is an example of a paragraph littered with too many quotations:

> According to McCullough, ''the groundswell of public opinion against the Japanese started in the early 1900s'' (191). This is when the United States Industrial Commission issued a report stating that the Japanese ''are more servile than the Chinese, but less obedient and far less desirable'' (Conrat 18). At about the same time, the slogan of politician and labor leader Dennis Kearney was ''the Japs must go!'' (10). The mayor of San Francisco wrote that ''the Japanese cannot be taken into the American culture because they are not the stuff of which American citizens are made'' (Daniels 9–10). In 1905, writes McCullough, ''the Japanese and Korean Expulsion League held its first meeting and spawned many other such similar organizations'' (102).

Here is an improved version, which deftly turns many of the quotations into summaries and paraphrases, resulting in a cleaner, less cluttered paragraph:

> The anti-Japanese movement in America goes back to the turn of the century, when the United States Industrial Commission claimed that the Japanese ''are more servile than the Chinese, but less obedient and far less desirable'' (Conrat 18). At about the same time, the slogan of politician and labor leader Dennis Kearney was ''The Japs must go!'' while the mayor of San Francisco insisted that it was impossible for the Japanese to assimilate into American culture and that they were ''not the stuff of which American citizens are made'' (Daniels 9-10). In this xenophobic atmosphere, the Japanese and Korean Expulsion League was formed in 1905 and a number of other anti-Japanese societies followed (McCullough 102).

Notice, by the way, that the improved version contains fewer references than the original. In the first version, the student was forced to document every quotation, even though successive quotations sometimes came from the same source. The blend of summaries, paraphrases, and quotations not only reduced clutter, but also cut down on the number of notes by combining references from the same source into a single sentence and under a single note.

b. Using brief quotations

Brief quotations (four lines or less) may be introduced with a simple phrase:

> Betty Friedan <u>admits</u> that it will be quite a while before women know ''how much of the difference between women and men is culturally determined and how much of it is real.''

''God is the perfect poet,'' said Browning in ''Paracelsus.''

Hardin Craig suggests that ''in order fully to understand and appreciate Shakespeare, it is necessary to see him as a whole.''

In Shakespeare's Antony and Cleopatra, Cleopatra prefers ''a ditch in Egypt'' as her grave to being hoisted up and shown to the "shouting varletry of censuring Rome."

According to David Halberstam, when McNamara began to take over the Vietnam problem, ''there was a growing split between the civilians and the military over the assessment of Vietnam.''

In contrast to Eichmann's concept of justice, Thoreau believed that ''a true patriot would resist a tyrannical majority.''

Note that if the quotation is grammatically part of the sentence in which it occurs, the first word of the quotation does not need to be capitalized, even if it is capitalized in the original.

Original quotation "Some infinitives deserve to be split."

Bruce Thompson

Quotation used as part of a sentence Bruce Thompson affirms what writers have always suspected, namely that ''some infinitives deserve to be split.''

Moreover, if the quotation is used at the end of a declarative sentence, it will be followed by a period whether or not a period is used in the original.

Original quotation "Love is a smoke rais'd with the fume of sighs; . . ."

Shakespeare

Quotation used in a declarative sentence In Act I Romeo describes love as ''a smoke rais'd with the fume of sighs.''

Finally, you should strive for variety in the introduction of quotations, rather than ploddingly serving them up with the same words and phrases. If you introduce one quotation with, "So-and-so says," try something different for the next, such as, "In the opinion of at least one critic," or "A view widely shared by many in the field affirms that," and so on.

c. *Using long quotations*

Unlike quotations of four lines or less, longer quotations need to be introduced by a formal sentence, placed in context, and properly explained. Moreover, long quotations must be set off from the text by triple spacing, indented ten spaces from the left margin, and typed with double spacing but without quotation marks (unless the quotation itself contains quotation marks). If two or more paragraphs are quoted, then the sentence beginning each paragraph should be indented three spaces. Each long quotation should be preceded by a colon. (See Figure 6-1, p. 78.) If the quotation consists of only a single paragraph, or if the opening sentence of the quotation is not the start of a paragraph, then the first line of the quotation need not be indented three spaces:

In his novel Lady Chatterley's Lover, D. H. Lawrence creates a mesmeric and ritualistic effect as he describes the love scene between Mellors and Connie:

> But he drew away at last, and kissed her and covered her over, and began to cover himself. She lay looking up to the boughs of the tree, unable as yet to move. He stood and fastened up his breeches, looking round. All was dense and silent, save for the awed dog that lay with its paws against its nose. He sat down again on the brushwood and took Connie's hand in silence. (150)

Lawrence has created a trancelike mood that conveys the symbolic importance of this scene.

Figure 6-1 A long quotation of two paragraphs

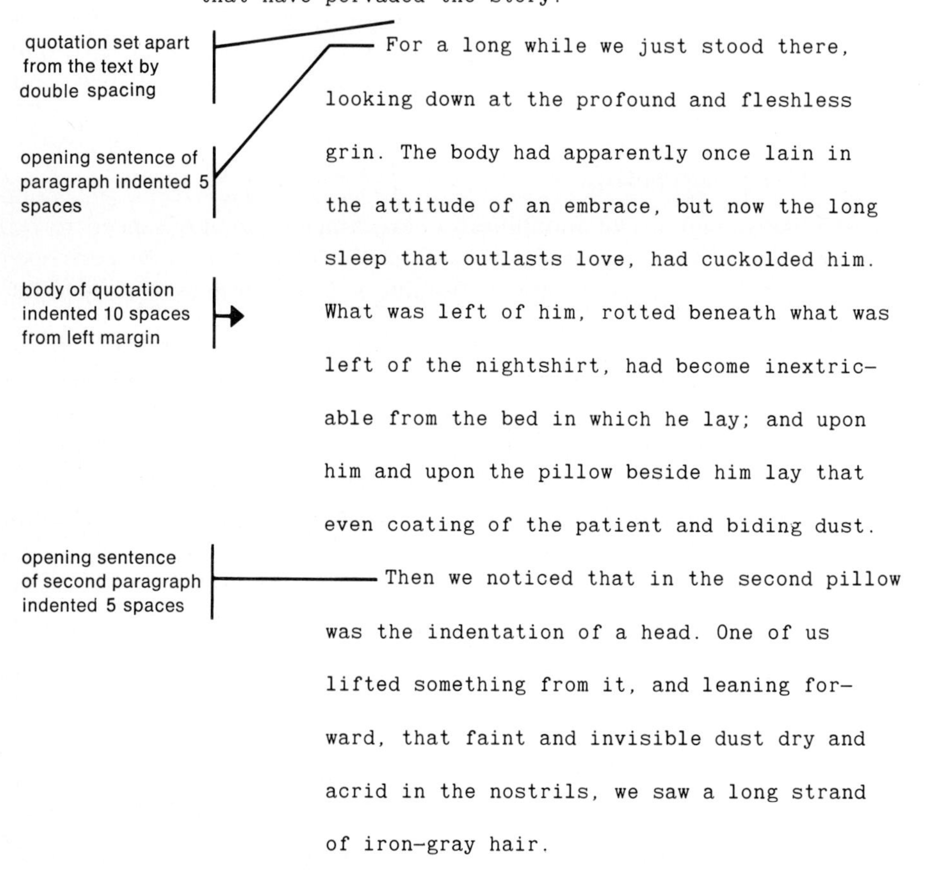

Notice how the author has provided a context for the quotation by alluding to it as "mesmeric and ritualistic"; how she has provided a formal introduction; and how, following the quotation, she has provided an explanation of why the quotation was presented.

d. Using quotations from poetry

Unless the stanzaic line needs to be preserved for stylistic emphasis, short passages of verse should be enclosed by quotation marks and incorporated into the text. Quotations of two or three lines may also be part of the text, but with the lines separated by a slash (/) with a space on each side of the slash:

> The line ''I have been half in love with easeful Death'' expresses a recurrent theme in Keats's poetry--the desire for permanent residence in a world free from pain and anguish.

> ''The raven's croak, the low wind choked and drear, / The baffled stream, the gray wolf's doleful cry'' are typical Romantic images used by William Morris to create a mood of idle despair.

Verse quotations that exceed three lines should be separated from the text by triple spacing, indented ten spaces from the left margin (or less, if the line is so long that it would cause the page to look unbalanced), double-spaced without quotation marks (unless the poem itself contains quotation marks), and introduced with a colon. The spatial arrangement of the original poem (indentation and spacing within and between lines) should be reproduced with accuracy:

> In the following lines from ''You Ask Me Why, Tho' Ill at Ease,'' Tennyson expresses the poet's desire for freedom to speak out:
>
> It is the land that freemen till,
>   That sober-suited Freedom chose,
>   The land, where girt with friends or foes
> A man may speak the thing he will.

The quotation beginning in the middle of a line of verse should be reproduced exactly that way and not shifted to the left margin:

> As Cordelia leaves her home, exiled by Lear's folly, she reveals full insight into her sisters' evil characters:
>
>   I know you what you are;
> And like a sister am most loath to call

Your faults as they are nam'd. Love well our father:
To your professed bosoms I commit him:
But yet, alas, stood I within his grace,
I would prefer him to a better place. (Lr. 1.1.272–77)

e. Using a quotation within another quotation

Use single quotation marks to enclose a quotation within another brief quotation:

Rollo May is further exploring the daimonic personality when he states that ''in his essays, Yeats goes so far as to specifically define the daimonic as the 'Other Will.'''

For quotations within long, indented quotations, use double quotation marks:

In his essay ''Disease As a Way of Life,'' Eric J. Cassell makes the following observation:

> As the term ''diarrhea–pneumonia complex'' suggests, infants in the Navajo environment commonly suffered or died from a combination of respiratory and intestinal complaints that are not caused by any single bacterium or virus.

f. Punctuating quotations

The rules for punctuating quotations are few and simple:

- Place commas and periods inside the quotation marks:

''Three times today,'' Lord Hastings declares in Act 3, ''my foot-cloth horse did stumble, and started, when he look'd upon the Tower, as loath to bear me to the slaughter-house.''

- Place colons and semicolons outside the quotation marks:

```
Brutus reassures Portia, ''You are my true and honourable wife, as
dear to me as are the ruddy drops that visit my sad heart''; conse-
quently, she insists that he reveal his secrets to her.
```

- Place question marks and exclamation marks inside the quotation marks if they are part of the quotation, but outside if they are not:

```
King Henry asks, ''What rein can hold licentious wickedness when
down the hill he holds his fierce career?''
```

But:

```
Which Shakespearean character said, ''Fortune is painted blind,
with a muffler afore her eyes''?
```

g. Interpolations in quoted material

Personal comments or explanations within a quotation must be placed in square brackets (not parentheses), which may be handwritten if no such key exists on your typewriter. The word "sic" within square brackets means that the quotation—including any errors—has been exactly copied.

```
The critical review was entitled ''A Cassual [sic] Analysis of
Incest and Other Passions.''
```

The "sic" indicates that "cassual" is reproduced exactly as it is spelled in the quotation.

Here is an explanatory interpolation, also set off in square brackets:

```
Desdemona answers Emilia with childlike innocence: ''Beshrew me if
I would do such a wrong [cuckold her husband] for all the whole
world.''
```

h. The ellipsis

The ellipsis—three dots (. . .) with a space before and after each dot—is used to indicate the omission of material from a quotation. Such omissions are necessary when only a part of the quotation is relevant to the point you are making. Use of the ellipsis, however, does not free a researcher from an obligation of remaining faithful to the intent of the author's original text. The following example illustrates the misuse of the ellipsis to distort an author's meaning:

Original Faulkner's novels have the quality of being lived, absorbed, remembered rather than merely observed.

Malcolm Cowley

Quotation Malcolm Cowley further suggests that ''Faulkner's novels have the quality of being . . . merely observed.''

If you are quoting no more than a fragment and it is clear that something has been left out, no ellipsis is necessary:

Malcolm Cowley refers to Faulkner's ''mythical kingdom.''

But when it is not clear that an omission has been made, the ellipsis must be used.

- *Omissions within a sentence* are indicated by three spaced dots:

Original Mammals were in existence as early as the latest Triassic, 190 million years ago, yet for the first one hundred and twenty million years of their history, from the end of the Triassic to the late Cretaceous, they were a suppressed race, unable throughout that span of time to produce any carnivore larger than cat-size or herbivore larger than rat-size.

Adrian Desmond

Quotation Adrian Desmond, arguing that the dinosaurs were once dominant over mammals, points out that ''mammals were in existence as early as the latest Triassic . . . yet for the first one hundred and twenty million years of their history . . . they were a suppressed race, unable to produce any carnivore larger than cat-size or herbivore larger than rat-size.''

Two omissions are made in the quotation, and both indicated by an ellipsis of three spaced dots.

- *Omissions at the end of a sentence* use a period followed by three spaced dots:

```
Adrian Desmond, arguing that the dinosaurs were once dominant over
mammals, points out that the mammals were, for millions of years,
''a suppressed race, unable throughout that span of time to pro-
duce any carnivore larger than cat-size. . . .''
```

Notice that the first dot is a period, and is placed immediately after the last word without an intervening space.

If the ellipsis is followed by parenthetical material at the end of a sentence, use three spaced dots and place the sentence period after the final parenthesis:

```
Another justice made the following, more restrictive, statement:
''You have the right to disagree with those in authority . . . but
you have no right to break the law . . .'' (Martin 42).
```

- *Omissions of a sentence or more* are also indicated by four dots, but with this proviso: that a complete sentence must both precede and follow the four dots. Here is an example:

Original *Manuscript Troana* and other documents of the Mayas describe a cosmic catastrophe during which the ocean fell on the continent, and a terrible hurricane swept the earth. The hurricane broke up and carried away all towns and forests. Exploding volcanoes, tides sweeping over mountains, and impetuous winds threatened to annihilate humankind, and actually did annihilate many species of animals. The face of the earth changed, mountains collapsed, other mountains grew and rose over the onrushing cataract of water driven from oceanic spaces, numberless rivers lost their beds, and a wild tornado moved through the debris descending from the sky.

Immanuel Velikovsky

Unacceptable use of four dots to mark an omission

```
That species of animals may have been made extinct by
some worldwide catastrophe is not unthinkable. Im-
```

> manuel Velikovsky states that according to ''Manuscript Troana and other documents. . . . The face of the earth changed, mountains collapsed, other mountains grew and rose over the onrushing cataract of water driven from oceanic spaces, numberless rivers lost their beds, and a wild tornado moved through the debris. . . .''

The quotation is unacceptably reproduced because the fragment "*Manuscript Troana* and other documents," rather than an entire sentence, is placed before the four dots. Here is an acceptable use of this material:

> That species of animals may have been made extinct by some worldwide catastrophe is not unthinkable. Immanuel Velikovsky states that ''Manuscript Troana and other documents of the Mayas describe a cosmic catastrophe. . . . The face of the earth changed, mountains collapsed, other mountains grew and rose over the onrushing cataract of water driven from oceanic spaces, numberless rivers lost their beds, and a wild tornado moved through the debris. . . .''

Complete sentences are reproduced before and after the four periods, which satisfies the convention.

- *Omissions of long passages*, such as several stanzas, paragraphs, or pages, are marked by a single typed line of spaced dots:

> Speaking through the prophet Amos, the God of the Israelites warns sternly:
>
> For you alone have I cared
> among all the nations of the world;

```
therefore will I punish you
for all your iniquities.
. . . . . . . . . .
An enemy shall surround the land;
your stronghold shall be thrown down
and your palaces sacked.
```

- *Omissions that immediately follow an introductory statement* require no ellipsis:

Acceptable In Booth's fantastic mind, his act was to be ''the perfect crime of the ages and he the most heroic assassin of all times.''

Unacceptable In Booth's fantasic mind, his act was to be ''. . . the perfect crime of the ages and he the most heroic assassin of all times.''

Although an omission has been made in the beginning of the quotation, the use of an ellipsis following the introductory remark is unnecessary.

6b-3 Using indirect quotations

There are times when you will want to quote an author indirectly. An indirect quotation reports what someone said or wrote but not in the exact words of the original passage. Indirect quotations should not appear in quotation marks. Study the following examples:

Direct quotation J. K. Galbraith makes the following statement: ''In the Affluent Society no useful distinction can be made between luxuries and necessaries.''

Indirect quotation J. K. Galbraith suggests that in an affluent society rich people don't make any useful distinction between luxuries and necessities.

Direct quotation After defining the qasida as a ''pre-Islamic ode,'' Katharine Slater Gittes comments: ''These wholly secular odes glorify the Bedouin life, the life of the wanderer.''

Indirect quotation According to Katharine Slater Gittes, the main purpose of the qasida, a pre-Islamic ode, is to glorify the life of the Bedouin wanderer.

The purpose of using indirect quotations is to avoid a choppy style that evolves when one uses a string of direct quotations. Indirect quotations maintain the continuity of the writer's own style, giving the text a smoother flow.

NOTE: Whether using a short, long, or indirect quotation, be sure to avoid vague pronoun references in your introductory phrasing:

Poor In one article it stated, ''Numerous victims. . . .''

Better In his article ''Anorexia Nervosa,'' Petersen states, ''Numerous victims. . . .''

Poor In the introduction they point out that the vote was 59 to 38 against the bill.

Better The Introduction points out that the vote was 59 to 38 against the bill.

6b-4 How to place and punctuate the page reference parentheses

This section applies only if your paper is documented in the parenthetical style used by the Modern Language Association (MLA) and the American Psychological Association (APA) (see Sections 7d and 7e).

a. Short quotations

When using a quotation of one sentence or less in your running text, place the page reference parentheses *after* the closing quotation mark but *before* the end punctuation, thus including the parentheses within your own sentence:

> Noyes, for example, insisted that ''there is a language in the Canticles which I could not apply to the Supreme Being . . . without feeling guilty of blasphemy'' (125).

b. Long quotations

When using a *long, indented quotation*, omit quotation marks and place the page reference parentheses *after* the final period with no period following the parentheses:

> Gail Sheehy characterizes certain successful males as wunderkinder:
>
> > The wunderkind often seems to possess a boundless capacity to bounce back from career failures. Business losses, power struggles, lost elections, even criminal charges are viewed as temporary setbacks; they merely stiffen his resolve to come out a winner. (191)

c. Quotations ending in an ellipsis

If the quotation (long or short) ends in an ellipsis, place the final period after the parentheses (see Section 6b-3*h*).

6b-5 Using personal comments

Students are expected to do more in a research paper than simply preside over the opinions of their sources. Naturally, the bulk of the paper will consist of material accumulated in research. But without the interpretation of the student, none of this material is likely to make any sense to a reader. A prime function of the personal comment, therefore, is to supply the reader with information otherwise unobtainable from the stark research data. Personal comments serve to interpret material, mark transitions from one idea to another, and draw conclusions. In a manner of speaking, the thesis statement can also be regarded as an elaborate personal comment in which the student enunciates a general design and focus for the entire paper.

The example below illustrates the use of the personal comment to interpret material. The student's paper is on the career of Pope Innocent III; the discussion in the preceding paragraph centered on a crusade that Innocent III had just called for. Interjecting a personal comment, the student interprets the motive of Innocent III in launching this crusade:

> Innocent III's call for this crusade shows that he was trying to establish that the Papacy was the temporal authority on earth. As the head of Christendom, he couldn't tolerate any philosophy that would divert attention away from the teaching of the Catholic church.

Personal comments are also used to establish smooth transitions as the discussion moves from one idea to another. Here is an example, taken from this same student paper. The preceding paragraph summarized the reaction of Innocent III to the heresy of the Cathars.

> The heresy of the Cathars was not the only anti-Catholic philosophy that Innocent III endeavored to crush. He desired to crush the heresy of the Moslems as well.

The paper then moves on to a discussion of the efforts of Pope Innocent III to crush the Moslems.

Finally, the personal comment is widely used to make summations and draw conclusions. The paper on Innocent III ends with this summation of the Pontiff's career:

> Innocent III's pontificate was the zenith of the medieval papacy. He involved himself in world affairs by endeavoring to stop heresy and by exerting his authority over kings. He crushed the Cathar heresy and brought the Greek church under his control. He used

the kings of Europe like pawns on a chessboard. Therefore one can conclude that Innocent III made the theory of papal theocracy into a reality.

6c

Writing the paper with unity, coherence, and emphasis

6c-1 Unity

The rhetorical principle of unity dictates that a paper should stick to its chosen thesis without rambling or digressing. If the thesis states that Japanese art influenced French Impressionism, the paper should cover exactly that subject and nothing more. If the thesis proposes to contrast the life styles of inner city residents and suburban dwellers, the paper should concisely pursue such a contrast, ignoring all side issues, no matter how personally fascinating to the writer.

To observe the principle of unity, a writer has merely to follow the lead of the thesis. Properly drafted, the thesis will predict the content of a paper, control its direction, and obligate the writer to a single purpose. The writer introduces only material relevant to the thesis, suppressing the urge to dabble in side issues or to stray from the point. Such admirable single-mindedness will produce a paper written according to the principle of unity, and consequently easier for a reader to follow.

The principle of unity should govern the progression of ideas within an individual paragraph as well as throughout the entire structure of an essay. Paragraphs should be written to scrupulously deliver exactly what the topic sentence promises, for the content of a paragraph is controlled by its topic sentence much as the structure and direction of an essay are determined by its thesis.

6c-2 Coherence

If unity means sticking to the point, coherence means "sticking together." A paragraph is said to be coherent if its sentences stick together in some obvious logical pattern that readers can follow. When writing is incoherent, on the other hand, a reader will have trouble following what a writer means and what the paragraph really says. Consider the following example:

In the past year it's been through times of extreme highs and lows in my emotional outlook on life. The trend of any life seems to follow this general pattern. Some of the high moments were meeting new people that turned out to be much more than mere acquaintances, having the newly-met person turn into a friend a person could know for the rest of one's life. Competing in sports and in the area of track and field and baseball was exhilarating. Meeting and going out with a few girls, which in our relationship between each other bloomed into a special kind of affection for ourselves.

This paragraph is incoherent because its sentences are devoted to separate and unrelated ideas instead of sticking together in some common overall purpose. To avoid incoherent writing, you must think of the paragraph as a single unit of expression to which individual sentences contribute increments of meaning. Here are four suggestions to help you achieve paragraph coherence:

- *Be precise about word reference.* Either repeat key words or make certain that the pronouns you use clearly hark back to them. In the passage that follows, notice how the key word *villain* is either repeated or replaced by a pronoun clearly referring to it:

The villain in science fiction movies is always the personification of evil. One way this concentration of evil is achieved is by surrounding the villain with numerous henchmen. Without henchmen, the villain would appear much less powerful. To accentuate his villainy, he surrounds himself by ruthless storm troopers, evil robots, slime monsters, or whatever. With these associates by his side, the eventual triumph of the hero over the villain takes place against a backdrop of overwhelming odds.

Repetition of the word *villain*, and of the pronouns *he* or *his* that refer to *villain*, provides a common thread connecting all five sentences.

- *Use parallel structures.* Deliberate repetition of certain words, phrases, or clauses in a paragraph can also provide sentences with a cohering rhythm and harmony, as repetition of *can* and a verb does in the following example:

> Fleas of various species can jump 150 times their own length; can survive months without feeding; can accelerate 50 times faster than the space shuttle; can withstand enormous pressure; and can remain frozen for a year and then revive.

- *Use transitional markers.* Transitional markers are words or phrases used to assert the relationships between the sentences of a paragraph. Common among these markers are the conjunctions *and, or, not, but,* and *for.* But other, lengthier connectives are also used to ensure coherence. Consider the italicized words in this passage:

> The type A person is forever nervous and uptight about coming events--always desiring success, but fearing failure. Type A's feel perpetually insecure and vulnerable because they suspect that they are flawed. As an illustration, consider Howard Hughes, the brilliant entrepreneur. He started a highly feasible car industry, but shut it down overnight when he reasoned that he had failed since his automobile was not perfect. Such reasoning is typical of type A personalities, who often set themselves up for failure because their best efforts never seem good enough. In contrast to type A persons, type B's pride themselves on their optimism and relaxed attitude. Type B's are the kinds of people who may study hours for an exam and do poorly; yet, they will still feel good about themselves because they did all that was possible. For instance, Doug Moe, coach of the Denver Nuggets, outlasted the average basketball coach tenure because he did not place unrealistic demands on his players, who in turn responded by performing to their highest potential.

The underlined transitional markers add to the coherent and smooth development of the ideas in a paragraph. Here are some of the most common transitional markers and how they are used:

Adding: Furthermore, in addition, moreover, similarly, also

Opposing: However, though, nevertheless, on the other hand, unlike

Concluding: therefore, as a result, consequently

Exemplifying: for example, for instance, to illustrate, that is

Intensifying: In fact, indeed, even, as a matter of fact

Sequencing: first, second, finally, in conclusion, to sum up, in short

- *Avoid mixed constructions.* Mixed constructions are sentences that begin in one kind of grammatical pattern but lurch off unexpectedly into another. Here are some examples, followed by a corrected version:

Mixed Whereas he was poor growing up caused him to be bitter in middle age.

Improved Because he was poor growing up, he became bitter in middle age.

Mixed With every new service on the part of government suggests that our taxes are going to be raised.

Improved Every new service on the part of government suggests that our taxes are going to be raised.

Mixed Meeting and going out with a few girls, which in our relationship between each other bloomed into a special kind of affection for ourselves.

Improved Meeting a few girls and going out with them fostered relationships that bloomed into special affections between us.

6c-3 Emphasis

The rhetorical principle of emphasis requires the expression of more important ideas in main or independent clauses, and of less important ideas in dependent or subordinate clauses. In sum, properly emphatic writing will attempt to rank ideas through grammatical structure. Here is an example of an unemphatic piece of writing:

Poor emphasis

The gifted child is a high achiever on a specific test, either the Otis or Binet I.Q. test. These tests are usually administered at the end of the second grade. They determine the placement of the child in third grade. These tests are characterized by written as well as verbal questions, so that the child has the opportunity to express himself creatively.

The grammatical treatment of ideas is altogether too egalitarian. A reader simply cannot distinguish between the important and the unimportant ideas, because they are all expressed in a similar grammatical structure. Here is the same passage made emphatic:

Improved emphasis

A child is considered gifted if he has achieved a high score on a specific test such as the Otis or Binet I.Q. test. Characterized by written as well as verbal questions so that the child has the opportunity to express himself creatively, these tests are administered at the end of the second grade in order to determine the proper placement of the child in third grade.

By placing subordinate ideas in subordinate clauses, the writer achieves a purposeful focus missing from the unemphatic version.

6d

Using the proper tense

6d-1 Maintain the present tense except when reporting an event that happened in the past.

In the following passage, note the appropriate shift from past to present.

> In the 1950s there was among the medical profession a sudden enthusiasm for the surgical removal of infected lung tissue, and expensive plans were made to build new surgical wards in many hospitals. But when streptomycin came along, much of this surgery became unnecessary. Thus huge amounts of money had been wasted. The truth is that a much higher priority needs to be given to basic research in biologic science. This is the best way of saving health care expenses in the long run.

Beginning with the sentence "The truth is . . . ," the shift from past to present is smoothly accomplished.

6d-2 Keep your tense or mood consistent.

Wrong The wildlife of the beaches would be contaminated in the event of an oil spill. The sand and water becomes covered with oil sludge and residue.

Right The wildlife of the beaches would be contaminated in the event of an oil spill. The sand and water would become covered with oil sludge and residue.

The writer began the idea in the conditional and must complete it in that mood.

6d-3 Use the present tense for most comments by authorities because they usually continue to be true and in print.

Thomas Jefferson supports the idea of . . .

Gilbert Highet criticizes . . .

Milton and Shakespeare, like Homer, acknowledge the desire . . .

"Art rediscovers . . . what is necessary to humanness," declares John Gardner.

But use the past tense for actions or events completed in the past.

When Horace wrote the Ars Poetica, . . .

The nationwide founding of the Brewers Association was a factor contributing . . .

In the 17th century, Seventh-day Baptists were among the followers of Oliver Cromwell.

6e

Aiming for a readable style

A clear and readable style is of utmost importance in any writing, but especially so in English research papers where the focus is often on interpreting the ideas of different disciplines. At the least, you should strive for a research writing style that allows you to make your points with economy and directness. For an example of the kind of style to avoid, consider this paragraph from a research paper dealing with the problems faced by minorities attempting a college education:

What is matriculation? It is a plan. Moreover, it is a collaborative, personal, representational effort reflecting the best and highest quality of the talents, skills, abilities, and processes needed and required to effectively operate in the changes of education in our highly technical information age. Now, these efforts include affiliations, relationships, courtesy, and cooperation with an eye on the end product of achieving goals, objectives, and effective results to meet the changing needs in today's underrepresented student population at a time when the great ship of education is drifting on shifting waters.

The wrongs of this paragraph are many and varied. First, it is cluttered with repetitions or imprecise words that are either unnecessary or wholly unrelated. For example, in the third sentence "personal" is at odds with "collaborative" and "representative." "Affiliations," "relationships," and "cooperation" in the fourth sentence are all words that mean "working together"; "courtesy" does not belong among them. The fifth sentence lumps together "goals," "objectives," and "results" in tiresome repetition. "Best" and "highest" as well as "needed" and "required" are redundant. In addition to being glutted with unnecessary words, the paragraph ends lamely on a hopelessly mixed metaphor, "great ship of education is drifting on shifting waters." After reading the paragraph, we are left with the impression that the writer only dimly understands the meaning of "matriculation."

The cardinal principle for cultivating a good research paper writing style and avoiding a bad one comes neither from grammar nor rhetoric, but from common sense: know and understand the researched topic. If you are unclear about the meaning of your research, you cannot possibly explain it to a reader. For example, here is a revision of the above paragraph written after the student had returned to the library and finally mastered the concept of matriculation. Notice the directness and added vigor of the new style:

What is matriculation? It is the process of creating a working partnership between the university and the student for the purpose of identifying and achieving the student's educational goals. In this partnership, the university will provide the instructional and support services needed, and the student will make use of these services in pursuit of his or her goals.

The increased clarity of the second paragraph over the first is largely due to the writer's improved mastery of the subject. A good style cannot wholly compensate for a weak grasp of content. Nor can a strong grasp of content completely overcome the defects of a bad style. In a writing project as complex as the research paper, style and mastery of content contribute equally to a successful outcome. To help you master a blend of good style and solid content in your own paper, we offer the following practical suggestions:

6e-1 Understand your sources.

Reread all difficult passages until you completely understand them. Don't pretend an understanding you do not really have, and don't quote a passage whose meaning you have not fully grasped. Paraphrasing an author's ideas is a useful way of testing your understanding of them.

6e-2 Be scrupulously accurate.

Be scrupulously accurate in transcribing the information you gather from your sources. One student began a research paper in political science with this blunder: "Benjamin Franklin's 'Declaration of Independence' is a perfect causal analysis, stating exactly why a young nation rebelled and overthrew a colonial master it considered tyrannical." The confusion of Benjamin Franklin with Thomas Jefferson not only got this paper off to a bad start, but also cast doubt on its overall validity. Accuracy is especially important in the use of names, dates, and statistics. To write that China must feed 500 million when its population is really over 800 million is to commit an inaccuracy that cannot be overcome by stylistic elegance.

6e-3 Be precise.

If your assertions are not made with precision, the value of your paper will be inevitably lowered. Precision is essential in any discussion of technical material, mainly for the sake of your reader's understanding. Notice the difference in precision between the following two paragraphs, taken from the first and second draft of a student paper on the origin of Indian castes:

Imprecise The occupations of the four major castes were spelled out in the Laws of Manu: The Brahmin were the highest, the Kshatriyas came second, the Vaishyas followed, and the Sudras were at the bottom of the pile.

The vagueness of this passage resulted from the writer's false assumption that readers would be already familiar with the general divisions of Indian castes. When the instructor pointed out that more information was needed, the student produced this revision:

More precise The occupations of the four major castes were spelled out in the Laws of Manu: The Brahmin were to teach, interpret the Vedas (holy scriptures), and perform the required ritual sacrifices. The Kshatriyas were to be the warriors and social governors (even kings). The Vaishyas were to tend the livestock and to engage in commerce in order to create wealth for the country. As for the Sudras, they were to become the servants of the three higher castes--doing their bidding without malice or resentment.

This greater precision adds immeasurably to the writer's style, making it seem less superficial and empty.

6e-4 Be concise.

Conciseness means using the least number of words necessary for clarity. Indeed, conciseness generally adds to clarity by ridding explanations of jargon and verbiage. The goal of concise writing is to delete any word that does not add significantly to meaning.

Not concise In the early years of 1970 the National Aeronautics and Space Administration conducted an investigation to find funds from Congress for this new concept of a reusable space vehicle. The Administration decided that the establishment of a careful approach on its part was an important necessity since some members of Congress would doubtless show a strong opposition to the replacement of the expendable Saturn rockets that had carried the Apollo astronauts to the moon. There was tremendous precision and careful documentation in the preparation and submission of the request to Congress.

Concise In the early 1970s the National Aeronautics and Space Administration (NASA) decided to see if Congress would fund their new concept of a reusable space vehicle. The Administration approached the problem carefully because some Congressional members had already opposed replacing the expendable Saturn rockets that had carried the Apollo astronauts to the moon. A precise and well-documented request was submitted to Congress.

The fuzziness of the first version comes from main ideas being couched in verb nominalizations: "conducted an investigation of" instead of "to see"; "the establishment of a careful approach was a necessity" instead of "The Administration approached the problem carefully"; and "the replacement of" instead of "replacing." It is always cleaner and clearer to express the action of a sentence in a verb rather than in a noun or a noun preceded by a preposition.

Three other common sources of wordiness are the use of redundant expressions, meaningless words or phrases, and snobbish diction.

- *Redundant expressions* occur when unnecessary words are used to repeat what has already been said. Here is an example:

During that time period the park area was populated with Indians who were sultry in appearance and made a living by working with silver metal.

That "time" is a "period," "park" an "area," "sultry" an "appearance," and "silver" a "metal," is already clear from the context of the sentence. It is enough to write:

During that time the park was populated with Indians who looked sultry and made a living by working with silver.

- *Meaningless words and phrases*, used incessantly, add murkiness to one's style. Consider the italicized words in the following passage:

The problem of world hunger is by and large a matter of business and politics. Basically, the two become virtually entwined until for all intents and purposes they cannot be addressed separately in any given city or country.

Getting rid of the useless modifiers produces a clearer idea:

The problem of world hunger is a matter of business and politics. The two become entwined until they cannot be addressed separately in any city or country.

- *Snobbish diction* consists of words used not to clarify, but to impress. One writer submitted this purple patch:

A person desirous of an interview must be cognizant of the fact that the interviewer may have dozens of other candidates to evaluate. A smart candidate will endeavor to utilize the time wisely and will facilitate the interviewer in ascertaining the candidate's qualifications.

Replacing the italicized words with their more common equivalents results in a sharper and less pompous style:

A person wanting an interview must be aware that the interviewer may have dozens of other candidates to evaluate. A smart candidate will try to use the time wisely and will help the interviewer find out the candidate's qualifications.

Here are some snobbish words followed by their more down-to-earth, and usually clearer, synonyms:

Contingent upon	depend on
termination	end
deem	think
eventuate	happen
utilize	use
transpire	happen
envisage	see, foresee
prior to	before

6e-5 Use the active voice.

Because the passive voice is erroneously associated with objectivity and detachment, many writers are tempted to use it in their research papers. But one may be objective and detached without sounding either textbookish or stilted. Consider the following excerpt from a student paper on the Great Pyramid at Giza:

> Who built the Great Pyramid? When? How? Throughout history students of archaeology have been baffled by these questions. All sorts of mystical theories have been propounded by Egyptologists, but it has been concluded by most experts today that the Great Pyramid was built by Egyptian citizens using the simplest of tools and technology.

Notice the greater directness and vigor when the passage is recast in the active voice:

> Who built the Great Pyramid? When? How? Throughout history these questions have baffled students of archaeology. Egyptologists have propounded all sorts of mystical theories, but most experts today have concluded that the Great Pyramid was built by Egyptian citizens using the simplest of tools and technology.

There are only two exceptions that call for the passive voice: one, for an occasional change of pace—to add an inviting pleat in an otherwise seamless bolt of writing; two, for the sake of maintaining a certain focus, especially when the action is more important than the actor. An example of this second exception occurs in the last sentence of the excerpt. Since the Great Pyramid is the focus both of the research and the passage, it deserves the emphasis it receives from this passive construction. Compare the last passage, for example, with the following:

> Who built the Great Pyramid? When? How? Throughout history these questions have baffled students of archaeology. Egyptologists have propounded all sorts of mystical theories, but most experts today have concluded that Egyptian citizens using the simplest of tools and technology built the Great Pyramid.

Recasting the final sentence in the active voice removes the pyramid from center stage and replaces it with "Egyptian citizens." But the focus of the paragraph is on the Great Pyramid, not on "Egyptian citizens." The passive voice is therefore justified in this instance as the more emphatic choice.

6e-6 Take an objective stance.

Research papers consist mainly of information found in books, periodicals, and other sources on which the writer must occasionally pass personal judgments or offer clarification. In the past, most instructors insisted that students write such papers only from the third-person point of view, which was thought to stress the objectivity of the writer. Here are examples of the two points of view that are generally used:

First-person point of view In my research I found that the most extreme negative criticism of Jefferson Davis places the full weight of the Southern defeat on his head.

Third-person point of view Research indicates that the most extreme negative criticism of Jefferson Davis places the full weight of the Southern defeat on his head.

Lately, however, many prestigious journals have relaxed their rules. Authors are now allowed to use the "I" or "we" point of view when reporting research data or when drawing attention to their findings, as the following examples show:

> In this essay I do not assert that all Mexican-American houses display the traits that I describe.
>
> —Daniel D. Arreola, *Geographical Review*, July, 1988

> A complicating feature of marriage transactions in complex societies is that there may be variability by social status, wealth, region, or ethnic group. Where this problem has arisen in coding for this study, we selected the preferred form of the dominant stratum or ethnic group within the society.
>
> —Alice Schlegel and Rohn Eloul, *American Anthropologist*, June, 1988.

Should you ever use the first-person point of view ("I" or "we") in your research papers, and if so, when? If your instructor enforces an absolute ban on any but the objective third-person point of view, that, of course, is the rule you will have to follow. Otherwise, a safe rule of thumb is this: Use the first-person point of view only for expressing your own personal comments or judgments. Here are some examples:

```
    I have tested these assumptions on a body of data gathered
from three anthropologists.

    To produce a better fit with reality, I have made the fol-
lowing adjustments in my interpretations of the findings.

    Thus I theorized that. . . .

    My findings indicated the exact opposite.
```

Our advice to the beginning research writer is this: use the third-person point of view, but try not to sound stuffy.

6e-7 Avoid sexist language.

Over the last decades feminists have complained about elements in our language that reflect the values and biases of a male-dominated society. Publishers have reacted to this criticism by encouraging the use of sex-neutral generic pronouns and sex-neutral nouns in place of those that automatically, and perhaps even inaccurately, specify the male sex. We urge you to do likewise. For example, the statement "Every anthropologist involved in the dig agreed that his job was made easier . . ." can be easily replaced with "All anthropologists involved in the dig agreed that their jobs were made easier. . . ." If the subject cannot be made plural, identify the specific anthropologist by name: "In her fieldwork Margaret Meade found that she. . . ." Avoid the use of gender-biased words such as "mankind," "chairman," "congressman," "poetess," "woman surgeon," or "actress." These can be changed to inoffensive equivalents of "humankind," "chair," "member of congress," "poet," "surgeon," "actor." Certainly sexist language is entirely inappropriate in a research paper.

6f

Writing the abstract

An abstract, a summary of the major ideas contained in your research paper, is usually required for papers written in the natural or social sciences, but not in the humanities. While the abstract replaces an outline, we still suggest for the sake of logical progression and balance in the paper that you write an outline, even if you are not required to submit one.

In writing the abstract, use no more than one page. Center the title "Abstract" (without quotation marks) one inch from the top of the page. (Remember that the whole point of abstracting is to condense.) The page containing the abstract must follow the title page but precede the actual body of the paper. It should have a running head and page number. Writing the abstract in coherent paragraphs will be relatively easy if you have outlined your paper. To produce a smooth abstract you need only link and condense the main ideas of the outline with appropriate commentary. See the sample student paper abstract on pp. 244–45 for an example.

7

Systems of Documentation

7a When to provide documentation

7b Types of documentation

7c Guide to systems of documentation

7d Parenthetical documentation: author and work (MLA style)

7e Parenthetical documentation: author and date (APA style)

7f Parenthetical documentation: numbers

7g Traditional documentation: footnotes/endnotes

7h Content notes

7i Consolidation of references

7a

When to provide documentation

General knowledge, common sayings, self-evident opinions, and conclusions do not neet do be documented. The rule of thumb is simply this: if the idea, opinion, or conclusion is of the kind that any well-read person is likely to know, then no documentation is necessary. For instance, the assertion that the Nazi regime under Hitler committed atrocities against the Jews is common knowledge and therefore requires no documentation. However, if you quote from eyewitness accounts of these atrocities, acknowledgment must be given in either a footnote, an endnote, or in parentheses. In sum, any idea, conclusion, information, or data specifically derived from the work of someone else must be acknowledged. (See also Section 4g, pp. 46–49—Plagiarism: what it is and how to avoid it.)

7b

Types of documentation

Documentation is the process by which you give credit to the appropriate sources for every borrowed idea used in your paper. Borrowed ideas may be incorporated into the paper either as direct quotations, summaries, or paraphrases. But no matter what form you use to incorporate the idea of another into your paper, you must give appropriate credit in a specific and conventional style that allows a reader to trace your sources and, if necessary, to investigate their accuracy or applicability. (See also Section 4f-2, pp. 41–46.)

Two basic styles of documentation are now used in research: (1) note citations and (2) parenthetical citations. The older style, note citations, calls for footnotes or endnotes. This style is preferred by two major fields, the humanities (but *not* language and literature) and the fine arts (music, art, and dance). Footnotes and endnotes both require superscript numbers within the text and corresponding documentary notes either at the bottom of the page (footnotes) or at the end of the paper (endnotes). For example, a paper on Salvador Dali's religious paintings might include the following passage:

> One of Dali's most popular paintings, Christ of Saint John of the Cross, pictures the crucified Christ suspended over Iligat Bay, a port on the east coast of Spain. Christ is symbolized as the nucleus of the atom, that is, the unity of the universe.[3]

In the footnote style, the superscript *3* would have the following corresponding footnote at the bottom of the same page on which the superscript *3* appeared:

> [3] Salvador Dali, Dali, trans. Eleanor R. Morse (New York: Abrams, 1968) 33.

The endnote style requires the same reference note (only double-spaced within and between notes) in numerical order according to the superscripts, in a separate section entitled "Notes" at the end of the paper. (See p. 124.)

The note citation style also requires a separate bibliography at the end of the paper in which all sources used are listed alphabetically by the surnames of the authors or, in cases where there is no author, by the first significant word of the title of the work:

> Dali, Salvador. Dali. Trans. Eleanor R. Morse. New York: Abrams, 1970.

Each source will therefore be documented at least twice: in a footnote or endnote, and in a bibliography entry. Slight differences exist in the format of each kind of documentation—differences which must be observed. Footnotes or endnotes cannot simply be transferred to the bibliography page of the paper; nor can a bibliography entry serve as a note.

A second style of documentation, which uses parenthetical citations, now dominates in the sciences as well as in language and literature. Here references are placed not in endnotes or footnotes but in parentheses within the text itself. The parenthetical note refers the reader to a bibliography entry, which includes complete publication details on the source. Let us assume, for instance, that a paper on the history of passive resistance alludes to a work by Ralph Templin. In the new parenthetical documentation style, all of the important documenting information would appear in the text, with only a short reference in parentheses:

> As Ralph Templin notes (253), nonviolence does not simply ignore evil so that peace can be maintained.

or

> Nonviolence does not simply ignore evil so that peace can be maintained (Templin 253).

For the full Templin reference, the reader then consults the bibliography section at the end of the paper—labelled "Works Cited" or "Reference List." Simplicity is the main virtue of this new style. In the past, beleaguered students had to perform double labor in documenting their papers. First, they had to laboriously type out footnotes on the bottoms of their pages, often ruining otherwise good pages because they had miscounted the number of lines a note required. Next, they had to repeat the nearly identical information in a bibliography citation. The use of endnotes required the same double labor. But the new style calls for only one complete citation—the bibliography entry. Within the text itself the parenthetical reference consists of author and page (or, in the case of scientific papers, author and date). This text favors parenthetical documentation, and that is the style it explains in detail. However, for those students whose teachers still prefer the traditional note style, summary guidelines to it, with examples, are provided as well.

7c

Guide to systems of documentation

The following list can help you decide which type of documentation your paper requires. Disciplines are listed alphabetically within each group.

GUIDE TO SYSTEMS OF DOCUMENTATION

Author/Work (MLA) (See Section 7d.)	Language Literature	
Author/Year (APA) See Section 7e.)	Agriculture Anthropology Archaeology Astronomy Biology Botany Business Education	Geology Home Economics Linguistics Physical Education Political Science Psychology Sociology
Traditional (Footnote/Endnote) (See Section 7g.)	Art Dance History Music	Philosophy Religion Theater
Numbers (See Section 7f.)	Chemistry Computer Science Health	Mathematics Medicine Nursing

7d

Parenthetical documentation: author and work (MLA style)

College research papers in the field of language and literature have long followed the style laid down by the Modern Language Association (MLA). In 1983 the MLA announced its decision to change to the parenthetical style of documentation. Other changes in style proposed by the MLA are as follows:

- Use of Arabic numerals for everything except titles (*Henry IV*) or preliminary pages of a text traditionally numbered with Roman numerals (i, ii, iv, x, etc.).
- Omission of "p." or "pp." for page numbers.
- Omission of "l." or "ll." in favor or "line" or "lines" until lineation is established in the paper.
- A new form for journal entries, as follows:

    Sherry, James J. ''Tennyson and the Paradox of the Sign.'' Victo-
    rian Poetry 17 (1979): 204-16.

  Note the omission of the comma after the journal title, the changed order of entries, and the colon following the year to separate the volume and page.
- Changing the heading of the bibliography section to "Works Cited."

7d-1 Reference citations in the text

The new MLA style simplifies the reader's job by suggesting the following rules for in-text citations.

a. Introducing the authority

Introduce paraphrases or quotations by giving the authority's name. Use both the first name and the surname the first time the authority is used:

Robert M. Jordan suggests that Chaucer's tales are held together by seams that are similar to the exposed beams supporting a Gothic cathedral (237-38).

Subsequent citations will refer simply to the authority's surname:

Jordan further suggests:

b. Identifying the source

Whenever possible, identify what makes the source important:

Noam Flinker, Lecturer in English at the Ben-Gurion University of the Negev in Israel, an authority on Biblical literature, repeatedly suggests . . .

c. Documenting without mention of authority

When the authority is not mentioned in the introduction to a paraphrase or quotation, place in parentheses the authority's name, followed by a page reference:

Democracy is deemed preferable to monarchy because it protects the individual's rights rather than his property (Emerson 372).

d. Material by two authors

When referrring to material written by two authors, mention the names of both authors:

Christine E. Wharton and James S. Leonard take the position that the mythical figure of Amphion represents a triumph of the spiritual over the physical (163).

Subsequent references would refer simply to Wharton and Leonard.

e. Material by more than two authors

For a work with more than three authors or editors, use the first name followed by "et al." or "and others" (without a comma following the name):

G. B. Harrison et al. (Major British Writers) provide an excellent overview of the best in English literature.

f. Mentioning both author and work

When it can be accomplished smoothly, mention both the author and the work in your introduction:

> In his essay ''Criticism and Sociology,'' David Daiches insists that ''sociological criticism can help to increase literary perception as well as to explain origins'' (17).

g. Anonymous author

When a work is listed as anonymous, mention the fact that it is anonymous in the text and place the title of the work from which the piece was taken, or an abbreviated version if the title is very long, in parentheses:

> Another anonymous poem, "Driftwood" (Driftwood 130–31), also damns the city for its thoughtless pollution of the environment.

h. No author

When a work has no author, cite the first two or three significant words from the title:

> Spokane's The Spokesman Review (''Faulkner Dies'') gets at the heart of America's greatest fiction writer when it states that...

i. More than one work by the same author

When more than one work by the same author is referred to in the paper, provide a shortened version of the title in each citation. Citing only author and page may confuse the reader since "Works Cited" will contain two references to the same author. The following passage is an example of how to handle two works by the same author:

> Feodor Dostoevsky declares that the ''underground'' rebel is representative of our society (Underground 3). He seems to confirm this view in Raskolnikov's superman speech (Crime 383–84), where he identifies . . .

j. Work in a collection

When citing a work in a collection, state the name of the person who wrote the words to which you are referring:

Lionel Trilling's "Reality in America" does not consider V. L. Parrington a great intellect.

"Works Cited" would then contain the following entry:

Trilling, Lionel. "Reality in America." Twentieth Century American Writing. Ed. William T. Stafford. New York: Odyssey, 1965. 564–77.

k. Multivolume works

When referring to a specific passage in a multivolume work, give the author, the volume number followed by a colon and a space, and the page reference:

Other historians disagree (Durant 2: 25) . . . .

When referring to an entire volume, give the name of the author, followed by a comma, and the abbreviation "vol.," followed by the volume number: (Durant, vol. 2).

l. Double reference—a quotation within a cited work

As Bernard Baruch pointed out, "Mankind has always thought to substitute energy for reason" (qtd. in Ringer 274).

"Works Cited" would then contain the following entry:

Ringer, Robert J. Restoring the American Dream. New York: Harper, 1979.

m. Short passages of poetry

When short passages of poetry are incorporated into your text, observe these rules:

- Set off the quotation with quotation marks.
- Use a slash (with a space before and after the slash) to indicate separate lines of poetry.
- Place the proper documentation in parentheses immediately following the quotation and inside the period, because the reference is part of your basic sentence. The reference will be to the lines of the poem.

Study the following example:

> Byron's profound sense of alienation is echoed in Canto 3 of <u>Childe Harold's Pilgrimage</u>: ''I have not loved the World, nor the World me: / I have not flattered its rank breath, nor bowed / To its idolatries a patient knee'' (190–91).

n. Using Arabic numerals

Use Arabic numerals for books, parts, volumes, and chapters of works; for acts, scenes, and lines of plays; for cantos, stanzas, and lines of poetry.

IN-TEXT CITATIONS

Volume 2 of *Civilization Past and Present*
Book 3 of *Paradise Lost*
Part 2 of *Crime and Punishment*
Act 3 of *Hamlet*
Chapter 1 of *The Great Gatsby*

PARENTHETICAL DOCUMENTATION

(*Tmp.* 2.2.45-50)	for act 2, scene 2, lines 45-50 of Shakespeare's *Tempest* (See Section 10g-2*c* for abbreviating titles of Shakespeare's plays.)
(*GT* 2.1.3)	for part 2, chapter 1, page 3 of *Gulliver's Travels* by Swift
(*Jude* 15)	for page 15 of the novel *Jude the Obscure* by Hardy
(*PL* 7.5-10)	for book 7, lines 5-10 of *Paradise Lost* by Milton
(*FQ* 1.2.28.1-4)	for book 1, canto 2, stanza 28, lines 1-4 of *The Faerie Queene* by Spenser

7d-2 Varying your introductions

Use variety in your introductions to in-text citations. As you achieve fluency and sophistication in writing, you will find ways to introduce authors and their works smoothly and without boring repetitions. Some possibilities are listed here, but you can create many more:

Lionel Trilling, the noted critic and editor, has championed this idea (108).

In The Coming of Age, Simone de Beauvoir contends that the decrepitude accompanying old age is ''in complete conflict with the manly or womanly ideal cherished by the young and fully grown'' (25).

William York Tindall describes this segment as ''the densest part of the Wake'' (171).

This attitude is central to the archetypal approach of interpreting poetry (Fiedler 519).

Richard Chase argues that Billy Budd is a sort of Adam ''as yet untainted by the 'urbane serpent''' (745).

In his eloquent guidebook Style, F. L. Lucas points out that revision in writing is ''a means not only of polishing, but also of compressing'' (261).

Others, like Booth (51) and Warren (33), take the opposite point of view.

7e

Parenthetical documentation: author and date (APA style)

Established by the American Psychological Association (APA), this style is used by the social sciences, business, anthropology, and some of the life sciences (see Section 7c for a list of the disciplines using it). The APA style favors a system of parenthetical citations within the text much like the style now recommended by MLA. But there is a significant difference between the two. An in-text citation done in the APA style mentions only the author and date of the cited publication, not the author and work.

7e-1 Reference citations in the text

On the whole, scientific papers favor a parenthetical style of documentation that briefly identifies the source of a quotation or a piece of information so that the reader can find it in the alphabetical list of references at the end of the paper. Because in scientific research the date of publication is often crucial, APA emphasizes the date by placing it in parentheses following the name of the author. All notes are so treated except for content notes (see Section 7h). This system, like the new MLA system, simplifies the job of documentation by eliminating all reference notes at the bottom of the paper or at the end of the paper, requiring instead only a final "Reference List."

APA distinguishes between a *reference list*, which is a list of works specifically used in the research and preparation of your paper, and a *bibliography*, a list of works used for background reading or for further reading on the subject. A paper in the sciences, therefore, will end with a reference list, not with a bibliography.

a. One work by a single author

The APA style sheet requires an author-date method of citation; that is, the surname of the author and the year of publication are inserted in the text of the paper at the appropriate point:

```
Johnson (1983) discovered that children were more suscep-

tible. . . .
```

or

```
In a more recent study (Johnson, 1983), children were found to be

more susceptible. . . .
```

or

```
In 1983 Johnson did another study that indicated children were

more susceptible. . . .
```

If the name of the author appears as an integral part of your sentence, then cite only the year of publication in parentheses, as in the first example. Otherwise, show both the author and the date of publication in parentheses, as in the second example. If, however, both the year and the author are cited in the textual discussion, then nothing need appear within parentheses, as in the third example.

b. Subsequent references

If you continue to refer to the same study within a paragraph, subsequent references do not need to include the year as long as the study cannot be confused with other studies in your paper:

```
In a more recent study, Johnson (1983) found that children were
more susceptible. . . . Johnson also found that. . . .
```

c. One work by two or more authors

Scientific papers commonly reflect multiple authorship because so much of scientific research involves teamwork or cooperative studies.

When a work has two authors, always mention both names each time the reference occurs in your text:

```
In a previous study of caged rats (Grant & Change, 1958) the sur-
prising element was . . .
```

or

```
Much earlier, Grant and Change (1958) had discovered . . .
```

Notice that each time you refer to a work by two authors, you must name both authors.

d. One work by up to six authors

For works with up to six authors, mention all authors the first time the reference occurs; however, in subsequent citations, include only the surname of the first author followed by "et al." (not underlined and without a period after "et") and the year of publication:

First citation:

```
Holland, Holt, Levi, and Beckett (1983) indicate that . . .
```

Subsequent citation:

```
Holland et al. (1983) also found . . .
```

An exception occurs when two separate references have the same first author and same date and would thus shorten to the same reference. For example, Drake, Brighouse, and High (1983) and Drake, High, and Guilmette (1983) would both shorten to Drake et al. (1983). In such a case always cite both references in full to avoid confusion. Also, all multiple-author citations in footnotes, tables, and figures should include the surnames of all authors every time the citations occur.

e. Work by six or more authors

When a work has six or more authors, name only the surname of the first author followed by "et al." (not underlined and without a period after "et") and the year, in the first as well as in subsequent citations. In the final reference list, the names of all authors will appear in full. An exception occurs when two separate references would shorten to the same form. In such a case, list as many authors as are necessary to distinguish the two references, followed by "et al." For instance,

```
Cotton, Maloney, Brauer, Martin, Rodiles, and Tscharner (1970)
```

and

```
Cotton, Maloney, Jenkins, Martin, Rodiles, and Tscharner (1970)
```

would be cited as follows in the text:

```
Cotton, Maloney, Brauer, et al. (1970)
```

and

```
Cotton, Maloney, Jenkins, et al. (1970)
```

NOTE: In your running text, join the names of multiple-author citations by the word *and*; however, in parenthetical material, in tables, and in the final reference list, join the names by an ampersand (&), as follows:

```
Anderson and Raoul (1984) demonstrated clearly that . . .
```

but

```
As was clearly demonstrated earlier (Anderson & Raoul, 1984), cer-

tain factors remain . . .
```

f. Corporate authors

Sometimes a scientific work is authored by a committee, an institution, a corporation, or a governmental agency. The names of most such corporate authors should be spelled out each time they appear as a reference source in your text. Occasionally, however, the name is spelled out in the first citation only and is abbreviated in subsequent citations. The rule of thumb for abbreviating is that you must supply enough information in the text for the reader to track down this source in your final reference list. In the case of long and cumbersome corporate names, abbreviations are acceptable in subsequent citations as long as the name is recognized and understood.

First citation in the text:

```
(National Institutes of Mental Health [NIMH], 1984)
```

Subsequent citations:

```
(NIMN, 1984)
```

First citation in the text:

```
(Santa Barbara Museum of Natural History [SBMNH], 1984)
```

Subsequent citations:

```
(SBMNH, 1984)
```

If the name is short or its abbreviation would not be understood easily, spell out the name each time the reference occurs:

```
(Harvard University, 1984)

(Russell Sage Foundation, 1984)

(Bendix Corporation, 1984)
```

The point is that the names of all of these corporate authors are simple enough to be written out each time they are cited.

g. Works by an anonymous author or no author

When the author of a work is listed as "Anonymous," show the word "Anonymous" in parentheses in the text, followed by a comma and the date:

```
(Anonymous, 1984)
```

In your final reference list, the work will be alphabetized under "A" for "Anonymous."

When a work has no author, simply show, in parentheses, the first two or three words from the title of the book or article, followed by a comma and the year:

```
. . . as seen in most cases (''Time graphs,'' 1983)
```

```
The study shows that 55% of seniors (College bound seniors, 1979)

have serious difficulty with . . .
```

In the final reference list, works without authors are alphabetized according to the first significant word in the title. Articles (*the, a, an*), prepositions (*from, between, behind*, etc.), and pronouns (*this, those, that*, etc.) do not count. References to statutes and other legal materials are treated like references to works without authors; that is, you will cite the first few words of the reference and the year. Note that court cases cited in the text must be underlined.

```
(Baker v. Carr, 1962)

(National Environmental Protection Act, 1970)

(Civil Rights Act, 1964)
```

h. Authors with the same surname

If your paper includes two or more authors with the same surname, include the authors' initials in all text citations even if the date differs. In this way you will be sure to avoid confusion:

```
D. L. Spencer (1965) and F. G. Spencer (1983) studied both as-

pects of . . .
```

i. Two or more works within the same parentheses

Sometimes your paper may require that you cite within parentheses two or more works supporting the same point. In such a case, you will list the citations in the same order in which they appear in the reference list and according to reference list guidelines (see Section 8a-1). The following rules will be helpful:

- *Two or more works by the same author(s)* are arranged in the same order by year of publication. If a work is in press (in the process of being published) cite it last:

  Research of the past two years (Jessup & Quincy, 1983, 1984) has revealed many potential . . .

  or

  Past studies (Eberhard, 1980, 1981, in press) reveal . . .

  Different works by the same author that have the same publication date must be identified by "a," "b," "c," etc.:

  According to these studies (Rodney & Campbell, 1980a, 1980b, in press) the prevalent attitude is . . .

- *Two or more works by different authors* cited within the same parentheses should be listed alphabetically according to the first authors' surnames. Use semicolons to separate the studies:

  Three separate studies (Delaney & Rice, 1980; Rodney & Hollander, 1980; Zunz, 1981) tried to build on the same theory, but . . .

j. References to specific parts of a source

Anytime you refer to a specific quotation, figure, or table, you must supply the appropriate page, figure number, or table number:

(Spetch & Wilkie, 1983, pp. 15-25)

(Halpern, 1982, Fig. 2)

Note that the words *page* and *Figure* are abbreviated.

k. Personal communications

Personal communications include such items as letters, memos, and telephone conversations. Since they do not represent recoverable data, such items will not be reflected in your reference list. You will cite them in your text only. Give the initials and the surname of the communicator, and the date on which the communication took place:

```
(R. J. Melrose, personal communication, November 19, 1984)
```

or

```
R. J. Reiss (personal communication, November 19, 1984) provided
considerable insight on . . .
```

l. Citation as part of a parenthetical comment

When a citation appears as part of a parenthetical comment, use commas rather than brackets to set off the date:

```
(See also Appendix A of Jenkins, 1983, for additional proof)
```

7e-2 Minimizing awkward placement of references

Many scholars favor the APA system of documentation because it helps the reader identify authority and date immediately without looking to the bottom of the page or flipping to the end of the article. However, you should guard against having so many references on one page that they become intrusive and hamper readability. The following passage, for example, is cluttered with parenthetical information:

```
The protocol itself was faulty (Jacobson, 1950); thus the result-
ing research was also seriously flawed (Zimmerman, 1955; Masters,
1956; Lester, 1956), and millions of dollars in time and equipment
were wasted (Smith, 1957).
```

To avoid this kind of congestion, some references can be given in the text:

```
In 1950, Jacobson acknowledged that the original protocol was
faulty, so that when Zimmerman (1955), Masters (1956), and Lester
```

(1956) performed their experiments, these too were flawed. The consequent loss of thousands of dollars in time and equipment has been well documented (Smith, 1957).

A prudent mixture of parenthetical and in-text references is best when a page threatens to become gorged with research citations.

7f

Parenthetical documentation: numbers

We shall make only brief mention of the numbers system, used mainly in the applied sciences (chemistry, computer science, mathematics, and physics) and in the medical sciences (medicine, nursing, and general health). Simply stated, this system requires an in-text number in place of an author, work, or page reference. That number will be used each time the source is cited within the text and will also appear in front of the work listed in "Works Cited." Observe the following rules, when using number citations in your text:

- Place the citation enclosed within parentheses, immediately after the authority's name:

  Caffrey's (1) first description of child abuse included . . .

  An alternate style is to place the citation as an elevated numeral:

  Zimmerman et al.[4] found cerebral infarctions in 50% of the cases.

- If your running text does not use the authority's name, insert both the name and number within parentheses:

  Table 3 (Kaplan 4) displays the response distribution . . .

  Alternate style:

  Table 3 (Kaplan[4]) displays the response distribution . . .

- If necessary, add specific data to the entry:

```
The self-reported symptoms as analyzed by Wynder (3 Table 6) indi-
cate a significant increase . . .
```

(The reference is to Table 6 on page 3).

Alternate style:

```
The self-reported symptoms3. Table 6
```

- If you are citing more than one authority in your text, use the following format:

```
Other authors have confirmed Caffrey's observations concerning
the pathogenesis of the injuries (4-6).
```

Alternate style:

```
Other authors have confirmed Caffrey's observations concerning
the pathogenesis of the injuries.4-6
```

The reference is to three sources in "Works Cited": 4, 5, and 6.

7g

Traditional documentation: footnotes/endnotes

Notes serve two purposes in a research paper: (1) They acknowledge the source of a summary, paraphrase, or quotation; (2) they add explanatory comments that would otherwise interrupt the flow of the paper. Explanatory notes are often called "content notes" (See Section 7h).

Some teachers require that notes be typed at the bottom of the page on which the source is cited; others prefer that all notes appear in a separate listing at the end of the paper, before the bibliography. A *foot*note appears at the *foot* of the page whereas an *end*note appears at the *end* of the paper.

The examples in this section follow the new MLA guidelines for documentation, insofar as those guidelines are applicable to traditional footnotes and endnotes. Note that your instructor may want you to use a documentation style that differs in some ways from these examples. To avoid extra work, consult your instructor before your paper is typed in final form.

7g-1 Format for endnotes

Endnotes occur in the following format, and are typed together on a separate sheet at the end of the paper:

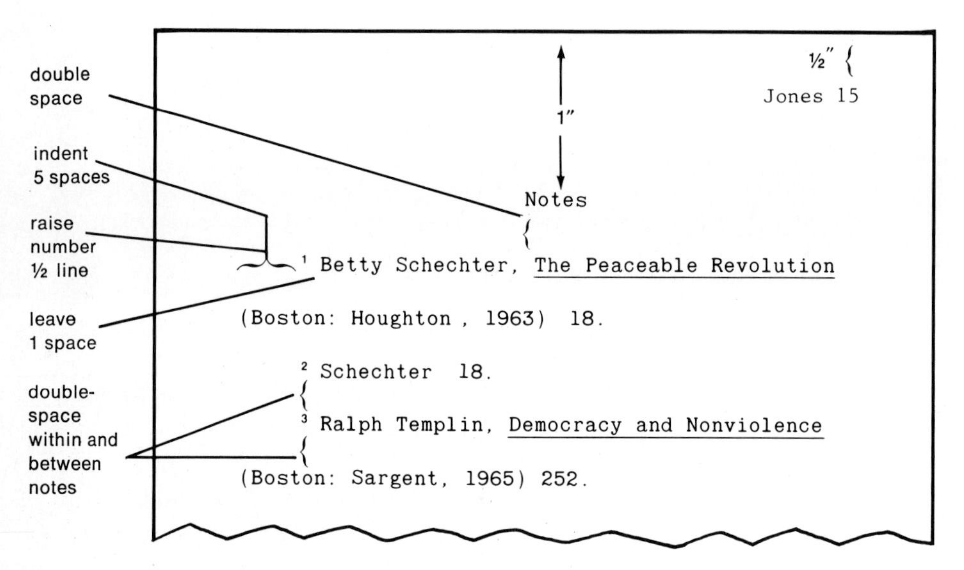

Figure 7-1 Format for endnotes

7g-2 Format for footnotes

Footnotes are placed at the bottom of the page on which the cited source occurs, and in the format shown in Figure 7-2.

7g-3 Numbering of notes

Notes are numbered by Arabic numerals elevated one half space above the line and placed as close as possible to the end of the material cited. All notes should be numbered consecutively throughout the paper (1, 2, 3, etc.). Note numbers are not followed by periods or enclosed in parentheses. Moreover, they follow without space all punctuation marks except the dash.

7g-4 Proper placement of note numbers

The prime rule is that a note number should be placed as near as possible to the *end* of cited material.

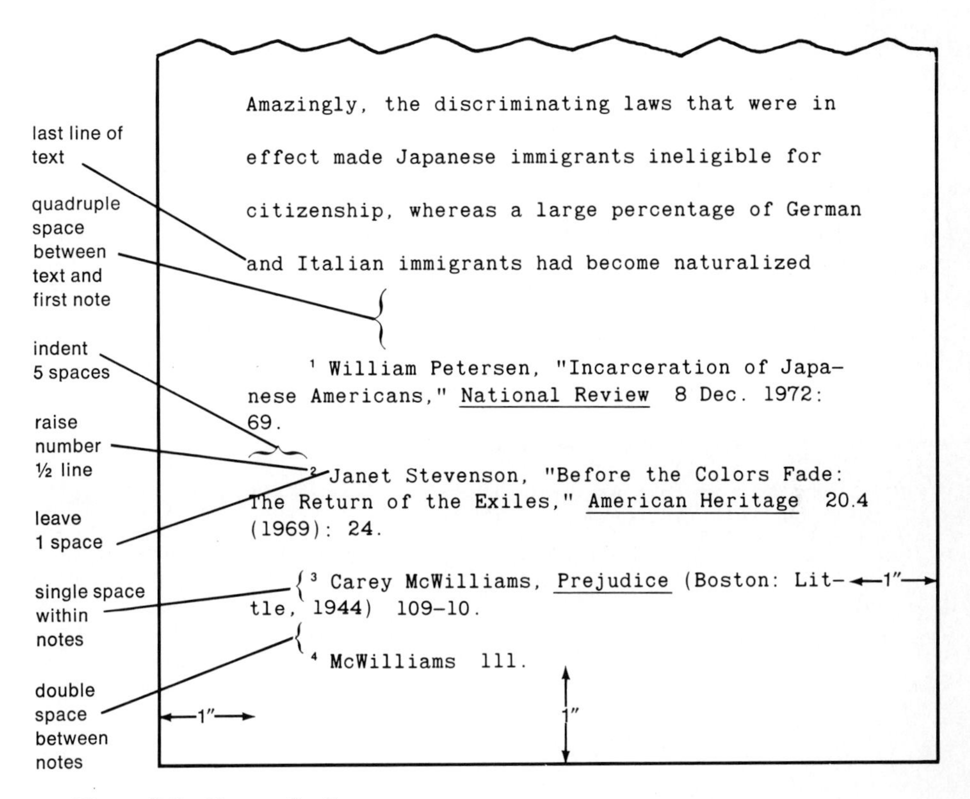

Figure 7-2 Format for footnotes

Wrong In A Matter of Life Bertrand Russell emphasizes that law ''substitutes a neutral authority for private bias,''[13] and he believes this to be the main advantage of the law.

Better In A Matter of Life Bertrand Russell emphasizes that law ''substitutes a neutral authority for private bias,'' and he believes this to be the main advantage of the law.[13]

However, if cited material is followed by material quoted or paraphrased from another source, then each note should be placed immediately after the material to which it refers.

Whereas Herbert Read suggests passive resistance as ''the weapon of those who despair of justice,''[14] Ralph Templin warns that non-violence must never overlook evil for the sake of peace.[15]

(In the preceding example, note 14 cites quoted material from one source, while note 15 cites paraphrased material from another source.)

Finally notes should not be placed immediately after an author's name, or immediately after the verb or colon that introduces a documented passage:

Wrong Justice Abe Fortas[1] states, for example, that civil disobedience should be directed only against ''laws or practices that are the subject of dissent.''

Wrong Justice Abe Fortas states,[1] for example, that civil disobedience should be directed only against ''laws or practices that are the subject of dissent.''

Right Justice Abe Fortas states, for example, that civil disobedience should be directed only against ''laws or practices that are the subject of dissent.''[1]

7g-5 Sample footnotes for books

Below you will find examples of most of the kinds of notes you will be using in your research paper if you do not use an in-text parenthetical style for citations. These samples, however, cannot anticipate every conceivable kind of citation. If you need to cite a source for which this book provides no model, use your common sense. Bear in mind, moreover, that the purpose of documentation is to allow a reader to reconstruct your research and thinking. You should therefore provide enough information to enable a reader to easily locate any cited source.

All samples are given in the footnote format, with single spacing. They can easily be converted to endnotes by double spacing within each note and between notes. Study each entry carefully to determine the proper punctuation, spacing, and underlining.

a. *Book by a single author*

[1] Fawn M. Brodie, Thomas Jefferson: An Intimate History (New York: Norton, 1974) 181.

b. *Book by two or more authors*

Cite all authors (up to three) in order of appearance on the title page. For a book written by more than three authors, use in full the first name listed, followed by "et al." with no comma in between:

[2] John C. Bollens and Grant B. Geyer, Yorty: Politics of a Constant Candidate (Pacific Palisades: Palisades Pub., 1973) 73.

[3] Gordon W. Allport, Philip E. Vernon, and Gardner Lindzey, Study of Values (New York: Houghton, 1951) 12.

[4] Ruth Brown et al., Agricultural Education in a Technical Society: An Annotated Bibliography of Resources (Chicago: American Library Assn., 1973) 220.

c. *Book by a corporate author*

Organizations that author books are treated like authors:

[5] American Institute of Physics, Handbook, 3rd ed. (New York: McGraw, 1972) 10.

d. *Book by an anonymous or pseudonymous author*

When the author of a book is anonymous, merely list the title. Neither "anonymous" nor "anon." needs to be added:

[6] Current Biography (New York: Wilson, 1976) 20–22.

The name of an author who writes under a pseudonym (or *nom de plume*) may be given in brackets:

[7] George Eliot [Mary Ann Evans], Daniel Deronda (London, 1876) 58.

NOTE: Since the book was published before 1900, no publisher has to be named.

e. Work in several volumes or parts

In a reference to a multivolume work in its entirety, state the number of volumes after the title:

[8] T. Walter Wallbank and Alastair M. Taylor, Civilization Past and Present, 2 vols. (New York: Scott, 1949).

Since the reference is to the entire work, no page is cited.

If the reference is to a specific page in a specific volume, the number of volumes is still given after the title. Then the volume number must be listed again in Arabic numerals after the facts of publication and separated from the page number(s) by a colon and a space:

[9] T. Walter Wallbank and Alastair M. Taylor, Civilization Past and Present, 2 vols. (New York: Scott, 1949) 2: 217.

For multivolume works published over a number of years, show the total number of volumes and the range of years as well as information on specific volumes used:

[10] LeRoy Edwin Froom, The Prophetic Faith of Our Fathers. 4 vols. (Washington: Review and Herald, 1950–54) 1: 16–17.

For individual volumes of a multivolume work with separate titles, use the following form:

[11] Paul Jacobs, Saul Landen, and Eve Pell, Colonials and Sojourners, vol. 2 of To Serve the Devil (New York: Random, 1971) 37–39.

f. Collections: anthologies, casebooks, and readers

For a work included in a casebook, anthology, essay collection, or the like—that is, a collection of different pieces by different authors—use the following form:

[12] Eudora Welty, ''The Wide Net,'' Story: An Introduction to Prose Fiction, ed. Arthur Foff and Daniel Knaff (Belmont: Wadsworth, 1966) 166.

g. Double reference—a quotation within a cited work

Use the following form for referring to a quotation within a cited work:

[13] Lin Piao as quoted in Jean Daubier, A History of the Chinese Cultural Revolution, trans. Richard Seaver (New York: Random, 1974) 83.

h. Reference work

For signed articles in well-known encyclopedias, supply name of author, title of entry, name of encyclopedia, and year of edition:

[14] Albert George Ballert, "Saint Lawrence River," Encyclopaedia Britannica, 1963 ed.

The authors of articles in reference works are usually identified by initials that are decoded in a special index volume. If the article is unsigned, begin with the title entry:

[15] "House of David," Encyclopedia Americana, 1974 ed.

[16] "Telegony," Dictionary of Philosophy and Psychology, 1902 ed.

i. Work in a series

[17] Louis Auchincloss, Edith Wharton, University of Minnesota Pamphlets on American Writers 12 (Minneapolis: U of Minnesota P, 1961) 17.

j. Edition

The word *edition* can be understood in three different ways: it can mean: (1) a revised printing of a work; (2) a collection of items edited by one or several authors; (3) the edited version of one or more works by an editor or editors. The proper forms to use in each of these cases are as follows:

(i) FOR A REVISED EDITION:

[18] Porter G. Perrin and Jim W. Corder, Handbook of Current English, 4th ed. (Glenview: Scott, 1975) 304-05.

(ii) FOR AN EDITED COLLECTION:

[19] Charles Clerc, "Goodbye to All That: Theme, Character and Symbol in Goodbye, Columbus," Seven Contemporary Short Novels, ed. Charles Clerc and Louis Leiter (Glenview: Scott, 1969) 107.

The reference here is to an editorial critique on one of the novels in the collection.

(iii) FOR THE WORK OF AN EDITOR:

[20] Hardin Craig and David Bevington, eds., The Complete Works of Shakespeare, rev. ed. (Glenview: Scott, 1973) 31–38.

Because the reference is to the editorial work of Craig and Bevington, the names of these editors are listed in place of the author's. But when the paper deals with the work of the original author, rather than with the work of an editor or translator, the author's name must then be listed first:

[21] Sylvia Plath, Letters Home, ed. Aurelia Schober Plath (New York: Harper, 1975) 153–54.

k. Translation

[22] Benvenuto Cellini, Autobiography of Benvenuto Cellini, trans. John Addington Symons (New York: Washington Square, 1963) 75–79.

l. Pamphlet

Citations of pamphlets should conform as nearly as possible to the format used for citations of books. Give as much information about the pamphlet as is necessary to help a reader find it:

[23] Calplans Agricultural Fund, An Investment in California Agricultural Real Estate (Oakland: Calplans Securities, n.d.) 3.

m. Government publication or legal reference

Because of their complicated origins, government publications can be difficult to document. Generally, the citation of a government publication should list first the author or agency, then the title of the publication (underlined), followed by the publication facts (place, publisher, date) and the page reference. Although no standard format exists for all such publications, we have tried to supply samples for the kinds of government sources most often cited in undergraduate papers.

(i) THE CONGRESSIONAL RECORD

A citation to the *Congressional Record* requires only title, date, and page(s):

> 24 Cong. Rec., 15 Dec. 1977: 19740.

(ii) CONGRESSIONAL PUBLICATIONS

The authors are listed either as "U.S. Cong., Senate," "U.S. Cong., House," or "U.S. Cong., Joint":

> 25 U.S. Cong., Senate, Permanent Subcommittee on Investigations of the Committee on Government Operations, Organized Crime—Stolen Securities, 93rd Cong., 1st sess. (Washington: GPO, 1973) 1-4.

"GPO" is the accepted abbreviation for "U.S. Government Printing Office."

> 26 U.S. Cong., House, Committee on Foreign Relations, Hearings on S. 2793, Supplemental Foreign Assistance Fiscal Year 1966—Vietnam, 89th Cong., 2nd sess. (Washington: GPO, 1966) 9.

The titles of government publications, although long and cumbersome, must nevertheless be accurately cited.

(iii) LEGAL PUBLICATIONS

> 27 Office of the Federal Register, "The Supreme Court of the United States," United States Government Manual (Washington: GPO, 1976) 67.

Names of laws, acts, and the like are generally neither underlined nor placed within quotation marks: Constitution of the United States, Declaration of Independence, Bill of Rights, Humphrey-Hawkins Bill, Sherman Anti-Trust Act. Citations of legal sources usually refer to sections rather than to pages. Certain conventional abbreviations are also used in such citations:

[28] U.S. Const., art. I, sec. 2.

[29] 15 U.S. Code, sec. 78j(b) (1964).

[30] U.C.C., art. IX, pt. 2, par. 9-28.

Names of law cases are abbreviated, and the first important word of each party is spelled out: Brown v. Board of Ed. stands for Oliver Brown versus the Board of Education of Topeka, Kansas. Cases, unlike laws, are italicized in the text but not in the notes. Text: *Miranda v. Arizona*. Note: Miranda v. Arizona. The following information must be supplied in a citation of a law case: (1) the name of the first plaintiff and the first defendant; (2) the volume, name, and page (in that order) of the law report cited; (3) the name of the court that decided the case; (4) the year in which the case was decided:

[31] Richardson v. J. C. Flood Co., 190 A. 2d 259 (D.C. App. 1963).

Interpreted, this footnote means that the Richardson v. J. C. Flood Co. case can be found on page 259 of volume 190 of the Second Series of the *Atlantic Reporter*. The case was settled in the District of Columbia Court of Appeals during the year 1963. For further information on the form for legal references, consult *A Uniform System of Citation*, 12th ed. (Cambridge: Harvard Law Review Association, 1976).

n. Classical works

In citing a classical work that is subdivided into books, parts, cantos, verses, and lines, specify the appropriate subdivisions so that a reader using a different edition of the work can easily locate the reference:

[32] Homer, The Iliad, trans. Richmond Lattimore (Chicago: U of Chicago P, 1937) 101 (3.15-20).

[33] Dante Alighieri, The Inferno, trans. John Ciardi (New York: NAL, 1954) 37 (2.75-90).

Books or parts have traditionally been indicated by large Roman numerals, cantos or verses by small Roman numerals, and lines by Arabic numerals. However, the modern trend is toward Arabic numerals for everything (see Section 7d-1*k*).

o. The Bible

Because the King James Bible is such a familiar document, only the appropriate book and verse need be cited. Translations other than the King James must be indicated within parentheses.

King James Bible:

[34] Isaiah 12:15. or [34] Isaiah 12.15.

Other translation:

[35] 2 Corinthians 2:10 (Revised Standard Version).

or

[35] 2 Corinthians 2.10 (Revised Standard Version).

7g-6 Sample footnotes for periodicals

a. Anonymous author

[1] "Elegance Is Out," Fortune 13 Mar. 1978: 18.

Most periodical articles are written by unidentified correspondents.

b. Single author

[2] Hugh Sidey, "In Defense of the Martini," Time 24 Oct. 1977: 38.

c. More than one author

[3] Clyde Ferguson and William R. Cotter, "South Africa—What Is to Be Done?" Foreign Affairs 56 (1978): 254.

The format of a citation to a multiple-authored magazine article is the same as for a multiple-authored book. For three authors, list the names of the authors exactly as they appear in the article. Separate the first and second name by a comma, and the second and third by a comma followed by the word "and." For more than three authors, list the name of the first author followed by "et al." with no comma in between.

d. Journal with continuous pagination throughout the annual volume

[4] Anne Paolucci, ''Comedy and Paradox in Pirandello's Plays,'' Modern Drama 20 (1977): 322.

Since there is only one page 322 throughout volume 20 of 1977, it is unnecessary to add the month.

e. Journal with separate pagination for each issue

[5] Claude T. Mangrum, ''Toward More Effective Justice,'' Crime Prevention Review 5 (Jan. 1978): 7.

[6] Janet Stevenson, ''Before the Colors Fade: The Return of the Exiles,'' American Heritage 20.4 (1969): 24.

Since each issue of these journals is paged anew, page 7, for example, will occur in all issues of volume 5; therefore, the addition of the month is necessary. Some journals use numbers to distinguish different issues. Footnote 6, for example, refers the reader to issue 4 of volume 20. Follow the style of the individual journal:

[7] Robert Brown, ''Physical Illness and Mental Health,'' Philosophy and Public Affairs 7 (Fall 1977): 18–19.

Since this journal is published quarterly and in volumes that do not coincide with the year, adding the season of publication makes the source easier to locate.

f. Monthly magazine

[8] Flora Davis and Julia Orange, ''The Strange Case of the Children Who Invented Their Own Language,'' Redbook Mar. 1978: 113, 165.

Note the split page reference to the article, which began on one page and was continued at the back of the magazine.

g. Weekly magazine

[9] Suzy Eban, ''Our Far-Flung Correspondents,'' The New Yorker 6 Mar. 1978: 70-72.

h. Newspaper

[10] James Tanner, ''Disenchantment Grows in OPEC Group with Use of U.S. Dollar for Oil Pricing,'' Wall Street Journal 9 Mar. 1978: 3, cols. 3-4.

See also footnote 13 below.

Listing the columns as well as the page makes the article easier to locate; however, listing the column(s) is optional.

NOTE: If the first word of a newspaper's title is an article, the article is deleted. For example, above, *The Wall Street Journal* becomes *Wall Street Journal.*

[11] Daniel Southerland, ''Carter Plans Firm Stand with Begin,'' Christian Science Monitor 9 Mar. 1978, western ed.: 1, 9.

Supply the edition or section when available.

i. Editorial

Signed:

[12] William Futrell, ''The Inner City Frontier,'' editorial, Sierra 63.2 (1978): 5.

Unsigned:

[13] ''Criminals in Uniform,'' editorial, Los Angeles Times 7 Apr. 1978, pt. 2: 6.

Listing the part as well as the page makes this newspaper article easier to locate.

j. Letter to the editor

[14] Donna Korcyzk, letter, Time 20 Mar. 1978: 4.

k. Critical review

[15] Peter Andrews, rev. of The Strange Ride of Rudyard Kipling: His Life and Works, by Angus Wilson, Saturday Review 4 Mar. 1978: 24.

7g-7 Sample footnotes for special items

Citation samples of other sources commonly used in research papers are given below. For citation forms on sources not covered here, consult your instructor. Bear in mind that the prime rule of documentation is to provide the information necessary for a reader to trace any cited source.

a. Lecture

As minimum information cite the speaker's name, the title of the lecture in quotation marks, the sponsoring organization, the location, and the date. If the presentation has no title, use an appropriate label, such as lecture, speech, or address:

[1] Gene L. Schwilck, ''The Core and the Community,'' Danforth Foundation, St. Louis, 16 Mar. 1978.

[2] Jesse Jackson, address, Democratic National Convention, San Francisco, 17 July 1984.

b. Film

Film citations should include the title of the film (underlined), the director's name, the distributor, and the year of release. Information on the producer, writer, performers, and size or length of the film may also be supplied, if necessary to your study:

[3] The Turning Point, dir. Herbert Ross, with Anne Bancroft, Shirley MacLaine, Mikhail Baryshnikov, and Leslie Brown, Twentieth Century-Fox, 1978.

c. Radio or television program

Citations should include the title of the program (underlined), the network or local station, and the city and date of broadcast. If appropriate, the title of the episode is listed in quotation marks before the title of the program, while the title of the series, neither underlined nor in quotation marks, comes after the title of the program. The name of the writer, director, narrator, or producer may also be supplied, if significant to your paper:

[4] ''Diving for Roman Plunder,'' narr. and dir. Jacques Cousteau, The Cousteau Odyssey, KCET, Los Angeles, 14 Mar. 1978.

[5] World of Survival, narr. John Forsythe, CBS Special, Los Angeles, 29 Oct. 1972.

d. Recording (disc or tape)

For commercially available recordings, cite the following: composer or performer, title of recording or of work(s) on the recording, artist(s), manufacturer, catalog number, and date of issue (if not known, state "n.d."):

[6] The Beatles, ''I Should Have Known Better,'' The Beatles Again, Apple Records, SO-385, n.d.

(This is a reference to one of several songs on a disc.) A citation of a recording of classical music may omit the title of the recording and instead list the works recorded. Musical compositions identified by form, key, and number are neither underlined nor placed within quotation marks:

[7] Johann Sebastian Bach, Toccata and Fugue in D minor, Toccata, Adagio, and Fugue in C major, Passacaglia and Fugue in C minor; Johann Christian Bach, Sinfonia for Double Orchestra, Op. 18, No. 1, cond. Eugene Ormandy, The Philadelphia Orchestra, Columbia, MS 6180, n.d.

(When two or more composers and their works are involved, a semicolon separates each grouping.) Citations of recordings of the spoken word list the speaker first:

[8] Swift Eagle, The Pueblo Indians, Caedmon TC 1327, n.d.

For a recording of a play, use the following form (the participating actors are listed):

[9] Shakespeare's Othello, with Paul Robeson, Jose Ferrer, Uta Hagen, and Edith King, Columbia, SL-153, n.d.

In addition to the speaker and title, a citation to a noncommercial recording should state when the recording was made, for whom, and where. The title of the recording is not underlined:

[10] Michael Dwyer, Readings from Mark Twain, rec. 15 Apr. 1968, Humorist Society, San Bernardino, CA.

e. Personal letter

Published letters are treated as titles within a book. Add the date of the letter, if available:

[11] Oscar Wilde, ''To Mrs. Alfred Hunt,'' 25 Aug. 1880, The Letters of Oscar Wilde, ed. Rupert Hart-Davis (New York: Harcourt, 1962) 67-68.

For letters personally received, use the following form:

[12] Gilbert Highet, letter to the author, 15 Mar. 1972.

f. Interview

Citations of interviews should specify the kind of interview, the name (and, if pertinent, the title) of the interviewed person, and the date of the interview:

[13] Dr. Charles Witt, personal interview, 23 Mar. 1976.

[14] Telephone interview with Edward Carpenter, librarian at Huntington Library, 2 Mar. 1978.

7g-8 Subsequent references to footnotes/endnotes

Subsequent citations to an already identified source are given in abbreviated form. The rule is to make subsequent citations brief but not cryptic. Ordinarily the author's last name or a key word from the title, followed by a page number, will do. Latin terms such as "op. cit." ("in the work cited"), "loc. cit." ("in the place cited"), and "ibid." ("in the same place") are no longer used.

First reference:

[1] John W. Gardner, Excellence (New York: Harper, 1961) 47.

Subsequent reference:

[2] Gardner 52.

If two or more subsequent references cite the same work, simply repeat the name of the author and supply the appropriate page numbers. Do not use "ibid.":

[3] Gardner 83.

[4] Gardner 198.

If, however, your paper also contains references to Gardner's other book, *Self-Renewal*, the two books should be distinguished by title in subsequent references:

[5] Gardner, Excellence 61.

[6] Gardner, Self-Renewal 62.

If two of the cited authors share the same last name, subsequent references should supply the full name of each author:

[7] Henry James 10.

[8] William James 23-24.

For a subsequent reference to an anonymous article in a periodical, use a shortened version of the title.

First reference:

[9] "The Wooing of Senator Zorinsky," Time 27 Mar. 1978: 12.

Subsequent reference:

[10] "Zorinsky" 13.

For subsequent references to unconventional or special sources, you may need to improvise.

7h

Content notes

Content notes consist of material that is relevant to your research but that does not need to interrupt the flow of your text. Such notes may consist of an explanation, additional information, reference to other sources, information about procedures used to gain information, or acknowledgment of special assistance. The format of content notes is the same no matter which style of documentation is used in the paper. Some instructors insist that all content notes be gathered together on a page entitled "Notes," placed after the text of the paper but before the "Works Cited" page. Other instructors prefer to have them placed at the foot of the appropriate page so that the reader can look down and read them as they occur. The following rules should be observed when typing content notes:

- Indent the first line of each note 5 spaces.
- Double-space content notes gathered at the end of the paper (see sample student paper, p. 240), but single-space those shown at the foot of a page. In the latter case be sure to allow for enough space for the entire note. Begin the note four lines below the text. Do *not* type a solid line between the text and the note since this would indicate a note continued from the previous page when space ran out. Single-space the note but double-space between notes if there is more than one note.
- In your text, roll up a half space at the relevant place and strike your note number, as in the following example:

  The centaur, being half horse and half man, symbolized both the wild and benign aspect of nature. Thus the coexistence of nature and culture was expressed.[12]

  The note at the foot of the page then adds the following comment without interrupting the flow of the text:

  [12] It should be noted that the horse part is the lower and more animalistic area whereas the human portion is the upper, including the heart and head.

- Provide complete documentation to content footnote sources in "Works Cited" or in "Reference List," but do *not* provide complete documentation in the note itself. For instance, the following content footnote might appear in a biology paper:

  [10] Harvey (1980) disagrees with this aspect of Johnson's interpretation of handwriting.

  The following full reference would then appear in "Reference List":

  Harvey, O. L. (1980). The measurement of handwriting considered as a form of expressive movement. Quarterly Review of Biology, 55, 231–249.

NOTE: An exception is the traditional footnote or endnote style, which provides full documentation in the note as well as in "Works Cited."

Study the following sample content notes:

7h-1 Content note explaining a term

[1] The "Rebellion of 1837" refers to December of 1837, when William Lyon Mackenzie, a newspaper editor and former mayor of Toronto, led a rebellion intended to establish government by elected officials rather than appointees of the British Crown.

7h-2 Content note expanding on an idea

[2] This pattern of development was also reflected in their system of allocation: only a small percentage of tax money was used for agriculture, whereas great chunks were apportioned to industry.

7h-3 Content note referring the reader to another source

[3] For further information on this point, see King and Chang (124–35).

NOTE: The "Works Cited" or "Reference List" must provide full documentation for this source:

King, Gilbert W., and Hsien Wu Chang. ''Machine Translation of Chinese,'' Scientific America 208.6 (1963): 124–35.

7h-4 Content note explaining procedures

[4] Subjects were classed according to their smoking history as never smokers, cigar and/or pipe smokers exclusively, ex-cigarette smokers (smoked cigarettes regularly in the past but not

within the year prior to the time of interview), and current cigarette smokers (smoked cigarettes regularly at the time of the interview for at least one year).

7h-5 Content note acknowledging assistance

[5] The authors wish to acknowledge the assistance of the Montreal Children's Hospital in providing access to their Hewlett Packard 3000 computer.

7i

Consolidation of references

If a substantial part of your paper is based on several sources that deal with the same idea, consolidating the references into a single note may save space and prevent repetition. The format for handling consolidation of references differs according to the documentation style being used.

7i-1 Footnote using author-work style (MLA)

[1] For this idea I am indebted to Holland (32), Folsom (136–144), and Edgar (15–17).

NOTE: A "Works Cited" or "Reference List" at the end of the paper must provide full documentation for these sources.

7i-2 Footnote using author-date style (APA)

[2] On this point see Hirsbrunner (1981), Florin (1981), and Frey (1981).

NOTE: A "Works Cited" or "Reference List" at the end of the paper must provide full documentation for these sources.

7i-3 Footnote using numbers style

[3] This section reflects the conclusions reached by Kuller (3), Thompson (4), Copley (7), Eisenberg (8), and Weaver (17).

NOTE: A "Works Cited" or "Reference List" list at the end of the paper must provide full documentation for these sources.

7i-4 Footnote using traditional style

[4] For this idea I am indebted to Laurence Bedwell Holland, The Expense of Wisdom (Princeton: Princeton UP, 1964) 32; James K. Folsom, ''Archimago's Well: An Interpretation of The Sacred Fount,'' Modern Fiction Studies 7 (1961): 136-44; and Pelham Edgar, Henry James: Man and Author (1927; New York: Russell, 1964) 15-17.

NOTE: Separate the individual citations with a semicolon. The "Works Cited" list must repeat the documentation for these sources.

8

The Bibliography

8a The bibliography

8b Works Cited (MLA and traditional styles)

8c Reference List (APA style)

8d Works Cited (numbers sytem)

8a
The bibliography

The last part of the research paper is a bibliography—a list in alphabetical order of the sources actually used in the paper. The purpose of this list is to allow the reader to identify and retrieve any source used. Every reference cited in the text must therefore appear in the bibliography; conversely, every work appearing in the bibliography must have been used in the text.

Differences in the format of the bibliography are minor among the various documentation styles. Under the MLA and traditional footnote/endnote styles, the bibliography is titled "Works Cited." The APA style labels it a "Reference List." This chapter concentrates on explaining the formats required in these bibliographies; it also gives examples of the format used in the numbers system.

8a-1 Alphabetizing bibliographic entries

Arrange the entries in your "Works Cited" or "Reference List" in alphabetical order according to the surname of the first author, keeping in mind the following rules:

- Alphabetize letter by letter. Notice, however, that nothing always precedes something. For instance, Rich, Herman B. precedes Richmond, D. L.
- The prefixes *M'*, *Mc*, and *Mac* must be alphabetized literally, not as if they were all spelled *Mac*. Disregard the apostrophe: MacKinsey precedes McCuen, and MacIntosh precedes M'Naughton. If the name of an author includes an article or preposition such as *de, la, du, von, van*, the rule is that when the prefix is part of the surname, then alphabetize according to the prefix (Von Bismarck precedes Vonnegut). If the prefix is not part of the name, treat it as part of the first and middle names (Bruy, Cornelis J. de). When in doubt, consult the biographical section of *Webster's New Collegiate Dictionary* (1981).
- Single-author entries precede multiple-author entries beginning with the same surname:

```
Hirsch, E. D.

Hirsch, E. D., and O. B. Wright.
```

Entries by the same author or authors in the same order are arranged alphabetically by the title, excluding *A* or *The*.

- A row of three hyphens followed by a period replaces the name of the repeated author(s):

Kissinger, Henry Alfred. The Necessity for Choice.

---. Nuclear Weapons and Foreign Policy.

- Works by authors with the same surname are alphabetized according to the first letter of the Christian name:

Butler, Alban

Butler, Samuel

- Corporate authors—associations, government agencies, institutions—are alphabetized according to the first significant word of the name. Use the full name, not an abbreviation:

Brandeis University (not B.U.)

Southern Asian Institute (not SAI)

- A parent body precedes a subdivision:

Glendale Community College, Fine Arts Department

- When a work is anonymous, its title moves into the author's place and is alphabetized according to the first significant word in the title.
- Alphabetize legal references by the first significant word:

Marbury v. Madison

National Labor Relations Act

8a-2 Sample bibliography page

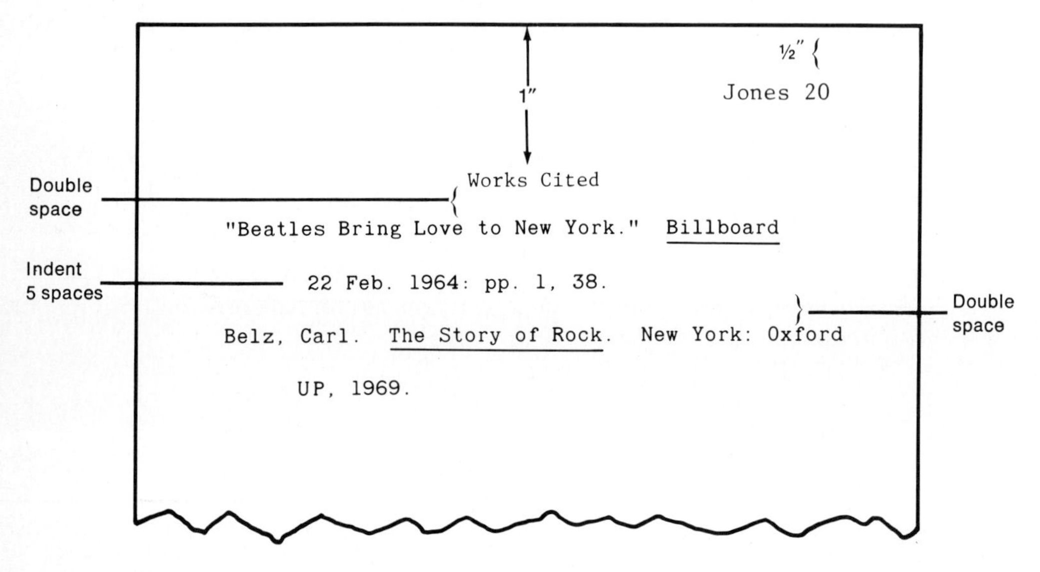

Figure 8-1 Sample bibliography page (MLA style)

(See also the sample student papers, pp. 241, 262, and 271.) For details on the form for various bibliographic entries, see Sections 8b and 8c. For rules on alphabetizing the entires, see Section 8a-1.

8b

Works Cited (MLA and traditional styles)

If you were careful in copying your sources accurately on the bibliography cards, preparing the bibliography will be mainly a matter of transcribing information. But you must still observe the following:

- The bibliography must occupy a separate page.
- Center the title, "Works Cited," one inch from the top of the page. Leave two spaces between the title and the first entry (see Fig. 8-1).
- List all entries in alphabetical order by first author (see Section 8a-1). Anonymous works are listed alphabetically according to the first word of the title, disregarding *a, an,* or *the* if such a word begins the title.
- Place the author's last name first. In case of two or more authors, all authors' names except the first retain their normal order.

- Second and subsequent entries by the same author(s) are listed with a line of three hyphens followed by a period:

```
Lewis, Sinclair.  Babbitt.  New York: Harcourt, 1922.

---. Main Street.  New York: Harcourt, 1920.
```

- Indent the second line of each entry five spaces.
- Double-space throughout the "Works Cited" list.

Study "Works Cited" at the end of two sample student papers (pp. 241 and 271). Note, however, that for a paper for a course in a field other than the modern languages or literature, your instructor may want you to use a documentation style that differs in some ways from the examples shown in this chapter and in the sample student papers in Chapter 11. To avoid extra work, consult your instructor before the final draft of your paper is typed.

8b-1 General order for bibliographic references to books in "Works Cited"

Bibliographic references to books list items in the following order:

a. Author

The name of the author comes first, alphabetized by surname. If more than one author is involved, invert the name of only the first and follow it by a comma:

```
Brown, Jim, and John Smith
```

For more than three authors, use the name of the first followed by "et al.":

```
Foreman, Charles, et al.
```

In some cases the name of an editor, translator, or compiler will be cited before the name of an author, especially if the actual editing, translating, or compiling is the subject of discussion (see Section 8b-1*c*).

b. Title

Cite the title in its entirety, including any subtitle, exactly as it appears on the title page. A period follows the title unless the title ends in some other mark, such as a question mark or an exclamation mark. Book titles are underlined; titles of chapters are set off in quotation marks. The initial word and all subsequent words (except for articles and short prepositions) in the title are capitalized. Ignore any unusual typographical style, such as all capital letters, or any peculiar arrangement of capitals and lower-case letters, unless the author is specifically known to insist on such a typography. Separate a subtitle from the title by a colon:

D. H. Lawrence: His Life and Work.

c. Name of editor, compiler, or translator

The name(s) of the editor(s), compiler(s), or translator(s) is given in normal order, preceded by "Ed(s).," "Comp(s).," or Trans.":

Homer. The Iliad. Trans. Richard Lattimore.

However, if the editor, translator, or compiler was listed in your textual citation, then his name should appear first, followed by "ed.," "trans.," or "comp." and a period:

Textual citation:

Gordon's Literature in Critical Perspective offers some . . .

"Works Cited" entry:

Gordon, Walter K., ed. Literature in Critical Perspective. New
York: Appleton, 1968.

If you are drawing attention to the translator, use the following format:

Textual citation:

The colloquial English of certain passages is due to Ciardi's
translation.

"Works Cited" entry:

Ciardi, John, trans. The Inferno. By Dante Alighieri. New York:
NAL, 1961.

d. Edition (if other than first)

The edition being used is cited if it is other than the first. Cite the edition in Arabic numerals (3rd ed.) without further punctuation. Always use the latest edition of a work, unless you have some specific reason of scholarship for using another:

Holman, C. Hugh. A Handbook to Literature. 3rd ed. Indianapolis: Odyssey, 1972.

e. Series name and number

Give the name of the series, without quotation marks and not underlined, followed by a comma, followed by the number of the work in the series in Arabic numerals, followed by a period:

Unger, Leonard. T. S. Eliot. University of Minnesota Pamphlets on American Writers 8. Minneapolis: U of Minnesota P, 1961.

f. Volume numbers

An entry referring to all the volumes of a multivolume work cites the number of volumes *before* the publication facts:

Durant, Will, and Ariel Durant. The Story of Civilization. 10 vols. New York: Simon, 1968.

An entry for only selected volumes still cites the total number of volumes after the title. The volumes actually used are listed *after* the publication facts:

Durant, Will, and Ariel Durant. The Story of Civilization. 10 vols. New York: Simon, 1968. Vols. 2 and 3.

For multivolume works published over a number of years, show the total number of volumes, the range of years, and specific volumes if not all of them were actually used:

Froom, LeRoy Edwin. The Prophetic Faith of Our Fathers. 4 vols. Washington: Review and Herald, 1950–54. Vol. 1.

g. Publication facts

Indicate the place, publisher, and date of publication for the work you are citing. A colon follows the place, a comma the publisher, and a period the date unless a page is cited.

You may use a shortened form of the publisher's name as long as it is clear: Doubleday (for Doubleday & Company), McGraw (for McGraw-Hill), Little (for Little, Brown), Scott (for Scott, Foresman), Putnam's (for G. Putnam's Sons), Scarecrow (for Scarecrow Press), Simon (for Simon and Schuster), Wiley (for John Wiley & Sons), Holt (for Holt Rinehart & Winston), Penguin (for Penguin Books), Harper (for Harper & Row). For example:

Robb, David M., and Jessie J. Garrison. Art in the Western World. 4th ed. New York: Harper, 1963.

But list university presses in full (except for abbreviating "University" and "Press") so as not to confuse the press with the university itself: Oxford UP, Harvard UP, Johns Hopkins UP.

Gohdes, Clarence. Bibliographical Guides to the Study of Literature of the U.S.A. 3rd ed. Durham: Duke UP, 1970.

If more than one place of publication appears, give the city shown first on the book's title page.

If more than one copyright date is given, use the latest unless your study is specifically concerned with an earlier edition. (A new printing does not constitute a new edition. For instance, if the title page bears a 1975 copyright date but a 1978 fourth printing, use 1975.) If no place, publisher, date, or page numbering is provided, insert "n.p.," "n.p.," "n.d.," or "n. pag.," respectively. "N. pag." will explain to the reader why no page numbers were provided in the text citation. If the source contains neither author, title, or publication information, supply in brackets whatever information you have been able to obtain:

Photographs of Historic Castles. [St. Albans, England]: N.p., n.d. N. pag.

Farquart, Genevieve. They Gave Us Flowers. N.p.: n.p., 1886.

Dickens, Charles. Master Humphrey's Clock. London: Bradbury and Evans, n.d.

h. Page numbers

Bibliographical entries for books rarely include a page number; however, entries for shorter pieces appearing within a longer work—articles, poems, short stories, and so on, in a collection—should include a page reference. In such a case, supply page numbers for the entire piece, not just for the specific page or pages cited in the text:

Daiches, David. "Criticism and Sociology." Literature in Critical Perspective. Ed. Walter K. Gordon. New York: Appleton, 1968. 7–18.

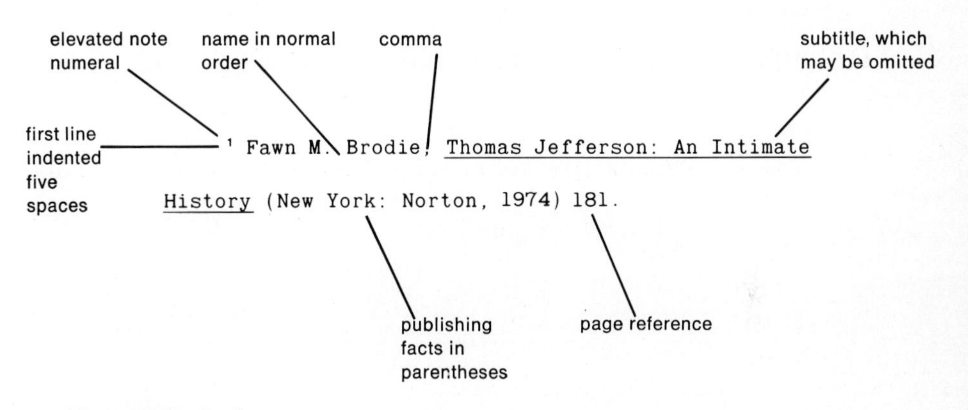

Figure 8-2 Endnote

Figure 8-3 Bibliographic entry

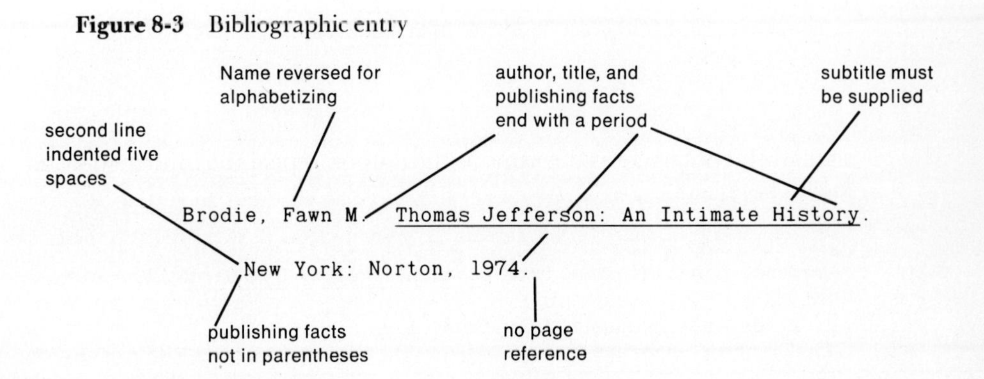

i. Differences between endnotes and bibliographic entries

Endnotes and bibliography entries contain the same information, with the exception of page numbers, but differ considerably in form, as the following examples make clear:

8b-2 Sample bibliographic references to books

a. Book by a single author

Brodie, Fawn M. Thomas Jefferson: An Intimate History. New York: Norton, 1974.

b. Book by two or more authors

Bollens, John C., and Grand B. Geyer. Yorty: Politics of a Constant Candidate. Pacific Palisades: Palisades Publ., 1973.

Allport, Gordon W., Philip E. Vernon, and Gardner Lindzey. Study of Values. New York: Houghton, 1951.

Brown, Ruth, et al. Agricultural Education in a Technical Society: An Annotated Bibliography of Resources. Chicago: American Library Assn., 1973.

c. Book by a corporate author

American Institute of Physics. Handbook. 3rd ed. New York: McGraw, 1972.

NOTE: If the publisher is the same as the author, repeat the information, as shown here:

Defense Language Institute. Academic Policy Standards. Monterey: Defense Language Institute, 1982.

d. Book by an anonymous or pseudonymous author

No author listed:

Current Biography. New York: Wilson, 1976.

If you are able to research the author's name, supply it in brackets:

[Stauffer, Adlai]. *Cloudburst*. Knoxville: Review and Courier Publishing Assn., 1950.

The name of an author who writes under a pseudonym (or *nom de plume*) may also be given in brackets:

Eliot, George [Mary Ann Evans]. *Daniel Deronda*. London, 1876.

e. Work in several volumes or parts

When citing the whole multivolume work:

Wallbank, T. Walter, and Alastair M. Taylor. *Civilization Past and Present*. 2 vols. New York: Scott, 1949.

When citing a specific volume of a multivolume work:

Wallbank, T. Walter, and Alastair M. Taylor. *Civilization Past and Present*. 2 vols. New York: Scott, 1949. Vol. 2.

When citing a multivolume work whose volumes were published over a range of years:

Froom, LeRoy Edwin. *The Prophetic Faith of Our Fathers*. 4 vols. Washington: Review and Herald, 1950–54.

When citing a multivolume work with separate titles:

Jacobs, Paul, Saul Landen, and Eve Pell. Colonials and Sojourners. Vol. 2 of To Serve the Devil. 4 vols. New York: Random, 1971.

f. Work within a collection of pieces, all by the same author

Johnson, Edgar. ''The Keel of the New Lugger.'' The Great Unknown. Vol. 2 of Sir Walter Scott. 3 vols. New York: Macmillan, 1970. 763–76.

Selzer, Richard. ''Liver.'' Mortal Lessons. New York: Simon, 1976. 62–77.

NOTE: The MLA no longer recommends the use of the word "In" preceding the title of the collection or anthology.

g. Chapter or titled section in a book

Goodrich, Norma Lorre. ''Gilgamesh the Wrestler.'' Myths of the Hero. New York: Orion, 1960.

NOTE: List the chapter or titled section in a book only when it demands special attention.

h. Collections: anthologies, casebooks, and readers

Welty, Eudora. ''The Wide Net.'' Story: An Introduction to Prose Fiction. Ed. Arthur Foff and Daniel Knapp. Belmont: Wadsworth, 1966. 159–77.

Cowley, Malcolm. ''Sociological Habit Patterns in Linguistic Transmogrification.'' The Reporter 20 Sept. 1956: 257–61. Rpt. in Readings for Writers. Ed. Jo Ray McCuen and Anthony C. Winkler. 2nd ed. New York: Harcourt, 1977. 489–93.

i. Double reference—a quotation within a cited work

Daubier, Jean. A History of the Chinese Cultural Revolution. Trans. Richard Seaver. New York: Random, 1974.

Only the secondary source is listed in "Works Cited." See Section 7d-1*l*, p. 112, for an example of how the source of such an entry would appear in text.

j. Reference works

(i) ENCYCLOPEDIAS

Ballert, Albert George. ''Saint Lawrence River.'' Encyclopaedia Britannica. 1963 ed.

''House of David.'' Encyclopedia Americana. 1974 ed.

Berger, Morroe, and Dorothy Willner. ''Near Eastern Society.'' International Encyclopedia of the Social Sciences. 1968 ed.

(ii) DICTIONARIES AND ANNUALS

''Barsabbas, Joseph.'' Who's Who in the New Testament (1971).

''Telegony.'' Dictionary of Philosophy and Psychology (1902).

k. Work in a series

(i) A NUMBERED SERIES

Auchincloss, Louis. Edith Wharton. University of Minnesota Pamphlets on American Writers 12. Minneapolis: U of Minnesota P, 1961.

(ii) AN UNNUMBERED SERIES

Miller, Sally. The Radical Immigrant. The Immigrant Heritage of America Series. New York: Twayne, 1974.

l. Reprint

Babson, John J. History of the Town of Gloucester, Cape Ann, Including the Town of Rockport. 1860. New York: Peter Smith, 1972.

Thackeray, William Makepeace. Vanity Fair. London, 1847–48. New York: Harper, 1968.

m. Edition

Perrin, Porter G., and Jim W. Corder. Handbook of Current English. 4th ed. Glenview: Scott, 1975.

Rowland, Beryl, ed. Companion to Chaucer: Studies. New York: Oxford UP, 1979.

n. Edited work

If the work of the editor(s) rather than that of the author(s) is being discussed, place the name of the editor(s) first, followed by a comma, followed by "ed." or "eds.":

Craig, Hardin, and David Bevington, eds. The Complete Works of Shakespeare. Rev. ed. Glenview: Scott, 1973.

If you are stressing the text of the author(s), place the author(s) first:

Clerc, Charles. "Goodbye to All That: Theme, Character and Symbol in Goodbye, Columbus." Seven Contemporary Short Novels. Ed. Charles Clerc and Louis Leiter. Glenview: Scott, 1969. 106–33.

o. Book published in a foreign country

Vialleton, Louis. L'Origine des êtres vivants. Paris: Plon, 1929.

Ransford, Oliver. Livingston's Lake: The Drama of Nyasa. London: Camelot, 1966.

p. Introduction, preface, foreword, or afterword

Davidson, Marshall B. Introduction. The Age of Napoleon. By J. Christopher Herold. New York: American Heritage, 1963.

q. Translation

Symons, John Addington, trans. Autobiography of Benvenuto Cellini. By Benvenuto Cellini. New York: Washington Square, 1963.

r. Book of illustrations

Janson, H. W. History of Art: A Survey of the Major Visual Arts from the Dawn of History to the Present. With 928 illustrations, including 80 color plates. Englewood Cliffs: Prentice and Abrams, 1962.

s. Foreign title

Use lower case lettering for foreign titles except for the first word and proper names:

Vischer, Lukas. Basilius der Grosse. Basel: Reinhard, 1953.

Supply a translation of the title or city if it seems necessary. Place the English version in brackets immediately following the original, not underlined:

Bruckberger, R. L. Dieu et la politique [God and Politics].
Paris: Plon, 1971.

8b-3 General order for bibliographic references to periodicals in "Works Cited"

Bibliographic references to periodicals list items in the following order:

a. Author

List the author's surname first, followed by a comma, followed by the first name or initials. If there is more than one author, follow the same format as for books (see Section 8b-2*b*).

b. Title of the article

List the title in quotation marks, followed by a period inside the quotation marks unless the title itself ends in a question mark or exclamation mark.

c. Publication information

List the name of the periodical, underlined, with any introductory article omitted, followed by a space and a volume number, followed by a space and the year of publication within parentheses, followed by a colon, a space, and page numbers for the entire article, not just for the specific pages cited:

Smith, Irwin. ''Ariel and the Masque in The Tempest.''
Shakespeare Quarterly 21 (1970): 213-22.

Journals paginated anew in each issue require the issue number following the volume number, separated by a period:

```
Beets, Nicholas.  "Historical Actuality and Bodily Experience."
      Humanitas 2.1 (1966): 15-28.
```

Some journals may use a month or season designation in place of an issue number:

```
2 (Spring 1966): 15-28.
```

Magazines that are published weekly or monthly require only the date, without a volume number:

```
Isaacson, Walter.  "After Williamsburg."  Time 13 June 1983:
      12-14.
```

Newspapers require the section or part number, followed by the page:

```
Rumberger, L.  "Our Work, Not Education, Needs Restructuring."
      Los Angeles Times, 24 May 1984, pt. 2: 5.
```

d. Pages

If the pages of the article are scattered throughout the issue (for example, pages 30, 36, 51, and 52), the following formats can be used:

30, 36, 51, 52	(This is the most precise method and should be used when only three or four pages are involved.)
30 and passim	(page 30 and here and there throughout the work)
30ff.	(page thirty and the following pages)
30+	(beginning on page thirty)

8b-4 Sample bibliographic references to periodicals

a. Anonymous author

```
"Elegance Is Out."  Fortune 13 Mar. 1978: 18.
```

b. Single author

Sidey, Hugh. ''In Defense of the Martini.'' Time 24 Oct. 1977: 38.

c. More than one author

Ferguson, Clyde, and William R. Cotter. ''South Africa--What Is to Be Done.'' Foreign Affairs 56 (1978): 254-74.

If three authors have written the article, place a comma after the second author, followed by "and" and the name of the third author. If more than three authors have collaborated, list the first author's name, inverted, followed by a comma and "et al."

Enright, Frank, et al.

d. Journal with continuous pagination throughout the annual volume

Paolucci, Anne. ''Comedy and Paradox in Pirandello's Plays.'' Modern Drama 20 (1977): 321-39.

e. Journal with separate pagination for each issue

When each issue of a journal is paged separately, include the issue number (or month or season); page numbers alone will not locate the article since every issue begins with page 1.

Cappe, Walter H. ''Humanities at Large.'' The Center Magazine 11.2 (1978): 2-6.

Mangrum, Claude T. ''Toward More Effective Justice.'' Crime Prevention Review 5 (Jan. 1978): 1-9.

Brown, Robert. ''Physical Illness and Mental Health.'' Philosophy and Public Affairs 7 (Fall 1977): 18-19.

f. Monthly magazine

Miller, Mark Crispin. ''The New Wave in Rock.'' Horizon Mar. 1978: 76–77.

Davis, Flora, and Julia Orange. ''The Strange Case of the Children Who Invented Their Own Language.'' Redbook Mar. 1978: 113, 165–67.

g. Weekly magazine

Eban, Suzy. ''Our Far-Flung Correspondents.'' The New Yorker 6 Mar. 1978: 70–81.

''Philadelphia's Way of Stopping the Shoplifter.'' Business Week 6 Mar. 1972: 57–59.

h. Newspaper

Tanner, James. ''Disenchantment Grows in OPEC Group with Use of U.S. Dollar for Oil Pricing.'' Wall Street Journal 9 Mar. 1978: 3.

List the edition and section of the newspaper if specified, as in the examples below:

Southerland, Daniel. ''Carter Plans Firm Stand with Begin.'' Christian Science Monitor 9 Mar. 1978, western ed.: 1, 9.

Malino, Emily. ''A Matter of Placement.'' Washington Post 5 Mar. 1978: L 1.

i. Editorial

If the section or part is labeled with a numeral rather than a letter, then the abbreviation "sec." or "pt." must appear before the section number. For example, see the unsigned editorial below.

Signed:

Futrell, William. "The Inner City Frontier." Editorial. Sierra 63.2 (1978): 5.

Unsigned:

"Criminals in Uniform." Editorial. Los Angeles Times 7 Apr. 1978, pt. 2: 6.

j. Letter to the editor

Korczyk, Donna. Letter. Time 20 Mar. 1978: 4.

k. Critical review

Andrews, Peter. Rev. of The Strange Ride of Rudyard Kipling: His Life and Works, by Angus Wilson. Saturday Review 4 Mar. 1978: 24–25.

Daniels, Robert V. Rev. of Stalinism: Essays in Historical Interpretations, ed. Robert C. Tucker. The Russian Review 37 (1978): 102–03.

"Soyer Sees Soyer." Rev. of Diary of an Artist, by Ralph Soyer. American Artist Mar. 1978: 18–19.

Rev. of Charmed Life, by Diane Wynne Jones. Booklist 74 (Feb. 1978): 1009.

l. Published interview

Leonel J. Castillo, Commissioner, Immigration and Naturalization Service. Interview. Why the Tide of Illegal Aliens Keeps Rising. U.S. News and World Report 20 Feb. 1978: 33–35.

m. Published address or lecture

Trudeau, Pierre E. ''Reflections on Peace and Security.'' Address to Conference on Strategies for Peace and Security in the Nuclear Age, Guelph, Ont., Can., 27 Oct. 1983. Rpt. in Vital Speeches of the Day 1 Dec. 1983: 98–102.

8b-5 Sample bibliographic references to nonprint materials

Since nonprint materials come in many forms and with varied information, the rule to follow when dealing with them is to provide as much information as is available for retrieval.

a. Address or lecture

O'Banion, Terry. ''The Continuing Quest for Quality.'' Address to California Assn. of Community Colleges. Sacramento, 30 Aug. 1983.

Schwilck, Gene L. ''The Core and the Community.'' Lecture to Danforth Foundation. St. Louis, 16 Mar. 1978.

For how to handle the reprint of an address or lecture appearing in a periodical, see Section 8b-4*m*.

b. Artwork

Angelico, Beato. Madonna dei Linaioli. Museo de San Marco, Firenze.

For how to handle an illustration in a book of art, see Section 8b-6*a*.

c. Computer source

A computer citation will refer to either: (1) a computer program, that is, information received directly from a data bank, or (2) a written publication retrieved by a computer base.

(i) COMPUTER PROGRAM

First, list the primary creator of the database as the author. Second, give the title of the program underlined, followed by a period. Third, write "Computer software," followed by a period. Fourth, supply the name of the publisher of the program, followed by a comma and the date the program was issued. Finally, give any additional information necessary for identification and retrieval. This additional information should include, for example, the kind of computer for which the software was created, the number of kilobytes (units of memory), the operating system, and the program's form (cartridge, disk, or cassette):

Moshell, J. M., and C. E. Hughes. Imagination: Picture Programming. Computer software. Wiley, 1983. Apple II/IIe, 64KB, disk.

(ii) SOURCE RETRIEVED FROM A DATABASE

Entire articles and books are now being stored in huge data bases, with companies like ERIC, CompuServe, The Source, Mead Data Control (Nexis, Lexis), and many others providing the access service. These sources should be listed as if they appeared in print, except that you will also list the agency providing the access service. If possible, list any code or file associated with the source:

Cohen, Wilbur J. ''Lifelong Learning and Public Policy.'' Community Services Catalyst 9 (Fall 1979): 4-5. ERIC. 1982. Dialog file 1: item EJ218031.

d. Film

Film citations should include the director's name, the title of the film (underlined), the name of the leading actor(s), the distributor, and the date of showing. Information on the producer, writer, and size or length of the film may also be supplied, if necessary to your study:

Ross, Herbert, dir. The Turning Point. With Anne Bancroft, Shirley MacLaine, Mikhail Baryshnikov, and Leslie Brown. Twentieth Century-Fox, 1978.

e. Interview

Citations of interviews should specify the kind of interview, the name (and, if pertinent, the title) of the interviewed person, and the date of the interview:

Witt, Dr. Charles. Personal interview. 18 Feb. 1984.

Carpenter, Edward, librarian at the Huntington Library, Pasadena. Telephone interview. 2 Mar. 1978.

f. Musical composition

Whenever possible, cite the title of the composition in your text, for instance:

Bach's Well-Tempered Clavier is a principal keyboard . . .

However, when opus numbers would clutter the text, cite the composition more fully in "Works Cited":

Grieg, Edward. Minuet in E minor, op. 7, no. 3.

g. Radio or television program

Citations should include the title of the program (underlined), the net work or local station, and the city and date of broadcast. If appropriate, the title of the episode is listed in quotation marks before the title of the program, while the title of the series, neither underlined nor in quotation marks, comes after the title of the program. The name of the writer, director, narrator, or producer may also be supplied, if significant to your paper:

Diving for Roman Plunder. Narr. and dir. Jacques Cousteau. KCET, Los Angeles. 14 Mar. 1978.

"Chapter 2." Writ. Wolf Mankowitz. Dickens of London. Dir. and prod. Marc Miller. Masterpiece Theater. Introd. Alistair Cooke. PBS. 28 Aug. 1977.

Dead Wrong. CBS Special. 24 Jan. 1984.

h. Recording (disc or tape)

For commercially available recordings, cite the following: composer, conductor, or performer; title of recording or of work(s) on the recording; artist(s); manufacturer; catalog number; and year of issue (if not known, state "n.d."):

Beatles, The. "I Should Have Known Better." The Beatles Again. Apple Records, SO-385, n.d.

Bach, Johann Sebastian. Toccata and Fugue in D minor, Toccata, Adagio, and Fugue in C major, Passacaglia and Fugue in C minor; Johann Christian Bach. Sinfonia for Double Orchestra, op. 18, no. 1. Cond. Eugene Ormandy. Philadelphia Orchestra. Columbia, MS 6180, n.d.

Eagle, Swift. The Pueblo Indians. Caedmon, TC 1327, n.d.

Shakespeare's Othello. With Paul Robeson, Jose Ferrer, Uta Hagen, and Edith King. Columbia, SL-153, n.d.

Dwyer, Michael. Readings from Mark Twain. Rec. 15 Apr. 1968. Humorist Society. San Bernardino.

D. K. Wilgus. Irish Folksongs. Rec. 9 Mar. 1969. U of California, Los Angeles, Archives of Folklore. T7-69-22. 7½ ips.

Burr, Charles. Jacket notes. Grofe: Grand Canyon Suite. Columbia, MS 6003, n.d.

i. Theatrical performance

Theatrical performances are cited in the form used for films, with added information on the theater, city, and date of performance. For opera, concert, or dance productions you may also wish to cite the conductor (cond.) or choreographer (chor.). If the author, composer, director, or choreographer should be emphasized, supply that information first:

Getting Out. Dir. Gordon Davidson. By Marsha Norman. With Susan Clark. Mark Taper Forum, Los Angeles. 2 Apr. 1978.

This citation emphasizes the author:

Durang, Christopher. Beyond Therapy. Dir. John Madden. With John Lithgow and Dianne Wiest. Brooks Atkinson Theater, New York. 26 May 1982.

This citation emphasizes the conductor:

Conlon, James, cond. La Bohème. With Renata Scotto. Metropolitan Opera. Metropolitan Opera House, New York. 30 Oct. 1977.

This citation emphasizes the conductor and the guest performer:

Commissiona, Sergiu, cond. Baltimore Symphony Orchestra. With Albert Markov, violin. Brooklyn College, New York. 8 Nov. 1978.

This citation emphasizes the choreographer:

Baryshnikov, Mikhail, chor. Swan Lake. American Ballet Theatre, New York. 24 May 1982.

8b-6 Sample bibliographic references to special items

No standard form exists for every special item you might use in your paper. Again, as a general rule arrange the information in your bibliographic entry in the following order: author, title, place of publication, publisher, date, and any other information helpful for retrieval. Some examples of common citations follow:

a. Artwork, published

Healy, G. P. A. The Meeting on the River Queen. White House, Washington, DC. Illus. in Lincoln: A Picture Story of His Life. By Stefan Lorent. Rev. and enl. ed. New York: Harper, 1957.

For how to handle an art work you have actually experienced, see Section 8b-5*b*.

b. The Bible

When referring to the Bible, cite the book and chapter within your text (the verse, too, may be cited when necessary):

The city of Babylon (Rev. 18.2) is used to symbolize ...

or

In Rev. 18:2 the city of Babylon is used as a symbol of ...

In "Works Cited" the following citation will suffice if you are using the King James version:

The Bible

If you are using another version, specify which:

The Bible, Revised Standard Version

c. Classical works in general

When referring to classical works that are subdivided into books, parts, cantos, verses, and lines, specify the appropriate subdivisions within your text:

Ovid makes claims to immortality in the last lines of The Metamorphoses (3. Epilogue).

Francesca's speech (5.118–35) is poignant because ...

In "Works Cited" these references will appear as follows:

Ovid. The Metamorphoses. Trans. and introd. Horace Gregory. New York: NAL, 1958.

Alighieri, Dante. The Inferno. Trans. John Ciardi. New York: NAL, 1954.

d. Dissertation

Unpublished: The title is placed within quotation marks and the work identified by "Diss.":

Cotton, Joyce Raymonde. "Evan Harrington: An Analysis of George Meredith's Revisions." Diss. U of Southern California, 1968.

Published: The dissertation is treated as a book, except that the entry includes the label "Diss." and states where and when the dissertation was originally written:

Cortey, Teresa. Le Rêve dans les contes de Charles Nodier. Diss. U of California, Berkeley, 1975. Washington, DC: UP of America, 1977.

e. Footnote or endnote citation

A bibliographical reference to a footnote or endnote in a source takes the following form:

Faber, M. D. The Design Within: Psychoanalytic Approaches to Shakespeare. New York: Science House, 1970.

In other words, no mention is made of the note. However, mention of the note should be made within the text itself:

In Schlegel's translation, the meaning is changed (Faber
205, n. 9).

The reference is to page 205, note number 9, of Faber's book.

f. Manuscript or typescript

A bibliographical reference to a manuscript or typescript from a library collection should provide the following information: the author, the title or a description of the material, the material's form (ms. for manuscript, ts. for typescript), and any identifying number. If possible, give the name and location of the library or institution where the material is kept.

Chaucer, Geoffrey. Ellesmere ms., El26C9. Huntington Library, Pasadena.

The Wanderer. Ms. Exeter Cathedral, Exeter.

Cotton Vitellius. Ms., A. SV. British Museum, London.

g. Pamphlet or brochure

Citations of pamphlets or brochures should conform as nearly as possible to the format used for citations of books. Give as much information about the pamphlet as is necessary to help a reader find it. Underline the title:

Calplans Agricultural Fund. An Investment in California Agricultural Real Estate. Oakland: Calplans Securities, n.d.

h. Personal letter

Published:

Wilde, Oscar. "To Mrs. Alfred Hunt." 25 Aug. 1880. The Letters of Oscar Wilde. Ed. Rupert Hart-Davis. New York: Harcourt, 1962. 67-68.

Unpublished:

Thomas, Dylan. Letter to Trevor Hughes. 12 Jan. 1934. Dylan Thomas Papers. Lockwood Memorial Library. Buffalo.

Personally received:

Highet, Gilbert. Letter to the author. 15 Mar. 1972.

i. Plays

(i) CLASSICAL PLAY

In your text, provide parenthetical references to act, scene, and line(s) of the play:

Cleopatra's jealousy pierces through her words:

What says the married woman? You may go;

Would she had never given you leave to come:

Let her not say 'tis I that keep you here;

I have no power upon you; hers you are.

(1.3.20-23)

The reference is to Act 1, Scene 3, lines 20–23. In "Works Cited" the play will be cited as follows:

Shakespeare, William. Antony and Cleopatra. The Complete Works of Shakespeare. Ed. Hardin Craig and David Bevington. Rev. ed. Glenview: Scott, 1973. 1073-1108.

NOTE: When the play is part of a collection, list the pages that cover the entire play.

(ii) MODERN PLAY

Many modern plays are published as individual books:

Miller, Arthur. The Crucible. New York: Bantam, 1952.

However, if published as part of a collection, the play is cited as follows:

Chekhov, Anton, The Cherry Orchard. 1903. The Art of Drama. Ed. R. F. Dietrich, William E. Carpenter, and Kevin Kerrane. 2nd ed. New York: Holt, 1976. 134-56.

NOTE: The page reference is to the entire play.

j. Poems

(i) CLASSICAL POEM

Lucretius [Titus Lucretius Carus]. Of the Nature of Things. Trans. William Ellery Leonard. Backgrounds of the Modern World. Vol. 1 of The World in Literature. Ed. Robert Warnock and George K. Anderson. New York: Scott, 1950. 343–53.

Or, if published in one book:

Dante [Dante Alighieri]. The Inferno. Trans. John Ciardi. New York: NAL, 1954.

(ii) MODERN POEM

Modern poems are usually part of a larger collection:

Moore, Marianne. "Poetry." Fine Frenzy. Ed. Robert Baylor and Brenda Stokes. New York: McGraw, 1972. 372–73.

NOTE: Cite pages covered by the poem.

Or, if the poem is long enough to be published as a book, use the following format:

Byron, George Gordon, Lord. Don Juan. Ed. Leslie A. Marchand. Boston: Houghton, 1958.

k. Public documents

Because of their complicated origins, public documents often seem difficult to cite. As a general rule, follow this order: Government; Body; Subsidiary bodies; Title of document (underlined); Identifying code; Place, publisher, and date of publication. Most publications by the federal government are printed by the Government Printing Office, which is abbreviated as "GPO":

(i) THE CONGRESSIONAL RECORD

A citation to the *Congressional Record* requires only title, date, and page(s):

Cong. Rec. 15 Dec. 1977, 19740.

(ii) CONGRESSIONAL PUBLICATIONS

United States. Cong. Senate. Permanent Subcommittee on Investigations of the Committee on Government Operations. Organized Crime—Stolen Securities. 93rd. Cong., 1st sess. Washington: GPO, 1973.

United States. Cong. House. Committee on Foreign Relations. Hearings on S. 2793, Supplemental Foreign Assistance Fiscal Year 1966—Vietnam. 89th Cong., 2nd sess. Washington: GPO, 1966.

United States. Cong. Joint Economic Committee on Medical Policies and Costs. Hearings. 93rd Cong., 1st sess. Washington: GPO, 1973.

(iii) EXECUTIVE BRANCH PUBLICATIONS

United States. Office of the President. Environmental Trends. Washington: GPO, 1981.

United States Dept. of Defense. Annual Report to the Congress by the Secretary of Defense. Washington: GPO, 1984.

United States. Dept. of Education. National Commission on Excellence in Education. A Nation at Risk: The Imperative for Educational Reform. Washington: GPO, 1983.

United States. Dept. of Commerce. Bureau of the Census. Statistical Abstracts of the United States. Washington: GPO, 1963.

(iv) LEGAL DOCUMENTS

When citing a well-known statute or law, a simple format will suffice:

US Const. Art. 1, sec. 2.

15 US Code. Sec. 78j(b). 1964.

US CC Art. 9, pt. 2, par. 9–28.

Federal Trade Commission Act. 1914.

When citing a little-known statute, law, or other legal agreement, provide all the information needed for retrieval:

''Agreement Between the Government of the United States of America and the Khmer Republic for Sales of Agricultural Commodities.'' Treaties and Other International Agreements. Vol. 26, pt. 1. TIAS No. 8008. Washington: GPO, 1976.

Names of court cases are abbreviated and the first important word of each party is spelled out: "Brown v. Board of Ed." stands for "Oliver Brown versus the Board of Education of Topeka, Kansas." Cases, unlike laws, are italicized in the text but not in "Works Cited." Text: *Miranda v. Arizona*. "Works Cited": Miranda v. Arizona. The following information must be supplied in the order listed: (1) name of the first plaintiff and the first defendant; (2) volume, name, and page (in that order) of the law report cited; (3) the place and name of the court that decided the case; (4) the year in which the case was decided:

Richardson v. J. C. Flood Co. 190 A. 2d 259. D.C. App. 1963.

Interpreted, the above means that the Richardson v. J. C. Flood Co. case can be found on page 259 of volume 190 of the Second Series of the *Atlantic Reporter*. The case was settled in the District of Columbia Court of Appeals during the year 1963.

For further information on the proper form for legal citations, consult *A Uniform System of Citation*, 12th ed. (Cambridge: Harvard Law Rev. Assn., 1976).

l. Quotation in a book or article used as a source

(i) QUOTATION IN A BOOK

MacDonald, Dwight. As quoted in John R. Trimble. Writing With Style: Conversations on the Art of Writing. Englewood Cliffs: Prentice, 1975.

(ii) QUOTATION IN AN ARTICLE

Grabar, Oleg. As quoted in Katharine Slater Gittes. "The Canterbury Tales and the Arabic Frame Tradition." PMLA 98 (1983): 237-51.

m. Report

Titles of reports in the form of pamphlets or books require underlining. When a report is included within the pages of a larger work, the title is set off in quotation marks. The work must be identified as a report:

The Churches Survey Their Task. Report of the Conference on Church, Community, and State. London: Allen & Unwin, 1937.

Luxenberg, Stan. "New Life for New York Law." Report on New York Law School. Change 10 (Nov. 1978): 16-18.

n. Table, graph, chart, or other illustration

If the table, graph, or chart has no title, identify it as a table, graph, or chart:

National Geographic Cartographic Division. Graph on imports drive into U.S. market. National Geographic 164 (July 1983): 13.

NOTE: The descriptive label is not underlined or set off in quotation marks.

Benson, Charles S. ''Number of Full-Time Equivalent Employees, by Industry, 1929-1959.'' Table. _The Economics of Public Education_. Boston: Houghton, 1961. 208.

This time the table has a title, so it is set off in quotation marks.

NOTE: The in-text citation should refer to "Table A.1."

o. Thesis

See Section 8b-6*d*, "Dissertation."

8c

Reference List (APA style)

Your reference list will contain the following elements listed in this order: author, year of publication, title, place of publication, and publisher.

The job of preparing your reference list will be easy if you took care to copy your sources accurately onto your bibliography cards. The following rules must be observed:

- Start your reference list on a new page, regardless of how much blank space is left on the last page of your paper.
- Center the title "Reference List" on the page, two inches from the top. Leave four spaces between the title and the first entry (see Section 8a-2).
- List all entries in alphabetical order (see Section 8a-1). Anonymous works are listed alphabetically according to the first word of the title, omitting *a*, *an*, or *the* if one of these words begins the title.
- List the names of all initial authors in inverted order.
- Second and subsequent entries by the same author(s) are listed with a line of three hyphens followed by a period: - - -.
- Indent the second line of each entry three spaces.
- Double-space throughout the reference list.
- Place a period followed by one space between all units.

Study the reference list at the end of the sample student paper.

8c-1 General order for bibliographic references to books in "Reference List"

Your reference list for books will contain the following elements, listed in the order indicated below:

- Name(s) of author(s) in inverted order, with only the initials of first and middle names.

- Year of publication in parentheses, followed by a period.
- Title of the book, underlined, with only the initial letter of the first word capitalized, followed by a period. (In two-part titles separated by a colon, the initial letter of the first word in the second title is also capitalized.)
- Place of publication, followed by a colon.
- Name of publisher, followed by a period. (The name of the publisher is listed in as brief a form as is intelligible. Terms like *Publisher, Co.*, and *Inc.* are omitted. However, names of university presses and associations are spelled out.)

8c-2 Sample bibliographic references to books

a. Book by a single author

Jones, E. (1931). On the nightmare. London: Hogarth.

A period is placed after the author's name (the period following an initial serves this purpose), after the final parenthesis of the publication date, after the title, and at the end of the entry. A colon separates the city from the publisher.

b. Book by two or more authors

Terman, L. M., & Merrill, M. A. (1937). Measuring intelligence. Cambridge, Mass.: The Riverside Press.

With two names, use an ampersand before the second name and do not use a comma to separate the names. With three or more names, use an ampersand before the last name and use commas to separate the names (Bowen, B. M., Poole, K. J., & Gorky, A.). Give the surnames and initials of all authors, no matter how many there are. Separate the names with commas and use an ampersand (&) between the last two names.

c. Edited book

Friedman, R. J., & Katz, M. M. (Eds.). (1974). The psychology of depression: Contemporary theory and research. New York: Wiley.

Give the surname and initials of all editors, regardless of how many there are. Show "Ed." or "Eds." in parentheses after the name(s), followed by a period. When referring to an article or chapter in an edited book, use the following form:

Waxer, P. (1979). Therapist training in nonverbal behavior. In A. Wolfgang (Ed.), Nonverbal behavior: Applications and cultural implications (pp. 221–240). New York: Academic Press.

Precede the name of the editor(s) with the word "In." When an editor's name is not in the author position, *do not* invert his name. Place "Ed." or "Eds." in parentheses after the name(s), followed by a comma. The title of the article or chapter is *not* placed within quotation marks and only the initial letter in the title is capitalized. Give inclusive page numbers for the article or chapter, in parentheses after the title of the book. Precede the page number(s) by "p." or "pp."

d. Translated book

The translator of a book (name *not* inverted) is placed within parentheses after the book title and is followed by "Trans." with a period after the end parenthesis:

Rank, O. (1932). Psychology and the soul (William Turner, Trans.). Philadelphia: Univ. of Pennsylvania Press.

e. Book in a foreign language

Saint-Exupéry, A. de. (1939). Terre des hommes. Paris: Gallimard.

NOTE: Titles of foreign books are in lower case except for the initial letter.

f. Revised edition of a book

Give the edition ("rev. ed.," "4th ed.," etc.) in parentheses following the title. Place a period after the final parenthesis:

Boulding, K. (1955). Economic analysis (3rd ed.). New York: Harper.

g. Book by a corporate author

When a book is authored by an organization rather than a person, the name of the organization appears in the author's place:

Committee of Public Finance. (1959). <u>Public finance</u>. New York: Pitman.

When the corporate author is also the publisher, place the word "Author" in place of the publisher:

Commission on Intergovernmental Relations. (1955). <u>Report to the President</u>. Washington, DC: Author.

h. Multivolume book

When citing a multivolume source, place the number(s) of the volume(s) actually used in parentheses immediately following the title. Use Arabic numerals for the volume number(s).

Reusch, J. (1980). Communication and psychiatry. In H. I. Kaplan, A. M. Freedman, & B. J. Sadock (Eds.), <u>Comprehensive textbook of psychiatry</u> (Vol. 1). Baltimore: Williams & Wilkins.

If a multivolume book was published over a number of years, list the years in parentheses following the author's name:

Brady, V. S. (1978–82).

i. Unpublished manuscript

Treat an unpublished manuscript the way you would a book except that instead of the place of publication and publishers, you will write "Unpublished manuscript":

Hardison, R. (1983). <u>On the shoulders of giants</u>. Unpublished manuscript.

NOTE: For a publication of limited circulation, supply in parentheses, immediately after the title, an address where the publication can be obtained.

8c-3 General order for bibliographic references to periodicals in "Reference List"

Entries for periodicals in your reference list will contain the following elements, in the order indicated:

- Name(s) of author(s) in inverted order with only the initials of first and middle names.
- Year of publication in parentheses, followed by a period. (For magazines issued on a specific day or month, give the year followed by the month or by the month and day.)
- Title of article not enclosed in quotation marks and with only the initial letter of the first word capitalized, followed by a period.
- Name of the journal or magazine, underlined, with the first word and all other words except articles and prepositions capitalized, followed by a comma.
- Volume number, underlined, followed by a comma. (Do not give volume numbers of periodicals issued on a specific date.)
- Page references, followed by a period.

8c-4 Sample bibliographic references to periodicals

a. Journal article, one author

Harvey, O. L. (1980). The measurement of handwriting considered as a form of expressive movement. Quarterly Review of Biology, 55, 231–249.

b. Journal article, up to six authors

Rodney, J., Hollender, B., & Campbell (1983). Hypnotizability and phobic behavior. Journal of Abnormal Psychology, 92, 386–389.

Use an ampersand preceded by a comma in front of the last author. Name each author. If the article has more than six authors, use this shortened form for in-text parenthetical references:

(Frey et al. 1981).

c. Journal article, paginated anew in each issue

Rosenthal, G. A. (1983). A seed-eating beetle's adaptations to poisonous seed. Scientific American, 249(6), 56–67.

If the journal begins each issue with page 1, supply the volume number, underlined, followed immediately by the issue number in parentheses, a comma, and then the page number(s) and a period.

d. Journal with continuous pagination throughout the annual volume

Anthony, R. G., & Smith, N. S. (1977). Ecological relationships between mule deer and white-tailed deer in southeastern Arizona. Ecological Monographs, 47, 255–77.

Most scholarly journals are paginated continuously throughout the year, so volume and page numbers are all the reader requires for retrieval.

e. Magazine article, issued monthly

Canby, T. Y. (1983, September). Satellites that serve us. National Geographic, pp. 281–300.

In parentheses after the author, place the year followed by a comma and the month. Place a period after the closing parenthesis. Use "p." or "pp." in front of page number(s).

f. Magazine article, issued on a specific day

Andersen, K. (1983, September 5). Private violence. Time, pp. 18–19.

In parentheses after the author, place the year followed by a comma and the month and date. Place a period after the closing parenthesis. Use "p." or "pp." in front of page number(s).

g. Newspaper article

Goodman, E. (1983, December 23). Bouvia case crosses the "rights" line. Los Angeles Times, Part 2, p. 5.

Place the exact date in parentheses following the author and indicate the section and page(s) following the newspaper title. Use Arabic numerals throughout the entry. Use "p." or "pp." for page(s). If the newspaper article has no author, begin with the title or headline of the article. Alphabetize works with no author by the first significant word in the title:

"Sad plight of anorexics." (Full title is "The sad plight of anorexics.")

h. Editorial

Guion, R. M. (1983). Comments from the new editor [Editorial]. Journal of Applied Psychology, 68, 547.

When citing an editorial, place the word "Editorial," followed by a period, after the title of the editorial. If the editorial has no title, "Editorial" immediately follows the date. Otherwise, treat the entry like any other magazine or journal article.

i. Letter to the editor

Jones, L. (1983, November). Bite the bullet [Letter to the editor]. Psychology Today, p. 5.

NOTE: When the month of the magazine is given in parentheses after the author, use "p." or "pp." for page(s). Place "Letter to the editor" in brackets immediately following the title.

j. Review

Boorstein, J. K. (1983, November/December). On welfare [Review of Dilemmas of welfare policy: Why work strategies haven't worked]. Society, pp. 120-122.

Place "Review of," followed by the title of the work being reviewed, in brackets immediately following the title of the review.

8c-5 Sample bibliographic references to nonprint materials

Since nonprint materials come in many forms and with varied information, the rule to follow when dealing with them is to provide as much necessary information as is available.

a. Computer sources

List the primary creator of the database as the author, followed by the date (in parentheses) when the program was produced. Then give the title of the program and, immediately following the title, identify the source [in brackets] as a computer program. Supply the location and name of the publisher of the program. Finally, enclose in parentheses any additional information necessary for identification and retrieval. This additional information should include the kind of computer for which the software was created. Computer citations will refer to material of two kinds: (1) Computer programs—that is, information received directly from data banks—and (2) written publications retrieved by a computer base. Examples of both kinds of citations follow:

(i) COMPUTER PROGRAM

Poole, L., & Barchers, M. (1977). <u>Future value of an investment</u> [Computer program]. Berkeley, CA: Adam Osborne & Associates. (Basic for a Wang 2200).

Fernandes, F. D. (1972). <u>Theoretical prediction of interference loading on aircraft stores</u>. [Computer program]. Pomona, CA: General Dynamics, Electro Dynamics Division. (1650 card images, Fortran IV, for CDC-6000. Available through the University of Georgia, Athens, Georgia).

NOTE: To cite a manual for a computer program, give the same information as you would for a computer program, but in brackets after the title identify the source as a computer manual:

Move-it: Inter-computer communication system. (1982). [Computer manual]. Canoga Park, CA: Wolfe Software Systems.

(ii) SOURCE RETRIEVED FROM A DATA BANK

Ulmer, C. (1981). Competence based instruction. Community College Review, 8(4), 51-56. rpt. Los Angeles: ERIC, File 1, EJ27541.

Sources retrieved from a data bank are cited the way you would the original source. Follow the original source citation with a semicolon and "rpt.", followed by the city and company providing the computer source service. Add a code, file, or record number when applicable.

b. Film

Cotton, D. H. (Producer), & Correll, J. B. (Director). (1980). The Management of hypertension in pregnancies [Film]. Houston: University of Texas.

When citing a film, name the producer (title in parentheses), followed by the director (title in parentheses), followed by the date of production (in parentheses). Always specify the medium in brackets so that the material cannot be confused with a book or some other source.

c. Recording (cassette, record, tape)

Bronowski, J. (Speaker). (1983). The mind (Cassette Recording BB 4418.01). Los Angeles: Pacifica Tape Library, 5316 Venice Blvd., Los Angeles, CA 90019.

When citing a recording, name the primary contributor (Speaker, Narrator, Panel Chair, Forum Director, etc.), followed by the date of production. If the recording has a number, list it in parentheses after specifying the kind of recording. Finally, list the place of publication and the publisher, supplying an exact address if one is available.

8c-6 Sample bibliographic references to special items

Sources come in such varied forms that a sample cannot be supplied for every possibility. When listing a source for which there is no exact model, provide enough information to make it possible for your reader to trace the source. In general, follow this order: (1) person or organization responsible for the work; (2) year the work was published, produced, or released; (3) title of the work; (4) identifying code, if applicable; (5) place of origin; (6) publisher. Study the following samples:

a. Government documents

(i) CONGRESS

U.S. Cong. House. (1977). U.S. assistance programs in Vietnam. 92d Cong., 2d sess. Washington, DC: U.S. Government Printing Office.

U.S. Cong. Senate. (1970). Separation of powers and the independent agencies: Cases and selected readings. 91st Cong., 1st sess. Washington, DC: U.S. Government Printing Office.

U.S. Cong. Joint Committee on Printing. (1983). Congressional directory. 98th Cong., 1st sess. Washington, DC: U.S. Government Printing Office.

(ii) EXECUTIVE BRANCH

Johnson, L. B. (1968). Economic report of the President. Washington, DC: U.S. Government Printing Office.

Executive Office of the President. (1981). Environmental trends. Washington, DC: U.S. Government Printing Office.

b. Legal references

The only kinds of legal references a student paper is likely to cite are references to court cases or references to statutes. Since legal references can be complex, consult *A Uniform System of Citation*, 12th Edition (Cambridge: Harvard Law Review Association, 1976), if your paper relies heavily on legal references. For common kinds of citations, follow these sample entries:

(i) COURT CASE

In general, use the following order when citing court decisions: (1) plaintiff v. defendant; (2) volume, name, and page of law report cited; (3) in parentheses, the name of the court that decided the case.

Clark v. Sumner. 559 S.W.2d. 914 (Tex. civ. app. 1977).

Explanation: The case can be found in the second series, volume 559, beginning on page 914, of the *South Western Reporter.* The case was decided by the Texas Civil Court of Appeals in 1977.

(ii) STATUTE

When citing commonly known statutes or laws, a simple format will suffice:

U.S. Const. Art. III, sec. 2.

15 U.S. Code, sec. 78j. (1964).

Sherman Antitrust Act. (1890).

For lesser-known statutes, supply additional information:

90 U.S. Statutes at Large. 505 (1976).

Nuclear Waste Policy Act, Part I, sec. 112 (a).

Energy Conservation and Production Act, Title I, Part A, sec. 101, 42 U.S.C. 6901, 1976.

(iii) TREATY

"Technical Cooperation Agreement Between the Government of Royal Kingdom of Saudi Arabia and the Government of the United States of America." Treaties and Other International Agreements. Vol. 26, Part 1, TAIS No. 8072. Washington, D.C.: U.S. Government Printing Office, 1976.

8c-7 Sample bibliographic references to a report

Organization for Economic Cooperation and Development. (1983). Assessing the impacts of technology on society. (Report). Washington, D.C.: U.S. Government Printing Office.

Place "Report" in parentheses after the title. If a code has been assigned to the report, add it also:

(Report No. CSOS-R-292).

If the publisher is the same as the author, place the word "Author" where you would normally give the name of the publisher:

California Postsecondary Education Commission. (1982). Promises to keep: Remedial education in California's public colleges and universities. (Report). Sacramento, CA: Author.

8d

Works Cited (numbers system)

Your "Works Cited" list should be arranged in alphabetical order and numbered consecutively. Of course, the numbers will not appear in consecutive order in your text. (Some authorities prefer that you forego an alphabetical arrangement in favor of consecutive numbering according to the order in which the sources appear in the text for the first time.) Study the sample below excerpted from an alphabetical/consecutive number listing. In listing works, follow the APA "Reference List" format as explained in Section 8c.

Works Cited

1. Albert, N., & Beck, A. T. (1975). Incidence of depression in early adolescence: A preliminary study. Journal of Youth and Adolescence, 4, 301-306.

2. American Heart Association. (1978). Guidelines for a weight control component in a smoking cessation program [Pamphlet]. Dallas: Author.

3. Hankin, J. R., & Locke, B. Z. (1982). The persistence of depressive symptomatology among prepaid group practice enrollees: An exploratory study. American Journal of Public Health, 72, 1000–1007.

4. Kovacs, M., & Beck, A. T. (1977). An empirical-clinical approach toward a definition of childhood depression. In J. G. Schulterbrandt & A. Ranskin (Eds.), Depression in childhood. New York: Raven, 1–25.

5. Nunnaly, J. C. (1967). Psychometric theory. New York: McGraw-Hill.

6. Wahrheit, G. J., Holzer, C. E., & Schwab, J. J. (1973). An analysis of social class and racial differences in depressive symptomatology: A Community study. Journal of Health and Social Behavior, 14, 291–299.

NOTE: Each of the sources cited by number in the text will correspond to one of the numbered sources listed above.

9

Finished Form of the Paper

9a Finished form of the paper

9b Outline

9c Title page

9d Abstract

9e Text

9f Tables, charts, graphs, and other illustrative materials

9g Content notes and endnotes

9h Bibliography

9a

Finished form of the paper

In its finished form the paper consists of the following parts:

Outline (if required)
Title page
Abstract (if required)
Text of the paper
Content notes (if required)
Endnotes or footnotes (if required)
Works Cited (or Reference List)

The paper should be neatly typed on one side only of each page with a fresh black ribbon. Papers typed in script characters are frequently more difficult to read and therefore unacceptable. Use heavy (20-pound) 8½″ × 11″ white bond paper. Erasable bond smudges too easily for a teacher to pencil in corrections; therefore it should not be used. If you must use erasable bond, have the paper photocopied on plain (uncoated) paper and submit the photocopy. Do not staple the pages or submit the paper inside a folder. Simply clip the pages together with a paper clip and submit the paper as a loose-leaf manuscript. Give the paper a ruthless proofreading before submitting it to the teacher for evaluation.

9b

Outline

The outline that precedes the text of the paper should look uncluttered and balanced. Use small Roman numerals to paginate all pages of the outline. These are not included in the total count of the paper. Place your name, the instructor's name, the name of the course for which the paper was written, and the date in the upper left-hand corner of the paper, just as you are required to do on the title page (see Fig. 9-1).

9c

Title page

A separate title page is not required for papers following the MLA style. Instead, the first page should contain the full title of the paper, your name, the instructor's name, the course for which the paper was written, the date, and the opening text of your paper. The following facsimile of a typical opening page includes marginal measurements and line spacing. (See also the first page of the sample paper on page 221.)

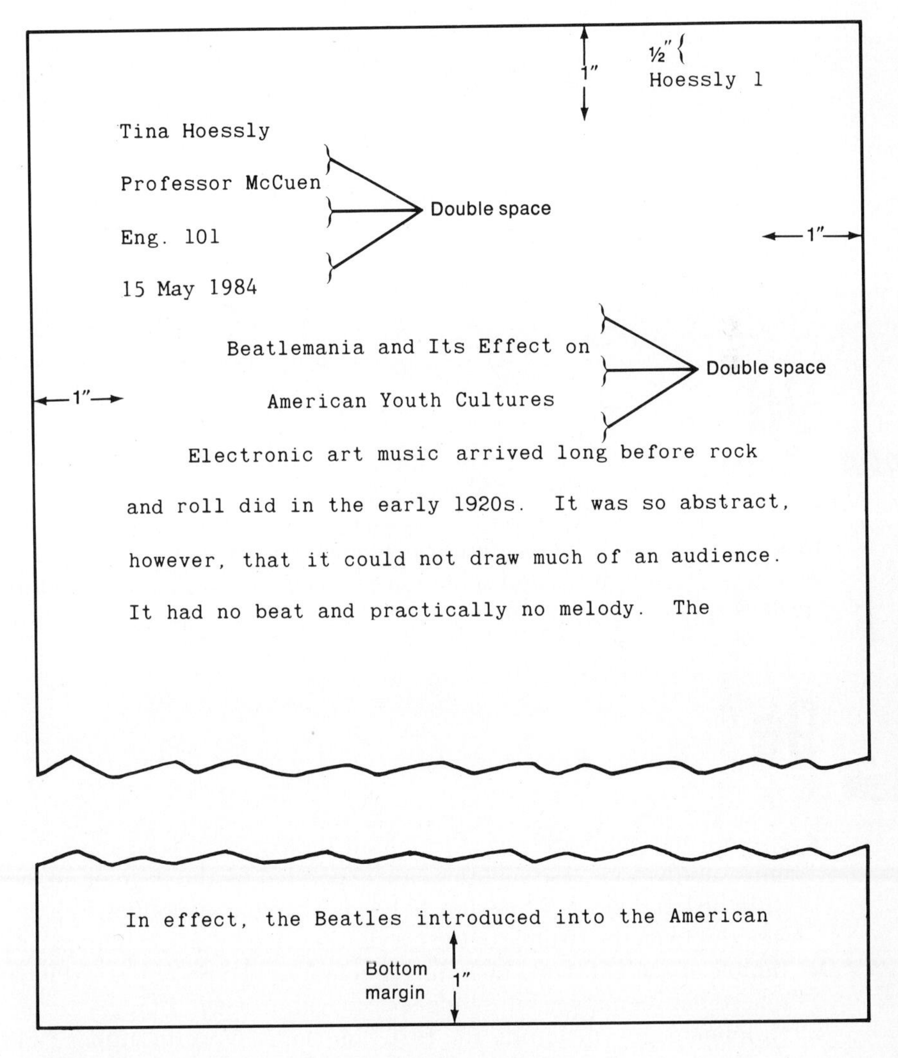

Figure 9-1 Sample student title page (MLA style)

This first page, and all subsequent pages, must contain one-inch margins on all sides. All pages, including the first, are numbered. From page 2 on, type your last name before the page number in case a page is misplaced. Except for titles of published works appearing within it, the title of the paper is neither underlined nor entirely placed in capitals. If the title takes up two or more lines, position the extra lines so as to form a double-spaced inverted pyramid, with each line centered on the page:

```
Early English Novels: The Development of a

New and Influential Stereotype

of the Feminine Role
```

Do not use a period at the end of the title.

Papers written in the APA style do require a title page. See the sample student paper on page 243 for specific directions on handling the title page.

9d
Abstract

Papers written for the social sciences require an abstract, that is a summary of the paper's major findings. The abstract must be written in coherent paragraph form and should not exceed one page. See the sample student paper on pages 244–45.

9e
Text

- Use normal paragraphing throughout the paper. If your paper contains subdivisions, use subtitles either centered on the page or aligned with the left margin. Underline but do not capitalize subtitles. Separate subtitles from the last line of the previous section by quadruple spacing.
- Double-space the text, including quotations. Footnotes are double-spaced between notes but single-spaced within (see p. 125).
- Number pages, including the first, consecutively in the upper right-hand corner of the paper. Numbers are not followed by hyphens, parentheses, periods, or other characters. "Notes" and "Works Cited" begin on new pages but are numbered as part of the general sequence (see sample student paper, pp. 221–42).
- Note that numerals are placed one half space above the line within the text of the paper. Each superscript numeral should be placed as near as possible to the end of the cited material to which it refers (see Section 7g-4).

- Unless otherwise indicated by your teacher, place each footnote on the bottom of the same page on which its numeral occurs. The first line of each footnote is indented five spaces; second and subsequent lines are aligned with the left margin. For both footnotes and endnotes use elevated numerals (a half space above the line) and follow the numerals with one space. (See p. 125.)
- For parenthetical citations, see Sections 7d and 7e.
- If possible use pica type, which is easier to read than elite. Script type and other artistic typefaces are often difficult to read and therefore unacceptable. If in doubt, consult your teacher.
- Avoid multiple corrections. If a correction is unavoidable, type it, or write it in legibly with black ink, *above* the line involved. Do not use the margins. If corrections are extensive, retype the page.
- We encourage all students to learn word processing on a computer. The advantage in terms of correcting, editing, revising, and producing a clean final copy are manifold.

9f

Tables, charts, graphs, and other illustrative materials

Papers in many fields frequently require tables, graphs, charts, maps, drawings, and other illustrations. For example, a paper on the decline of basic skills among high-school students may include a graph that plots this decline over the past five years. An economics paper may require charts that explain certain economic changes. An anthropology paper may include drawings of primitive artifacts. A history paper may illustrate some historic battle with a map. A biology paper may include drawings of enlarged cells. The possibilities are nearly endless. The general rule, however, is for all illustrative materials to appear as close as possible to the part of the text that they illustrate.

9f-1 Tables

Tables are usually labeled, numbered with Arabic numerals, and captioned. Both labels and captions are capitalized as you would a title (do not use all capital letters). The source of the table and accompanying notes should be placed flush left at the bottom of the table. If no source is listed, a reader will assume that the table is your original work. Indicate notes to tables with lower-case letters, or with asterisks and crosses if you need additional indicators, to avoid confusion with endnotes, footnotes, or other textual notes. (See Fig. 9-2, p. 196).

9f-2 Other illustrative materials

Other illustrative materials should be labeled "Fig." or "Figure" and numbered with Arabic numerals: Fig. 3. Each figure should be captioned and capitalized with a title:

Fig. 12. Chart Tracing the Development of the Alphabet

Again, the source of the illustration and any notes should be placed flush left immediately below the illustration. If no source is cited, a reader will assume that the illustration is your original work. Indicate notes to illustrations with lower-case letters, asterisks, and crosses, so as to avoid confusion with other footnote or endnote numbers in the text. A few sample illustrations follow:

Table 2

Significance of Differences Between Mean Grade Point Averages of Male Achievers and Underachievers from Grade One Through Eleven

	Mean grade point average					
Grade	Achievers	Under-achievers	F	P	t	P
1	2.81	2.56	1.97	n.s.†	1.44	n.s.
2	2.94	2.64	1.94	n.s.	1.77	n.s.
3	3.03	2.58	1.49	n.s.	2.83	.01*
4	3.19	2.72	1.03	n.s.	2.96	.01*
5	3.28	2.75	1.02	n.s.	3.71	.01*
6	3.33	2.67	1.33	n.s.	4.46	.01*
7	3.25	2.56	1.02	n.s.	5.80	.01*
8	3.36	2.50	1.59	n.s.	6.23	.01*
9	3.25	2.14	1.32	n.s.	10.57	.01*
10	3.13	1.87	1.30	n.s.	10.24	.01*
11	2.81	1.85	4.05	.02**	5.46	.01*

* Yields significance beyond the .01 level.

** Yields significance beyond the .02 level but below the .01 level.

† No significance.

Figure 9-2 Sample table

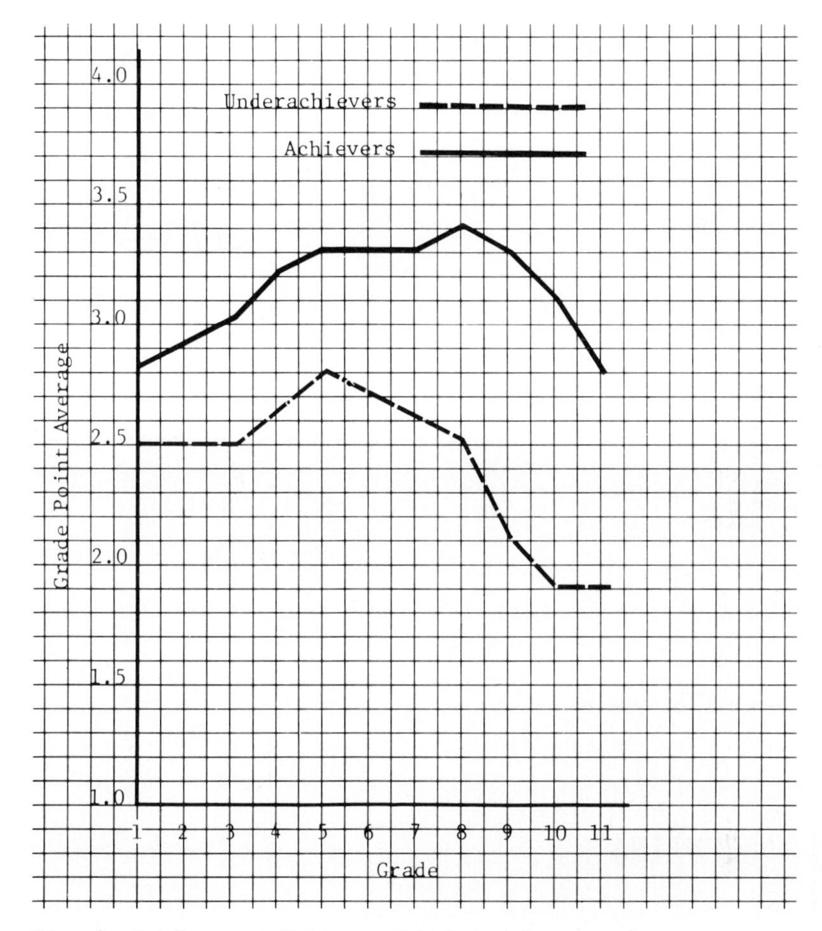

Fig. 1. Achievement Pattern of Male Achievers and Underachievers from Grades One Through Eleven

Figure 9-3 Sample line graph

9g

Content notes and endnotes

If you are using the parenthetical style of documentation, content notes, numbered consecutively, would appear at the end of the paper under the heading "Notes." If you are using endnotes, they appear on a separate page at the end of the paper, preceded by the heading "Notes." Any content notes appear either at the bottom of the appropriate page or on a separate page along with the endnotes. (See Section 7h, pp. 139–142.)

Fig. 2. African Doll (Akua'ba)
Source: American Museum of Natural History

Figure 9-4 Sample illustration

Figure 9-5 Sample map

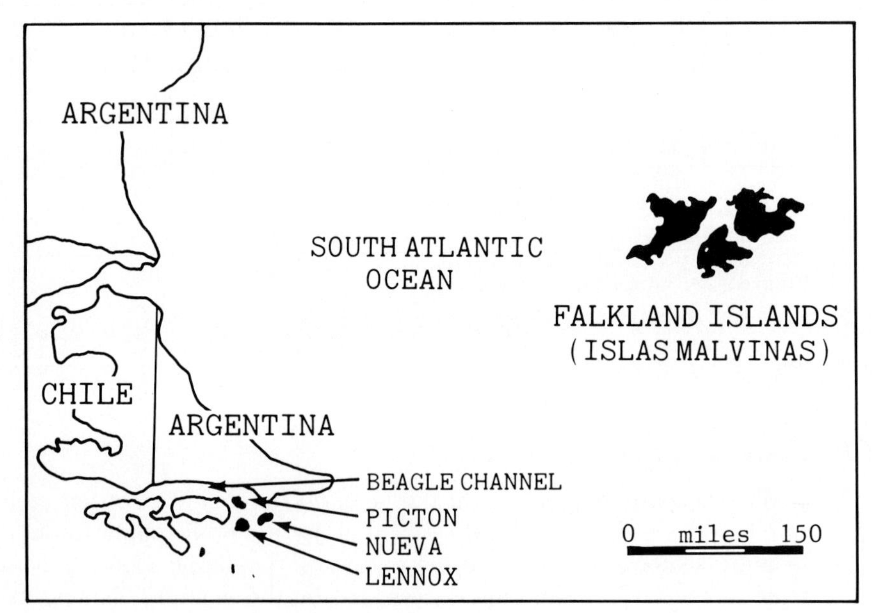

Fig. 3. Islands Involved in the Beagle Channel Dispute
Source: U.S. Government Printing Office, 1984

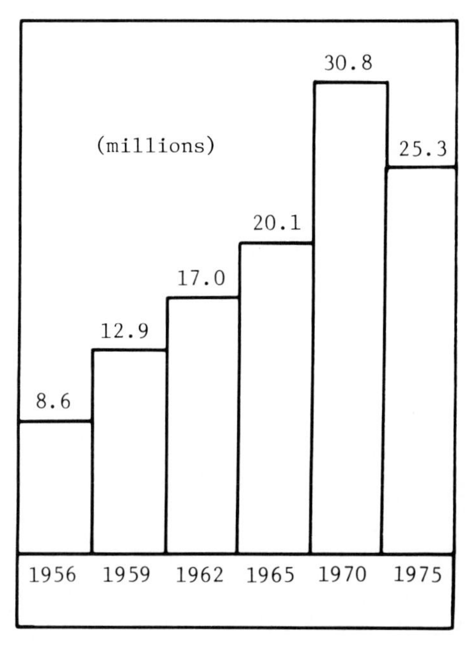

Fig. 4. Number of individuals owning shares in public corporations

Source: New York Stock Exchange

Figure 9-6 Sample bar graph

9h

Bibliography

The bibliography appears on a separate page at the end of your paper, marked by the centered heading "Works Cited" or "Reference List." (For sample "Works Cited" pages, see Fig. 8-1, p. 148, and student paper, p. 241; for sample "Reference List," see student paper, p. 262.)

10

Mechanics

10a Using numbers in the paper

10b Titles

10c Italics

10d Names of persons

10e Hyphenating words

10f Handling foreign-language words

10g Abbreviations

10a

Using numbers in the paper

10a-1 Numerals

The rule of thumb on the use of numerals is this: use a numeral only if the number cannot be spelled out in two words or less. The MLA prefers that writers spell out numbers from one to nine; use numerals for all numbers 10 and above. For the Roman numeral "one," use a Capital "I"; for the Arabic numeral "one," use either the number "1" on your typewriter keyboard, or the lower case letter "l." Dates and page numbers are usually *not* spelled out: "November 19" or "19 November," and "page 36," are preferred to "the nineteenth of November" and "the thirty-sixth page."

Wrong 25,500 voters hailed the passage of the bill.

Right The bill was hailed by 25,500 voters.

10a-2 Percentages and amounts of money

Figures of percentages or amounts of money are governed by the rule for numerals. Figures or amounts that can be written out in two words or less may be spelled out; otherwise, they must be expressed as numerals.

May be spelled out:	thirteenth percent	thirteen Deutsche Mark
	eighty-three percent	fifty British pounds
	ten francs	thirty-six dollars
Should be expressed as numerals:	133%	185 DM
	83.5%	£ 550
	103 fr	$366

10a-3 Dates

Consistency is the prime rule governing the treatment of dates in the paper. Write either "19 November 1929" or "November 19, 1929," but not a mixture of both. Write either "June 1931" or "June, 1931," but not both. (Note: if a comma is placed between the month and the year, a comma must also follow the year, unless some other kind of punctuation mark is necessary.) The MLA prefers that writers do not use a comma between the month and year. Centuries are expressed in lower-case letters:

```
in the thirteenth century
```

A hyphen must be added when the century is used as an adjective:

```
twelfth-century literature

seventeenth- and eighteenth-century philosophy
```

Decades can either be written out:

```
during the thirties
```

or expressed in numerals:

```
during the 1930s

during the '30s
```

The term "B.C." (meaning before Christ's birth) follows the year; "A.D." (meaning after Christ's birth) precedes the year. The MLA recommends omitting the periods in these abbreviations:

```
in 55 BC

in AD 1066
```

When using both a Western and a non-Western date, place one or the other in parentheses:

```
1912 (Year One of the Republic)
```

Both "in 1929–30" and "from 1929 to 1930" are correct, as is "from 1929–30 to 1939–40." However, do not write "from 1951–72"; confusion may result from the absence of the preposition "to" after 1951. Rather, write "1951 to 1972."

10a-4 Numbers connected consecutively

When connecting two numbers, give the second number in full for all numbers from one through ninety-nine. For numbers from one hundred on, give only the last two figures of the second number, if it is within the same hundred or thousand:

```
4-5

15-18
```

```
    106–07
    486–523
    896–1025
  1,860–1,930
  1,860–75
  1,608–774
 13,456–67
 13,456–14,007
```

The above examples follow the style of the *MLA Handbook*. However, APA and other styles tend to show all digits of the second number, in all cases.

10a-5 Roman numerals

The following require capital Roman numerals: major divisions of an outline (see Section 5b-1); people in a series, such as monarchs, who share a common name:

```
Henry VIII, King of England
```

The following no longer require capital Roman numerals: volumes, books, and parts of major works; acts of plays.

Use lower-case Roman numerals for pages from prefaces, forewords, or introductions to books:

The following no longer require lower-case Roman numerals: chapters of books, scenes of plays, cantos of poems, chapters of books from the Bible.

10b Titles

The rules that follow apply to titles used in your text. For how to handle titles in notes or bibliography, consult the section on the style you are using in Chapters 7 and 8. The APA, for example, has a special way of handling titles.

10b-1 Italicized titles

Certain titles must be italicized and therefore underlined in typewritten work. Underlined titles include the following:

Published books

`A Farewell to Arms`

Plays

`The Devil's Disciple`

Long poems

`Enoch Arden`

Pamphlets

`The Biology of Cancer: A Guide to Twelve College Lectures`

Newspapers

`Los Angeles Times`, *but* `Stoneham Gazette`

(Underline only those words that appear on the masthead of the paper.)

Magazines and journals

`U.S. News and World Report; Shakespeare Quarterly`

Classical works

`Plutarch's Parallel Lives`

Films

`Gone with the Wind`

Television and radio programs

`Sixty Minutes (CBS); The Music of Your Life (KNXT)`

Ballets

`The Sleeping Beauty`

Operas

`Carmen`

Instrumental music listed by name

`Brahms's Rinaldo`

NOTE: Instrumental music listed by form, number, and key is not underlined:

`Brahms's Piano Concerto no. 1, opus 15 in D minor`

Paintings

`Regnault's Three Graces`

Sculptures

`Michelangelo's Madonna and Child`

Ships

U.S.S. Charr

Aircraft

the presidental aircraft Airforce One

NOTE: An initial "a," "an," or "the" is italicized and capitalized when it is part of the title:

The Grapes of Wrath

After the use of the possessive case, delete "The," "A," or "An," in a title:

Henry James's Portrait of a Lady

(The full title is *The Portrait of a Lady*.)

10b-2 Titles within quotation marks

The following items should be placed within quotation marks:

Short stories

''The Black Cat''

Short poems

''The Road Not Taken''

Songs

''A Mighty Fortress Is Our God''

Newspaper articles

''It's Drag Racing without Parachutes''

Magazine or journal articles

''How to Cope with Too Little Time and Too Many Meetings''

Encyclopedia articles

''Ballet''

Subdivisions in books

''The Solitude of Nathaniel Hawthorne''

Unpublished Dissertations

''The Local Communications Media and Their Coverage of Local Government in California''

Lectures

''The Epic of King Tutankhamun: Archeological Superstar''

Television episodes

''Turnabout,'' from the program The World of Women

NOTE: Sacred writings, series, editions, societies, conventional titles, and parts of books neither use underlining nor are enclosed in quotation marks.

Sacred writings

the Bible, the Douay Version, the New Testament, Matthew, the Gospels, the Talmud, the Koran, the Upanishads

Series

Masterpiece Theater, the Pacific Union College Lyceum Series

Editions

the Variorum Edition of Spenser

Societies

L'Alliance française, the Academy of Abdominal Surgeons

Conventional titles

Kennedy's first State of the Union Address

Parts of books

Preface
Introduction
Table of Contents
Appendix
Index

10b-3 Titles within titles

If a title enclosed by quotation marks appears within an underlined title, the quotation marks are retained. If an underlined title appears within a title enclosed by quotation marks, the underlining is retained:

Book ''The Sting'' and Other Classical Short Stories

Article ''Textual Variants in Sinclair Lewis's Babbitt''

Single quotation marks are used with a title requiring quotation marks appearing within another title also requiring quotation marks:

Article ''Jonathan's Swift's 'Journal to Stella'''

A title that would normally be underlined, but that appears as part of another title, is neither underlined nor placed in quotation marks. For example, the title of the book, *The Great Gatsby*, would normally be underlined. But when this title forms part of the title of another book, such as *A Study of* The Great Gatsby, only "A Study of" is underlined:

A Study of The Great Gatsby

10b-4 Frequent reference to a title

If the research paper refers frequently to the same title, subsequent reference to the title may be abbreviated, once the full title has been initially used. In abbreviating, always use a key word:

Return *for* Return of the Native

Tempest *for* Tempest in a Teapot

''The Bishop'' *for* ''The Bishop Orders His Tomb at Saint Praxis''

UNESCO *for* United Nations Educational, Scientific, and Cultural Organization

For citation of titles in subsequent references in notes, see Section 7g-8.

10c
Italics

In typewritten work, italics are indicated by underlining. Words making up a phrase or title may be continuously, rather than separately, underlined.

- Underline phrases, words, letters, or numerals cited as linguistic examples:

One cannot assume that the Victorian word trump is an amalgamation of tramp and chump.

- Underline foreign words used in English texts:

It seems clearly a case of noblesse oblige.

He used the post hoc ergo propter hoc fallacy.

NOTE: Exceptions to the rule include quotations entirely in another language, titles of articles in another language, and words anglicized through frequent use, such as: détente, laissez faire, gestalt, et al. In papers dealing with the arts, foreign expressions commonly used in the field need not be underlined: hubris, mimesis, leitmotif, pas de deux.

See Section 10b-1 for italics in titles.

10d

Names of persons

- In general, omit formal titles (Mr., Mrs., Miss, Ms., Dr., Professor) when referring to persons, living or dead, by their last names. However, convention dictates that certain persons be referred to by title:

  Mme de Staël, Mrs. Humphry Ward

- It is acceptable to use simplified names for famous people:

  Dante *for* Dante Alighieri

  Vergil *for* Publius Vergilius Maro

  Michelangelo *for* Michelangelo Buonarroti

  It is also acceptable to use an author's pseudonym rather than the author's real name:

  George Sand *for* Amandine-Aurore-Lucie Dupin

  Mark Twain *for* Samuel Clemens

  Molière *for* Jean-Baptiste Poquelin

- The *von, van, van der,* and *de* of foreign names are usually not included in references to people:

  Goethe (Hans Wolfgang von Goethe)

  Frontenac (Louis de Frontenac)

  Ruysdael (Salman van Ruysdael)

However, certain names are traditionally not used with the last name alone:

Van Dyck *not* Dyck

De Gaulle *not* Gaulle

von Braun *not* Braun

O. Henry *not* Henry

10e Hyphenating words

- If possible, avoid dividing a word at the end of a typewritten line. But if a word must be divided for the sake of a balanced margin, make the division at the end of a syllable:

de-ter-mined	haz-ard-ous
i-vo-ry	grad-u-al
con-clud-ing	dress-er

Correct syllabification of words is listed in a dictionary. College dictionaries indicate the syllables of words with dots: bru · tal · i · ty; far · ci · cal.

- Never hyphenate a one-syllable word, such as "twelfth," "screamed," or "brought."
- Do not end or begin a line with a single letter:

a-mend, bur-y

- Make no division that might cause confusion in either the meaning or pronunciation of a word:

sour-ces, re-creation

- Divide hyphenated words only at the hyphen:

editor-in-chief, semi-retired

- Do not divide proper names, such as "Lincoln" or "Italy."
- Do not end several consecutive lines with a hyphen.

10f

Handling foreign-language words

Words or phrases from a foreign language must be reproduced with all their accent marks. If you are doing a lengthy paper on a foreign language or on comparative literature, consider renting a typewriter with an international keyboard. Otherwise, the accent marks of foreign words must be written in by hand. Pay special attention to the following:

- It is not necessary to accent the capital letters of French words:

  énormément, *but* Enormément *or* ENORMEMENT

- For German words with the umlaut, use two dots rather than an "e," even for initial capitals:

  Überhaupt *not* Ueberhaupt

  fröhlich *not* froehlich

- Proper names retain their conventional spelling:

  Boehm *not* Böhm

  Dürrenmatt *not* Duerrenmatt

- Digraphs (two letters that represent only one sound) can be typed without connection (ae, oe), can be written in by hand (æ , œ), or can be connected at the top ($\overline{\text{ae}}$, $\overline{\text{oe}}$). In American English, the digraph "ae" is being abandoned:

  archeology *not* archaeology

  medieval *not* mediaeval

  esthetic *not* aesthetic

10g

Abbreviations

Following is a list of abbreviations commonly encountered in research. The MLA favors dropping periods whenever possible.

10g-1 Abbreviations and reference words commonly used

AD, A.D. — *anno Domini* 'in the year of the Lord.' No space between; precedes numerals (AD 12).

anon. — anonymous

app.	appendix
art., arts.	article(s)
assn.	association
assoc.	associate, associated
b.	born
BC, B.C.	before Christ. No space between; follows numerals (23 BC).
bibliog.	bibliography, bibliographer, bibliographical
biog.	biography, biographer, biographical
bk., bks.	book(s)
©	copyright (© 1975)
c., ca.	*circa* 'about.' Used with approximate dates (c. 1851).
cf.	*confer* 'compare.' Do not use "cf." if "see" is intended.
ch., chs.	chapter(s)
chor., chors.	choreographed by, choreographer(s)
col., cols.	column(s)
comp., comps.	compiled by, compiler(s)
cond.	conducted by, conductor
Cong.	Congress
Cong. Rec.	*Congressional Record*
d.	died
dir., dirs.	directed by, director(s)
diss.	dissertation
E, Eng.	English
ed., eds.	edited by, editor(s), editions(s)
e.g.	*exempli gratia* 'for example.' Preceded and followed by a comma.
enl.	enlarged (as in "rev. and enl. ed.")
esp.	especially (as in "124–29, esp. 125")
et al.	*et alii* 'and others'
etc.	*et cetera* 'and so forth.' Do not use in text.
ex., exs.	example(s)
f., ff.	and the following (with no space after a numeral) page(s) or line(s). Exact references are preferable: 89–90 instead of 89f.; 72–79 instead of 72ff.
facsim. (or facs.)	facsimile
fig., figs.	figure(s)
fol., fols.	folio(s)
Fr.	French
front.	frontispiece
Ger.	German
Gk.	Greek
GPO	Government Printing Office, Washington, D.C.
hist.	history, historian, historical
ibid.	*ibidem* 'in the same place,' i.e., in the cited title. Avoid using. Cite instead the author's last name and the page number.
i.e.	*id est* 'that is.' Preceded and followed by a comma.
illus.	illustrated (by), illustrator, illustration(s)
intro. (or introd.)	introduced by, introduction
ips	inches per second (used on labels of recording tapes)
It.	Italian

jour.	journal
L., Lat.	Latin
l., ll.	line(s). MLA style now uses "line" or "lines" instead of "l" or "ll."
lang., langs.	language(s)
LC, L. C.	Library of Congress. Typed with a space between when periods are used.
loc. cit. (not l.c.)	*loco citato* 'in the place (passage) cited.' Avoid using. Repeat the citation in shortened form.
MA, M.A.	Master of Arts. No space between.
mag.	magazine
ME	Middle English
ms, mss (or ms., mss.)	manuscript(s). Capitalized and followed by a period when referring to a specific manuscript.
MS, M.S.	Master of Science. No space between.
n., nn.	note(s)
narr., narrs.	narrated by, narrator(s)
NB, N.B.	*nota bene* 'take notice, mark well.' Not spaced.
n.d.	no date (in a book's imprint). No space between.
no., nos.	number(s)
n.p.	no place (of publication); no publisher. Not spaced.
n. pag.	no pagination. Space between.
OE	Old English
op.	opus (work)
op. cit	*opere citato* 'in the work cited.' Avoid using. Repeat citation in shortened form.
p., pp.	page(s).
par., pars.	paragraph(s)
passim	'throughout the work, here and there' (as "84, 97, and passim")
PhD., Ph.D.	Doctor of Philosophy. No space between.
philos.	philosophical
pl., pls.	plate(s)
pref.	preface
prod., prods.	produced by, producer(s)
pseud.	pseudonym
pt., pts.	part(s)
pub., pubs.	published by, publication(s)
rept., repts.	reported by, report(s)
rev.	revised (by), revision; review, reviewed (by). Spell out "review," if there is any possibility of ambiguity.
rpm	revolutions per minute (used on recordings)
rpt.	reprinted (by), reprint
sc.	scene
sec., secs.	section(s)
ser.	series
sic	'thus, so.' Put between square brackets when used to signal an editorial interpolation.
soc.	society
Sp.	Spanish
st., sts.	stanza(s)
St., Sts.	Saint(s)
supp., supps.	supplement(s)

Tech rep.	Technical report
TLS	typed letter signed
trans. (or tr.)	translated by, translator, translation
ts.	typescript. Cf. "ms."
v., vs.	versus 'against.' Cf. "v., vv."
v., vv. (or vs., vss.)	verse(s)
vol., vols.	volume(s)

10g-2 The Bible and Shakespeare

Use the following abbreviations in notes and parenthetical references; do not use them in the text (except parenthetically).

a. The Bible

OLD TESTAMENT (OT)

Gen.	Genesis	Eccl.	Ecclesiastes
Exod.	Exodus	Song. Sol. (also Cant.)	Song of Solomon (also Canticles)
Lev.	Leviticus	Isa.	Isaiah
Num.	Numbers	Jer.	Jeremiah
Deut.	Deuteronomy	Lam.	Lamentations
Josh.	Joshua	Ezek.	Ezekiel
Judg.	Judges	Dan.	Daniel
Ruth	Ruth	Hos.	Hosea
1 Sam.	1 Samuel	Joel	Joel
2 Sam.	2 Samuel	Amos	Amos
1 Kings	1 Kings	Obad.	Obadiah
2 Kings	2 Kings	Jon.	Jonah
1 Chron.	1 Chronicles	Mic.	Micah
2 Chron.	2 Chronicles	Nah.	Nahum
Ezra	Ezra	Hab.	Habakkuk
Neh.	Nehemiah	Zeph.	Zephaniah
Esth.	Esther	Hag.	Haggai
Job	Job	Zech.	Zechariah
Ps.	Psalms	Mal.	Malachi
Prov.	Proverbs		

SELECTED APOCRYPHAL AND DUETEROCANONICAL WORKS

1 Esd.	1 Esdras	Bar.	Baruch
2 Esd.	2 Esdras	Song 3 Childr.	Song of the Three Children
Tob.	Tobit	Sus.	Susanna
Jth.	Judith	Bel and Dr.	Bel and the Dragon
Esth. (also Apocr.)	Esther Apocrypha	Pray. Man.	Prayer of Manasseh
Wisd. Sol. (also Wisd.)	Wisdom of Solomon (also Wisdom)	1 Macc.	1 Maccabees
Ecclus. (also Sir.)	Ecclesiasticus (also Sirach)	2 Macc.	2 Maccabees

NEW TESTAMENT (NT)

Matt.	Matthew	1 Tim.	1 Timothy
Mark	Mark	2 Tim.	2 Timothy
Luke	Luke	Tit.	Titus
John	John	Philem.	Philemon
Acts	Acts	Heb.	Hebrews
Rom.	Romans	Jas.	James
1 Cor.	1 Corinthians	1 Pet.	1 Peter
2 Cor.	2 Corinthians	2 Pet.	2 Peter
Gal.	Galatians	1 John	1 John
Eph.	Ephesians	2 John	2 John
Phil.	Philippians	3 John	3 John
Col.	Colossians	Jude	Jude
1 Thess.	1 Thessalonians	Rev. (also Apoc.)	Revelation (also Apocalypse)
2 Thess.	2 Thessalonians		

SELECTED APOCRYPHAL WORKS

G. Thom.	Gospel of Thomas	G. Pet.	Gospel of Peter
G. Heb.	Gospel of the Hebrews		

b. Shakespeare

Ado	*Much Ado about Nothing*	*MND*	*A Midsummer Night's Dream*
Ant	*Antony and Cleopatra*	*MV*	*The Merchant of Venice*
AWW	*All's Well That Ends Well*	*Oth.*	*Othello*
AYL	*As You Like It*	*Per.*	*Pericles*
Cor.	*Coriolanus*	*PhT*	*The Phoenix and the Turtle*
Cym.	*Cymbeline*	*PP*	*The Passionate Pilgrim*
Err.	*The Comedy of Errors*	Q	Quarto ed.
F1	First Folio ed. (1623)	*R2*	*Richard II*
F2	Second Folio ed. (1632)	*R3*	*Richard III*
Ham.	*Hamlet*	*Rom.*	*Romeo and Juliet*
1H4	*Henry IV, Part I*	*Shr.*	*The Taming of the Shrew*
2H4	*Henry IV, Part II*	*Son.*	*Sonnets*
H5	*Henry V*	*TGV*	*The Two Gentlemen of Verona*
1H6	*Henry VI, Part I*	*Tim.*	*Timon of Athens*
2H6	*Henry VI, Part II*	*Tit.*	*Titus Andronicus*
3H6	*Henry VI, Part III*	*Tmp.*	*The Tempest*
H8	*Henry VIII*	*TN*	*Twelfth Night*
JC	*Julius Caesar*	*TNK*	*The Two Noble Kinsmen*
Jn.	*King John*	*Tro.*	*Troilus and Cressida*
LC	*A Lover's Complaint*	*Ven.*	*Venus and Adonis*
LLL	*Love's Labour's Lost*	*Wiv.*	*The Merry Wives of Windsor*
Lr.	*King Lear*	*WT*	*The Winter's Tale*
Luc.	*The Rape of Lucrece*		
Mac.	*Macbeth*		
MM	*Measure for Measure*		

11

Sample Student Papers

11a **Entire paper using the author-work style of documentation (MLA)**

11b **Entire paper using the author-date style of documentation (APA)**

11c **Excerpt from a paper using footnote documentation (traditional)**

The following samples were researched and written by college freshmen. Except for a few minor corrections, they are reproduced as they were submitted. The accompanying marginal annotations clarify the format of the paper, explain specific problems, or draw attention to important aspects of research.

11a

Entire paper using the author-work style of documentation (MLA)

Double-space throughout the body of the outline.

The title, centered on the page, appears in the outline.

Place the thesis at the beginning of the outline, although it may not be the first sentence of the paper. The thesis in the outline may be worded more succinctly than in the paper.

The outline leaves out the details of the paper, mentioning only major points.

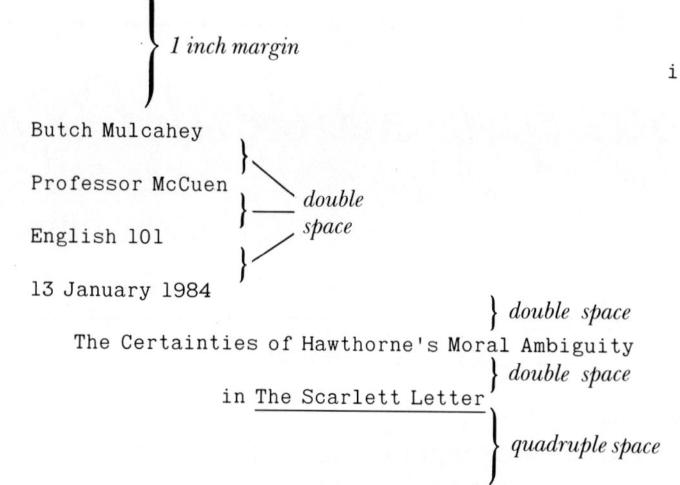

i

Butch Mulcahey

Professor McCuen

English 101

13 January 1984

The Certainties of Hawthorne's Moral Ambiguity
in The Scarlett Letter

Thesis: Hawthorne's moral ambiguity suggests certainties that transcend in importance the ambiguity, which several critics claim to be the novel's fault.

I. There are matters of interpretation of Hawthorne's concerns upon which most critics agree.

A. Most critics agree that Hawthorne concerns himself with the consequences of sin rather than with the sin itself.

B. Hypocrisy is generally believed to be what Hawthorne considered the most

Use small Roman numerals for paginating the outline.

Use standard outline symbols. For a full discussion of how to write the outline, see Section 5b.

ii

grave consequence of sin.

C. A common interpretation is that Hawthorne's moral seems to follow logically from his concern with the gravity of hypocrisy.

II. Beyond this level of generally accepted interpretation, however, some critics suggest that the value of the moral diminishes in the presence of ambiguity in the novel.

A. Some argue that Hawthorne's definition of sin itself is ambiguous and has at best only a cloudy, tentative meaning.

B. Some, especially Jeffrey Duncan, suggest that Hawthorne's plea that men ''be true'' is paradoxical.

C. Hyatt H. Waggoner questions whether salvation is possible from Hawthorne's proposed morality, observing the dark and uncertain conclusion that Hester and Dimmesdale seem to share.

III. Undoubtedly these ambiguities exist; however, they do not destroy the ''blossom'' of wisdom that Hawthorne wishes to convey, but

Neither the introduction nor the conclusion carries a special label.

iii

rather they enrich its meaning by implying important certainties in life.

A. Hawthorne defines sin ambiguously because he wants to show the absolute relativity of it in this world.

B. Hawthorne also asserts his belief that the existence of sin is certain.

C. Finally, he implies in his ambiguity the most important certainty that he wishes to present, the certainty of tragedy in life.

The name of the student, professor, and class, as well as the date, are repeated on the title page of the paper.

The title is centered (and double-spaced if more than one line).

A quotation from a primary source creates an effective opening.

Mulcahey 1

Butch Mulcahey

Professor McCuen

English 101

13 January 1984

The Certainties of Hawthorne's Moral Ambiguity in <u>The Scarlet Letter</u>

''Be true! Be True! Be True! Show freely to the world, if not your worst, yet some trait whereby the worst may be inferred!'' Nathaniel Hawthorne (242) impresses upon his readers this singular statement in order to ''relieve the darkening close of a tale of human frailty and sorrow'' (56). The tale, of course, is <u>The Scarlet Letter</u>, and the statement represents the ''sweet moral blossom'' which at the end of the first chapter Hawthorne promises to present to his readers. He hopes that this ''moral blossom'' will project a brightening ray of wisdom into the darkness of the fateful triangle of sin in which his three main characters seem tragically entrapped. Yet, despite Hawthorne's stated intention, several critics suggest that his ''blossom'' lacks the sweetness he wishes it to have, that his conclusion lacks

An elevated numeral indicates a content note. Such superscripts are not *used for in-text documentation.*

The thesis is placed in a classical position, at the end of the first paragraph.

A transitional paragraph alerts the reader to what is coming—matters upon which critics agree.

Mulcahey 2

moral value because of the ambiguity and paradox found in the development of Hawthorne's view of morality.[1] And, of course, the critics observing these ambiguities and paradoxes make valid points, for such moral uncertainty undeniably exists in The Scarlet Letter. However, Hawthorne's moral ambiguity is not the book's fault but its strength. It will be seen that Hawthorne's moral ambiguity actually enhances the wisdom, the ''blossom,'' which the reader is to receive. It does not confuse the meaning of Hawthorne's conclusion, but rather it redefines and enriches it by implying certainties concerning sin which transcend in importance the ambiguities.

Despite the controversy concerning Hawthorne's view of morality, there are nevertheless interpretations of his moral concerns upon which most critics agree.

One observation accepted almost without debate is that Hawthorne concerns himself with the consequences of sin rather than the action of sin. Several critics assert that, regardless of its background, the book obviously does not deal with the sin of adultery. Arlin Turner, for instance, draws attention to

A Latin expression is underlined to indicate italics.

Note the in-text citations to "Works Cited."

A word referred to as a word is underlined to indicate italics.

Since the author (Brownell) is named, only the page is cited within parentheses.

A direct quotation is smoothly introduced by "He comments."

Mulcahey 3

the fact that Hawthorne begins the novel *in medias res*, long after Hester Prynne and Arthur Dimmesdale have committed the initial sin of passion (Turner 56). Apparently, then, Hawthorne wishes to deal with the consequences of sin and to study them exclusively. As W. C. Brownell notes, the word *adultery* does not even appear in the text of the novel (245). Brownell further suggests that the entire book ultimately fails to support a study of original sin. He comments, ''As a story of illicit love its omissions are too great, its significance is not definite enough, its detail has not enough richness; the successive scenes of which it is composed have not an effective enough cohesion'' (246).

Certain critics of form indicate that the structure of the novel does support very well Hawthorne's study in consequences. Gordon Roper considers the entire progress of *The Scarlet Letter* to be divided into four separate parts, in each of which a single activating force affects three other forces in the novel (49–52). The initial sin is seen simply as the force which triggers the mechanism of the whole development of the book. What results is a study in the

Mulcahey 4

reactions of the three main characters to this sin. Another pattern observed by critic Roy Male is the symmetrical approach of the characters to their ends, as Hester Prynne becomes a repentant sinner, Dimmesdale a partially repentant sinner, and Chillingworth an unrepentant sinner (91). Both of these patterns uphold the presumption that Hawthorne places his major emphasis on the effects of sin on the characters.

Coherence is maintained by reminding the reader of the continuing topic at hand—common agreement.

Critics also commonly agree on what Hawthorne considers the most grave consequence of sin. Although interpretations of this consequence vary, Hawthorne is generally thought to concentrate much of his concern on the dangers of hypocrisy. Brownell interprets the novel as an attempt to study predominantly the problems resulting from concealment of sin, whereby concealment itself is considered a serious sin (247). And, of course, this form of hypocrisy pervades the novel, as all three of Hawthorne's main characters are continuously guilty of it. Hester is guilty because she refuses to reveal her partner in adultery; Dimmesdale is guilty because he conceals both his guilt in the adultery and his sin of concealment; and

Coherence is achieved by repeating the phrase "is guilty because."

Mulcahey 5

Chillingworth is guilty because he conceals both his identity and his vengeful purpose. More accurately, however, Hawthorne's study of hypocrisy stands as a study of human perfidy and especially self-delusion. Undoubtedly, Arthur Dimmesdale serves as the ultimate example of this type of hypocrisy. Religious and philosophical explanations would summarize Dimmesdale's dilemma as the ''skeptical predicament.'' Dimmesdale assumes that flesh and spirit are separate and different, that the sins of one are not necessarily the sins of the other. He lives a double life, damning his flesh while pridefully glorifying his spirit and maintaining his elevated ministerial image in the Puritan society. Consequently, he absolutely distorts his sense of which life is real, and his life becomes totally false (Davidson 86). He loses his sense of his true humanity. Here one can see, then, why Hawthorne considered hypocrisy such a dangerous sin.

A popular phrase is placed in quotation marks.

The clarity of Hawthorne's extensive study of hypocrisy emerges not only in Dimmesdale, whose hypocrisy is obvious, but also in Roger Chillingworth. Chillingworth practices the most intense forms of

Mulcahey 6

hypocrisy. He attempts to punish sin despite the fact that he himself is not free from it. He assumes the role of Dimmesdale's presumably helpful physician while, ironically, he knowingly inflicts the minister's harm (Turner 102). He thus becomes the most false of Hawthorne's characters, and he concludes the story as a demon, a dehumanized mortal. In this respect, Hawthorne's concern with the dangers of hypocrisy is once again reflected. As many critics have indicated, this concern seems ever-present.

Paraphrase and personal comment are nicely integrated.

From these interpretations of Hawthorne's concern with hypocrisy, his moral seems to follow logically. ''Be true'' is obviously the morality he prescribes for avoiding the terrible suffering of Dimmesdale as well as that of the other characters guilty of hypocritical sins. ''Being true,'' as Roy Male indicates, involves each character's direct confrontation of his own guilt (96). Each character who fulfills this requirement of Hawthorne's moral is believed to achieve salvation. Hester, of course, must embrace her guilt from the beginning of the novel. Her resulting ignominy is what makes her a heroine. It causes her to ''[stand] erect, and [think],'' ques-

Bracketed words help the reader to understand the quotation in proper context.

Van Doren's first name is cited so he will not be confused with Mark Van Doren, who is cited later.

Since two of Waggoner's works appear in "Works Cited," a key word from the title appears here.

Here the student writer moves to negative criticism of the novel's ambiguity.

Mulcahey 7

tioning her punishment and the society which inflicts it (Carl Van Doren 69-70). Her salvation is seen in her humbler spirit and her greater sympathy for human fault as well as her increased generosity. Dimmesdale appears to achieve his salvation in the final scaffold scene, where he confronts and resists Roger Chillingworth, the strong advocate of hypocrisy. In fact, his conclusion has been interpreted to be almost Christlike (Waggoner, The Presence 66). Pearl, who is Hawthorne's symbol of truth, reaches a proportionately happy conclusion, becoming ''the richest heiress of her day, in the New World'' (243). From these observations, Hawthorne's view of morality seems very beneficial, and indeed proves to be, without further interpretation, the ''sweet moral blossom'' the reader anticipates.

Beyond this level of interpretation, however, several critics suggest that the value of Hawthorne's proposed morality diminishes because of his ambiguity. They contend that his moral solution cannot possibly be useful in the definite sense he wishes it to be, because its meaning lacks certainty as a result of the novel's atmosphere of ambiguity and paradox.

Here sin *is referred to as a word.*

Direct quotation and paraphrase smoothly alternate, adding to the smooth flow of the paper.

Parenthetical documentation is placed inside the fourth period because the page citation is part of the context of the sentence.

Mulcahey 8

Some argue that Hawthorne's concept of sin itself is indefinite, that sin has at most only a cloudy, tentative meaning in the novel. Jeffrey Duncan asserts that Hawthorne entertains at least two possibilities about ''the essential nature'' of the reality of sin and evil. In one, sin is only ''committed in the flesh''; in the other, sin exists only in the human mind––in thoughts––and ''sins of the flesh'' only exist in the mind's interpretation of actions (61). Duncan concludes of Hawthorne's presentation of sin that ''reality [hangs] in the balance, a moot point, indeterminable'' (61). Thus it is argued that Hawthorne's sin cannot be definitely perceived, that what may be considered sin in one sense may not be considered sin in another sense. Arlin Turner observes this ambiguity to be especially true in the presentation of the sin of adultery: ''The transgression of Hester and Dimmesdale stands condemned by the laws of society but in an absolute sense is condemned only mildly if at all by the author and the reader . . .'' (Turner 59). The adultery of Hester and Arthur seems acceptable in the context of The Scarlet Letter, yet it is not condoned in a gener-

Mulcahey 9

al sense. According to this interpretation, the gravity of this sin is uncertain and almost arbitrary. The obvious implication of these arguments is that sin cannot be conquered if its true nature is unknown.

In a similar argument, Hawthorne's plea that man ''be true'' is proven to be inherently and irreconcilably paradoxical. Duncan indicates first of all that Hawthorne does not explain to what one should be true (Duncan 52). The perfect example of this ambiguity occurs in chapter 18 of the novel, when Hester discards her scarlet ''A'' and proposes that she and Dimmesdale flee from the Puritan community. As revealed in Pearl's disapproval of this act, Hawthorne censures the idea, showing Hester as trying to ignore the fact of her own sinfulness. Yet, as John Gerber notes, she is true to the natural passion that she has demonstrated throughout the book; therefore she does not in essence commit what Hawthorne considers a sin (107). Thus Hester can be considered a sinner or she can be absolutely justified, regardless of her actions. Likewise, Roger Chillingworth, the undisputed antagonist of the novel, can be considered

Mulcahey 10

totally justified in his actions, for he is true to his own antagonism throughout the novel.

Furthermore, Duncan contends that Dimmesdale's final moment of truth, his apparent salvation through confession, is ''perfectly ambiguous'' because of an endless paradox in his ''being true.'' Duncan proposes that the minister's confession may be interpreted in several different ways: (1) he may be false in his confession in the sense that he confesses in such a way as to appear to the Puritan community as the Christlike saint which he is not; (2) his confession may be as sincere and true as common interpretation contends; (3) he may be perfectly false in confession, in which case he is perfectly true to himself (69-70). An endless cycle of paradox results, which Duncan interprets to mean that Dimmesdale's truth may be false and his falsity may in fact be truth. Whether Dimmesdale gains his salvation from his ''being true'' is therefore indefinite and ultimately irreconcilable. Once more the usefulness of Hawthorne's morality is questioned.

In one essay, Hyatt H. Waggoner questions whether salvation ever comes about by Hawthorne's

Three ellipsis dots are used to indicate a word or words omitted at the start of the quotation.

Since the author (Waggoner) is mentioned twice earlier in the paragraph, only an abbreviated title is necessary.

Mulcahey 11

proposed morality, observing the dark and uncertain conclusion which both Hester and Dimmesdale appear to share. He asserts that neither Hester nor Dimmesdale achieves a glorious salvation: ''. . . For Hester there is no escape, only sublimation and self-control. For Dimmesdale there is only public confession of guilt and submission to a will he conceives as higher than his own'' (The Presence 69). Waggoner further declares that the final images of the novel are gloomy and pessimistic. He suggests that the imagery of the final tombstone inscription ''ON A FIELD, SABLE, THE LETTER A, GULES'' (Hawthorne 245) implies all of the negativeness of Hawthorne's dual symbols and none of the positiveness. The scene, he believes, is absolutely void of the relieving gleam of hope which Hawthorne had promised, and death or guilt seems to be all that is left to Hester and Arthur in the end (The Presence 70). ''Being true'' apparently has not brought them to a happier state than they had experienced without ''being true.'' Thus, Waggoner concludes that Hawthorne does not succeed in lightening the dark close of his story. He notes that both Hawthorne and his wife wept miserably

Mulcahey 12

when Hawthorne had read the conclusion aloud (The Presence 72). This reaction suggests to Waggoner that even Hawthorne himself tended to feel that ambiguity of his moral, that he also had doubts concerning the ultimate value of his "moral blossom."

These arguments have unanswerable validity. Such ambiguity undeniably exists in The Scarlet Letter, as Hawthorne's tears apparently attest. In fact, Hawthorne's ambiguity even serves as the cement which bonds the entire novel together, allowing illusions to assume a sense of reality and binding abstract ideas to materialistic symbols such as the scarlet "A." Contrary to what the critics cited suggest, however, the ambiguity does not destroy the true purpose of the story, nor does it confuse the "blossom" of wisdom which Hawthorne wishes to imply to the reader. Instead, it solidifies the certainties which Hawthorne had felt to be true throughout his life.

The student author now leads the reader back to his original thesis.

In Waggoner's opinion, Hawthorne defines sin ambiguously not because he doubted his own concept of sin but because he wished to show the relativity it assumes in this world. He used ambiguity as an ex-

Key words from Waggoner's other work are cited to avoid confusion.

Words are added in brackets to clarify the context.

Mulcahey 13

pression of his own ''existentially oriented'' religious beliefs, and he based his view of life on his own experience (''Art and Belief'' 67). Just as Hawthorne's convictions depended on his own perception of life, the reality of the nature of sin in The Scarlet Letter varies relative to the perception of the characters of the novel. As John Gerber states, ''Sin [in Hawthorne's novel] . . . is a violation of only that which the sinner thinks he violates.'' The inevitable conclusion of this statement is that a uniform definition of sin cannot exist and indeed is not supposed to exist in The Scarlet Letter. Hawthorne is certain that sin is relative and dependent on man himself. For instance, Hester Prynne realizes that she has sinned against the Puritan society, but she hardly views her adultery in the sense that the Puritan community views it. She does not consider it a breach of God's law, but a breach of the law of order and Puritan orthodoxy (Gerber 108). Although the society's and Hester's views are very different, both nevertheless have a sense of reality with respect to those who conceive them.[2] Hawthorne is certain, then, that man's concept of sin is definite only with respect to himself.

Thus Hawthorne's purpose is not to define sin but to juxtapose his characters' relative concepts of sin and let the reader observe the results. R. W. B. Lewis maintains that the novel is merely a showcase in which the characters and the Puritan society are measured against each other (74). It was therefore Hawthorne's intention to have the entire effect of the novel on the reader depend on the reader's determination of this measurement. For instance, a reader with a strong religious background might consider adultery a serious sin, while on the other hand a romantic might believe the act of passion to be totally justified.

Hawthorne does not intend to imply, however, that sin does not really exist because it is merely a formulation of each man's mind. Strongly implicit in _The Scarlet Letter_ is that sin is inevitable despite its relativity. As an American writer who partially refuted the ideas of Transcendentalism, Hawthorne was certain that sin and evil were real enough so that they could not be relinquished, as Ralph Waldo Emerson had thought, by ''self-reliance'' or by simply im-

Van Doren's full name is given to avoid confusing him with Carl Van Doren, cited earlier.

Mulcahey 15

agining that they did not exist (Mark Van Doren 137). He saw the certainty of the existence of sin not as a result of dogma, but as a direct implication of the relativity of sin. Men perceive sin with respect to their own convictions, and therefore their perceptions are necessarily various. And since men interact with each other in a society, they must perceive sin in each other and attempt to impress their concepts of sin upon others. Such is the case with the Puritan society of Hawthorne's novel, of which the adulterers are influenced members. ''In the minds of [Hawthorne's] characters, their sins are absolute, for they have broken God's laws; and they see themselves and their relations with people and institutions about them in the light of that assumption'' (Turner 57). The main characters are convinced that they are sinners, despite their ability to believe otherwise. That their sins depend on their own relative perceptions does not make these sins any less real to them. Therefore, Hawthorne's grand implication of sin's definite existence is finally revealed. Because he shows the nature of sin's reality to vary from man to man, sin must always exist; for if a man does not see sin in himself, he must surely see it in others, and vice versa. In either case, the existence of sin will be definite.

And if the certainty of sin does not lie in man's perception of it, Hawthorne implies that evil must exist in the punishment of sin and the resulting suffering of his characters. If it is certain that one can justify Hester's adultery in her naturally passionate and wild nature, then surely the Puritan society has sinned against her by punishing her action. In this case, the sin committed is that of human injustice, which occurs ''because men fumbled in their understanding of justice'' (Mark Van Doren 138). In either sense, some form of sin has occurred, and Hawthorne shows evil and suffering to be tragically inevitable.

These ideas concerning human beings and their perceptions of sin imply the most important certainty which Hawthorne wishes finally to give to his reader. This is the certainty of tragedy in life. In his study of the consequences of sin, Hawthorne asserts a belief that ''retribution for sin is certain,'' and apparent in the entire progress of the novel is an

A colon precedes long quotations. The quotation is double-spaced and indented 10 spaces. The final period is placed before the documentation parentheses. Double-space above and below the quotation.

Mulcahey 17

assumed inevitability, a fatefulness surrounding the destinies of the characters (Turner 58). Chillingworth serves as the constant symbol, or indeed the mechanism, of this fatefulness. It is he who makes Hester and Arthur tragic victims of destiny. This fact is clear in his statement to Hester in chapter 14:

double space

> It is not granted me to pardon. I have no such power as thou tellest me of. By thy first step awry thou didst plant the germ of evil; but since that moment, it has all been dark necessity. . . . It is our fate. Let the black flower blossom as it may. (167)

double space

double space

It is also made definite by the entrapment of Hester, Dimmesdale, and Chillingworth. For instance, the plans of Hester and Dimmesdale to escape by boat are spoiled by Chillingworth himself, who plans to board the same ship. All three characters are deterministically tied to their destinies, and the occurrence of tragedy in their conclusions is certain.

However, the certainty of tragedy in life that Hawthorne wishes to demonstrate is ironically most

Mulcahey 18

apparent in the ambiguity of the moral itself. The inevitable tragedy implied by the ambiguity of the moral exists in what Roy Male calls its ''eternal paradox.'' Man's knowledge, represented by the wisdom of Hawthorne's final moral, may be ''insanity to God,'' while celestial truth may likewise seem insane in the social world (Male 94). In this respect, tragedy exists in the fact that man cannot be absolutely sure of the nature of ultimate truth, that his worldly perceptions do not reflect necessarily the truths of the spirit. The ambiguity of Hawthorne's moral thus converts itself into an absolute certainty, the certainty that any of man's attempts to solve the eternal problem of sin, including that of Hawthorne, is unavoidably vested with tragic uncertainty. The weeping of Hawthorne which Waggoner notes is not for his ambiguous moral but for the impending tragedy which it implies.

The student author moves toward his conclusion.

The ''blossom'' which Hawthorne presents to the reader therefore reveals its highest meaning. It is not represented by definite moral advice but by tragic wisdom. It is the sad knowledge that the reader finally shares with Hester Prynne, the knowledge that

Mulcahey 19

sin is ''a problem for which there is no solution in life,'' the knowledge which makes ''the life of Hester [increase], not [diminish] . . .'' (Mark Van Doren 132). The ''blossom'' of wisdom serves for the reader the same purpose that Pearl serves for Hester, reminding her of her guilt and sin and causing her to ''look with warm sympathy into the hearts of sinners'' (Turner 61). Hawthorne's ''moral blossom'' therefore does not lose its value or its sweetness. It gives to readers a renewed hope that although they cannot conquer the problem of sin altogether, they can still benefit from its tragedy. At this point, the ''blossom'' is in full bloom.

Once again the thesis is emphasized.

The paper has come full circle, beginning with a reference to the "moral blossom" and ending with this same reference. The final sentence is a strong conclusion.

Content notes are on a separate page entitled "Notes."

Mulcahey 20

Notes

A reference to another work for comparison

[1] It is useful to compare Hawthorne's moral ambiguity and paradox with that of Milton in Paradise Lost.

A note of further explication

[2] Only in the forest (symbolizing a moral wilderness away from society) can Hester and Dimmesdale escape the strict Puritan code and acknowledge their bond.

Mulcahey 21

"Works Cited" must begin on a new page.

The title of the novel is not *underlined since it is part of a title that must be underlined (see Section 10b-3, p. 207).*

*Citation of a work within an edited collection (see Section 8b-2*h*, pp. 156–57).*

*Citation of a journal article (see Section 8b-4*d*, p. 162).*

*Citation of a book by a single author (see Section 8b-2*a*, p. 154).*

Works Cited

Brownell, W. C. ''This New England Faust.'' The Scarlet Letter: An Authoritative Text, Back-grounds and Sources, Criticism. Ed. Sculley Bradley and others. 2nd ed. New York: Norton, 1978. 291–293.

Davidson, Edward H. ''Dimmesdale's Fall.'' Twentieth Century Interpretations of The Scarlet Letter. Ed. John C. Gerber. Englewood Cliffs: Prentice, 1968. 82–105.

Duncan, Jeffrey L. ''The Design of Hawthorne's Fab-rications.'' The Yale Review 71 (Oct. 1981): 51–71.

Gerber, John C. ''Form and Content in The Scarlet Letter.'' The New England Quarterly 17 (1944): 25–55.

Hawthorne, Nathaniel. The Scarlet Letter. New York: NAL, 1959.

Lewis, R. W. B. ''The Return into Time: Hawthorne.'' Hawthorne: A Collection of Critical Essays. Ed. A. N. Kaul. Englewood Cliffs: Prentice, 1966. 72–95.

Male, Roy R. Hawthorne's Tragic Vision. New York:

Mulcahey 22

Norton, 1957.

Roper, Gordon. "The Four Part Structure." Twentieth Century Interpretations of The Scarlet Letter. Ed. John C. Gerber. Englewood Cliffs: Prentice, 1968. 49–52.

Turner, Arlin. Nathaniel Hawthorne: An Introduction and Interpretation. New York: Barnes, 1961.

Van Doren, Carl. The American Novel, 1789–1939. 2nd ed. New York: Macmillan, 1940.

Van Doren, Mark. "The Scarlet Letter." Hawthorne: A Collection of Critical Essays. Ed. A. N. Kaul. Englewood Cliffs: Prentice, 1966. 129–140.

Waggoner, Hyatt H. The Presence of Hawthorne. Baton Rouge: Louisiana State UP, 1979.

---. "Art and Belief." Twentieth Century Interpretations of The Scarlet Letter. Ed. John C. Gerber. Englewood Cliffs: Prentice, 1968. 67–72.

Citation of a book in its second edition (see Section 8b-2m, p. 158).

The line indicates a repetition of Hyatt H. Waggoner as author.

11b

Entire paper using the author-date style of documentation (APA)

A running head (an abbreviated version of the title) is placed at the top right-hand side of each page. Do not use more than 50 characters (including spaces) for the running head.

The page number is placed one double-spaced line below the running head, beginning with the title page and going on through the entire paper, including the reference pages.

The first page of the paper is the title page. It includes the full title of the paper, the name of the student, the name of the class, the name of the institution, and the date. All lines are centered on the page.

1

Passive Victims of Substance Abuse

Tracy Weed

English 101

Glendale Community College

June 2, 1989

Following the title page is the abstract, a brief summary of the paper's major ideas. The heading "Abstract" is centered at the top of the page. For a paper of ten pages or less, the abstract should be no longer than one page.

The abstract itself is written in coherent paragraph form but leaves out the minor points and details of the research.

Passive Victims

2

Abstract

For the past twenty years the United States has witnessed the proliferation of substance abuse, counteracted by treatment programs aimed at resolving addictions. Research indicates that addictive behavior affects all the people around the addict, most especially the spouses and the children. Every member of the addict's family is caught in the web of co-dependency, a behavioral syndrome characterized by an obsession with other people and other people's problems, and a denial of one's self and one's needs. Co-dependency is considered an illness that parallels the progressive deterioration in addiction. The most lamentable among the co-dependent victims are the children of addicts or alcoholics, termed CoAs. They develop coping and surviving skills that serve them well in childhood but can cripple their adult lives. There is no dispute about the fact that alcoholism and co-dependency are generational afflictions and that in order to stop the havoc they create, these innocent young victims must be identified. Only as society

Passive Victims

3

becomes aware of the patterns exhibited by these passive victims as a result of their dysfunctional home-lives can they be set free from the inevitable repetition of injurious patterns.

The body of the paper begins on page 3. The full title of the paper is centered at the top of the page. The text begins one double-spaced line below the title.

The introductory paragraph contains no documentation, as it is the student's own conclusion. The final sentence is the thesis of the paper.

Passive Victims

4

Passive Victims of Substance Abuse

Since the mid-nineteen sixties, the United States has witnessed an ever-increasing portion of its population involved with illegal street drugs, so-called recreational drugs, and the use and abuse of legal, mind-altering substances, such as alcohol and prescription drugs. The nineteen eighties have seen the creation of treatment programs, offered to assist substance abusers of every kind in overcoming their addictions. Missing in this rush to treat and resolve addiction problems is an awareness of the passive victims of substance abuse: the family members and significant others affected by their relationships to the abusers. The devastating impact of substance abuse on these passive victims is gradually coming to light, and the damage done to them urgently needs to be addressed. If we are to break this chain of substance abuse and addiction, all those touched must first be recognized and then helped to understand that they do not have to create an endless cycle of pernicious patterns.

Any addictive behavior, whether it involves the abuse of substances, such as alcohol and cocaine, or

Passive Victims

5

the excessive intake of high-calorie food resulting in extreme obesity "is one of the most pervasive and intransigent mental health problems facing society today" (Coleman, Butcher, & Carson, 1984, p. 367). It must be understood from the onset of this paper that all addictions evolve as ways to handle anxiety, conflict, and stress. All addictions provide a false sense of relief--"a quick fix"--and cause the build-up of tolerance so that when the substance is removed, withdrawal ensues (Peterson, 1987). The particular substance is not the critical factor. Disorders that have all the features of an addictive condition but do not involve addictive substances can be just as damaging and life threatening as those resulting from alcohol or other drugs. A person can develop an overpowering need or addiction to just about any substance or behavior. Witness the recovering alcoholic who becomes a workaholic (Capell-Sowder, 1984).

In 1938, Menninger described addiction as chronic suicide. Much later, Stanton Peele (in Capell-Sowder, 1984) stated that addictive disorders are not a sign of weak moral character; rather, they

The reference is to a quotation from a book by three authors. Always cite the specific page number of a quotation. Place the final period following the end parenthesis.

The reference is to an idea from one author. Only the author and date need to be cited.

Here the author and date are named in the body of the text; therefore, no parenthetical citation is

Passive Victims

6

represent disorders of self-control, a way of coping with the world and the self, a way of interpreting experience. Toby Rice Drews (1983) maintained that long-standing repression of feelings could lead to overeating, compulsive sexual behavior, compulsive spending, alcohol and drug use, obsessive or controling gestures, and other compulsive behaviors. Moreover, addicts often move from one addiction to another in a compulsive repetitiveness that aggravates and expresses denial (V., 1984). They are trapped in the illusion that they hold the power to control the fast high while in reality their lives are completely out of control.

The focus of this paper is on the families of alcoholics, particularly the children. Families of alcoholics are caught in a web of addiction that causes their members to become increasingly angry with the people they love the most. There is a generational link in alcoholism that was recognized as long ago as Aristotle and the philosopher Plutarch (Squires, 1987). According to a January, 1988, Newsweek article, at least 28 million Americans are either living with or have seen at least one of their

necessary. Since the statement by Stanton Peele was found in a book by Capell-Sowder, the word "in" precedes the parenthetical citation.

Citing an author in the body of the text and following the name with the year in parenthesis is the most common way of handling a citation in the APA style.

The reason the author's name is a mere initial ("V.") is that he or she is a member of Alcoholics Anonymous, an organization that insists on the anonymity of its members.

In the text the student writer names the year and title of the magazine used.

At the end of the idea, she provides the names of the two authors and the page reference within parentheses.

Passive Victims

7

parents in the throes of addictive behavior (Leerhsen & Nanuth, p. 62).

The hallmark of the alcoholic family is isolation from feelings, from other family members who do not talk about the problem, and from the world at large (Woititz, 1983). Not really wanting to confront reality is the biggest issue in the alcoholic home. The family is not conscious that isolation and non-confrontation provide the perfect environment for the alcoholic to continue in his or her entrapment. By trying to conceal their embarrassment, shame, and humiliation, the family clears the way for the progression of the disease. By protecting the alcoholic from the world, the family unwittingly sets in motion a cycle of addiction that can last for generations. Families of serious substance abusers have many commonalities. They are dysfunctional, chaotic, unpredictable, and inconsistent. They are also abusive, rigid, and neglectful. As the addictive disorder progresses, these families are trapped in a divisive atmosphere about the problem and become consumed with unspoken anger and feelings of guilt,

Passive Victims

8

shame, anxiety, confusion, and remorse (Squires, 1987). As the saying goes in alcohol treatment circles, "The alcoholic is addicted to alcohol, the non-drinking parent is addicted to the alcoholic, and the children are left to fend for themselves" (Squires, 1987, p. 15).

Neither author nor date is mentioned in the text. They are both placed within parentheses, followed by the page since a specific quotation is involved. As you can see, considerable flexibility exists for handling documentary citations. The main rule is to keep the body of the paper running smoothly.

These dysfunctional families are highly connected by their simultaneous denial of and loyalty to the family secret. They suffer undercurrents of tension and anxiety in the face of constant unpredictability and chaos. Their peculiar bonding, better described as being fused or enmeshed, is an unhealthy system of corroding the mental, emotional, and spiritual growth of each member. These shame-based families have rigid rules: don't ask questions; don't express your feelings; don't betray the family; focus on the troubled person's behavior to the exclusion of all else. This is known as the family syndrome. In these families there is a blurring of generational boundaries, a lack of consistent limits set by the parents, and a complete lack of structure. Perhaps

Passive Victims

9

the situation is best summarized by the venerable psychoanalyst Carl Jung (1983): "When an inner situation is not made conscious, it appears on the outside as fate" (p. 203).

The author is mentioned in the text; the quoted page is placed within parentheses following the quotation.

All the family members of the alcoholic are termed co-dependents, including the spouse or significant other adult and the children (Beattie, 1987). Co-dependency follows a remarkably parallel degenerative progression to the disease of the addict. What begins as a little concern may trigger isolation, depression, emotional or physical illness, and suicidal fantasies (Beattie, 1987). Adult co-dependents inevitably find their way into relationships with needy people because most co-dependents have been the victims of physical, sexual, or emotional abuse and have been neglected or abandoned in their families of origin. They adopt this caretaking role and develop a compulsion to ignore their own needs in order to anticipate and serve others. They feel responsible for other adults and compelled to solve others' problems. They may become so obsessed with others, that they

The next four references are to Beattie. Each time both the author and date are cited.

Passive Victims

10

abandon their own routines and gradually lose touch with the world outside their compulsion. These are the perfectionists who are never satisfied with themselves; yet, they build increasing tolerance to the unacceptable behavior of those around them. Their self-image deteriorates as they live through the addict's deteriorating behavior. They compromise their value system for the sake of clearly destructive relationships, becoming hopelessly entangled in others' lives and problems as if they had no choice. They let their lives become chaotic by always focusing outside themselves and living through and with people who are out of control (Beattie, 1987).

Co-dependents live in a profound state of denial as an instinctive reaction to pain, loss, and change. They use denial to shut themselves away from facts and events that are too disturbing to acknowledge (Beattie, 1987). They are reactionaries who forfeit their power to think, to feel, or to behave in their own best interest. They take other people's loathsome behavior to be a reflection of their own lives. Desperate to find love, they usually seek it from people incapable of giving or loving (Beattie, 1987). Ironically, they equate love with pain, and often tolerate abuse just to keep others close to them. This emotional insecurity is fueled by a form of self-torture, a nameless sense of being unfit for reality (Beattie, 1987), an antagonistic relationship to the self, and the shame of feeling their entire lives to be a dreadful mistake (Whitfield, 1987).

Alcoholic or co-dependent parents who are locked into their own narcissistic needs cannot provide a mirror for their child and therefore the child cannot develop an individual identity (V., 1987). Children from alcoholic homes are robbed of their individual identity and become subject to situational reinforcement or "people pleasing." Similar to co-dependents, they feel their very worth tied to their "performance," to the reactions and judgments of others, and to the outcome of situations. They are the forgotten victims of addiction, known in research circles as Children of Alcoholics, or CoAs. While adult co-dependents feel trapped in their relationship with the alcoholic,

Passive Victims

12

they could, in reality, leave. Unlike them, the CoA has neither the choice nor the mobility to enter or exit the relationship to either parent, and truly is trapped (Greenleaf, 1984). These children are not born with social skills, moral values or standards for evaluating behavior, but they implicitly learn from what they see in the environment into which they are born. In other words, they learn behavior from both the alcoholic and the co-dependent parent. Consequently, it is not sufficient to say that children are hurt by distorted parental behavior; what they learn becomes the model not only for their own behavior but their choice of future relation-ships (Greenleaf, 1984). "It is an unfounded platitude that children are resilient. The ability to bounce back into health from repeated, long-term psychological trauma requires a healthy, well-developed ego not present until adulthood. When childhood development is continually thwarted, there is nothing to bounce back to" (Greenleaf, 1984, p. 14).

CoAs span the social strata all the way from the White House to the welfare rolls. Often they appear as super achievers, honor roll students, or varsity players. But in reality they are masquerading behind the expertise of their long-practiced denial of what goes on (Squires, 1987). They have strong tendencies as children to look normal because they do not want to draw attention to themselves (Woititz, 1983).

Krisberg (1986) describes three levels of stress among CoAs that create responses that greatly resemble Post Traumatic Stress Disorder. "For a child moderate stress is caused by continual parental fighting; severe stress is caused by the parents' divorce and persistent, harsh parental discipline; and extreme stress is caused by repeated physical and sexual abuse" (Whitfield, 1987, p. 57). The traumas hardest to treat are of human origin and have existed for a period of six months or more. They appear in the child as the absence of feeling and as a decreased interest in important life activities.

Former Secretary of Health, Education, and Welfare, Margaret Heckler (1986, January), stressed that one of the issues most urgently needing to be

Here the student deftly mixes text and documentation. She names the magazine and author in the text, placing the year and month of the issue in parentheses following the title of the magazine. At the end of the quotation she cites the page number within parentheses.

The student writer smoothly integrates the author, title of work, and the date—all in her text. Do not attempt to crowd in so much information unless doing so will not mar the coherence of your text. The next three paragraphs are based on information from the source cited.

Passive Victims

14

addressed is the under-reported crimes of family violence. "These crimes," says Heckler, "are usually committed in an atmosphere where alcohol and drug abuse are present; they are, in fact, a by-product of such abuse" (p. 55).

Janet Geringer Woititz, President of the Institute for Counseling and Training, in Verona, New Jersey, commented on CoAs in Newsweek (1987, January): "Violence, incest, and sexual abuse are three times more common in alcoholic households than in the general population" (p. 65).

In her 1981 expose of the problems of CoAs, It Will Never Happen to Me, author Claudia Black describes the most common roles these children adopt early in life as a means of coping and surviving. One such role is that of the "responsible" child who seldom misbehaves, takes over household chores as the home deteriorates, and creates structure and organization. This child acts as an adult because the adults are not available to fill the child's needs. This child is never exposed to models of either setting or achieving long-term goals, and from the effort of keeping the home functioning from crisis to crisis, has only practiced immediate, short-term goals for survival. Such a child will grow into an adult who is completely unable to be spontaneous, who always needs to be in control, and who is not able to relate to others as equals. He or she will eventually become isolated from all intimate relationships.

Another common role is that of the "adjuster." This role is characterized as detachment from the deteriorating household. The child does not attempt to prevent or alleviate the chaotic situation and is not highly visible in the home. He or she copes by acting without thinking or feeling. This is the role most permeated with denial. As "adjusters" grow up, they continue to avoid central positions and often feel victimized and powerless. Their continued need for movement creates a total lack of continuity in their lives. They only know how to deal with chaos, not with their own feelings. They feel lonely, inadequate, and depressed.

A third common role is that of the "placater." The "placater" is adept at focusing attention away from him or herself by showing extreme sensitivity to others' feelings. The "placater" grows into a compulsive rescuer and caregiver, the most obviously co-dependent role, and as an adult will often take up a caregiving profession. These caregivers never consider what they want and need; instead they seek out situations with "takers" so that they can play out childhood roles.

Finally, there is the role of "acting out". The "acting out" child draws attention by negative, disruptive behavior. Because this child cannot be ignored, he or she is the most likely one to have his or her problem addressed early and to receive professional attention. Children who "act out" are often institutionalized, either in jail or in a mental hospital by their late teens. As adults, they are unable to interact with others or to express their needs in acceptable ways. Often their early behavior causes life-long complications.

CoAs may exhibit some or each of these adaptive roles, which are progressive and may change in adulthood. All children reared in alcoholic homes have problems in adulthood with control, trust, identity, dependency, and expression of feelings (Black, 1981).

CoAs will experience great gaps in their development, especially in the area of self-esteem. They suffer from a lack of identity and from severe discrepancies in their self-image. Because of their compulsion for control, they tend toward an all-or-nothing thinking and reacting style. They have no role models and no exposure to healthy problem solving, having grown up, literally, from crisis to crisis (Whitfield, 1987). They lock themselves into a course of action without giving serious consideration to alternatives. They live with a sense of urgency, silent desperation, always thinking that "this is my last chance, it's now or never" (Woititz, 1983). They are terrified of losing control, which is tied to their early dependence on unpredictable, inconsistent adults. They have an unusually high tolerance for inappropriate behavior in the people around them.

Since self-esteem is based on respectful acceptance and concerned treatment from significant others, the lack of these in an alcoholic home makes it impossible for CoAs to feel good about themselves (Woititz, 1983). CoAs have extreme problems with their self-images because they internalize the early parental messages that they are unimportant and not cared about. They translate these messages into the belief that somehow their very existence is wrong and shameful, that they do not merit the right to be alive. Because they confuse loyalty with love, they remain in destructive friendships, love affairs, and marriages long after they would be better dissolved. CoAs would rather endure known pain than face the uncertainty of starting fresh. Paradoxically, the only frame of reference CoAs have in terms of intimate relationships is the push/pull of "I want you, go away" (Woititz, 1983). Thus, their fear of abandonment, sparked to life in early childhood, overwhelms reason and leads them to deny their loveableness. Emotional insecurity urges them to maintain almost intolerable relationships (Beattie, 1987).

The conclusion of the paper is a strong appeal for action on the part of the psychological community and parents. It is a restatement of the original thesis.

Passive Victims

19

Changing CoAs' habitual behavior is extremely difficult because it is the only behavior they know and because it is interlocked with the unconscious of one or both parents (V., 1987). The seven million CoAs who are under the age of eighteen right now are the hardest to reach because their parents' denial keeps them from treatment. For these children, who never know what to expect when they come home from school each day, life is a state of constant anxiety (Woititz, p. 68) It should be a primary goal of the psychological community and society in general to identify these passive victims and to help them understand that they are not responsible for their parents' illness (Greenleaf, 1984). Only then can these children be saved from the bondage of a life sentence to a half-life of blindly repeating their parents' pain and misery.

Passive Victims

20

"Reference List" is centered at the top of a new page.

All of the references follow the APA rules for listing sources.

This anthology has no editor.

Reference List

Beattie, M. (1987). Co-dependent no more. Center City, MN.: Hazelden.

Black, C. (1987). It will never happen to me. Denver: M.A.C.

Blum, R. (1984). An argument for family research. In B.G. Ellis (Ed.), Drug abuse from the family perspective. (pp. 104–116). Washington, D.C.: U.S.G.P.O.

Capell-Sowder, K. (1984). On being addicted to the addict: co-dependent relationships. In Co-dependency: an emerging issue. (pp. 19–23). Deerfield Beach, FL: Health Communications.

Coleman, J.C., Butcher, J.N., & Carson, R.C. (1984). Abnormal psychology and modern life. Glenville, IL.: Scott, Foresman.

Ellis, B.G. (1980). Drug abuse from the family perspective. Washington, D.C.: U.S.G.P.O.

Greenleaf, J. (1984). Co-alcoholic/para-alcoholic: Who's who and what's the difference? In Co-dependency: an emerging issue. (pp. 1–17). Deerfield Beach, FL.: Health Communications.

Passive Victims

21

Jung, C.J. (1983). The development of personality. In Storr, A. (Ed.), _The essential Jung_. (pp. 191–228). Princeton, N.J.: Princeton University.

Leerhsen, C., & Namuth, T. (1988, January 18). Alcohol and the family. _Newsweek_, pp. 62–68.

Menninger, K.A. (1938). _Man against himself_. New York: Harcourt, Brace & World.

Peterson, N. (1986, November). What about the children? _McCalls_, 114(2) pp. 103–104; rpt. Pasadena, CA.: Microcomputer Index, Dialog File 47, 04459707.

Squires, S. (1987, December 15). For families, a long road to happiness. _Washington Post_, Health, pp. 15–16.

V., R. (1987). _Family secrets_. San Francisco: Harper & Row.

Weingarton, N. (1980). Treating adolescent drug abuse as a symptom of dysfunction in the family. In B.G. Ellis (Ed.), _Drug abuse from the family perspective_ (pp. 57–61). Washington, D.C.: U.S.G.P.O.

Whitfield, C.L. (1987). Healing the child within. Deerfield Beach, FL.: Health Communications.

Woititz, J.G. (1983). Adult children of alcoholics. Pompano Beach, FL.: Health Communications.

11c

Excerpt from a paper using footnote documentation (traditional)

1

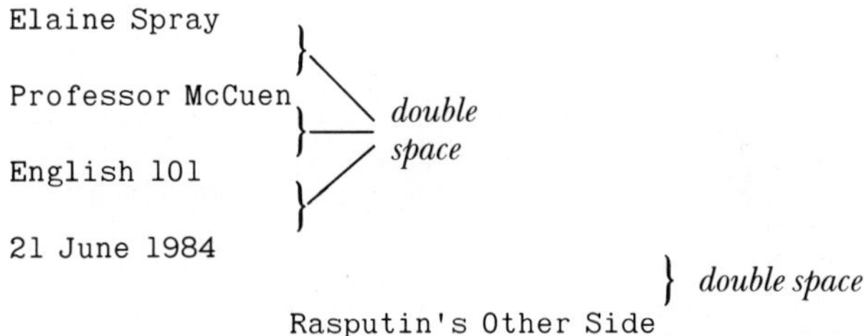

The title is centered on the page.

Rasputin's Other Side

quadruple space

The name ''Rasputin'' commonly evokes an image of unbridled, mystical evil. Few figures have fared as badly in the popular memory. In the 1930s, Lionel Barrymore transfixed thousands of movie goers by portraying him as a devilish, licentious, mysteriously hypnotic fiend. Hundreds of books published since his murder in 1916 unanimously agree on his subhumanity. Reporting a libel trial involving one of his murderers, United Press International in 1965 casually labeled Rasputin as mad, filthy, licentious, semiliterate, fiendish, and lecherous.[1] After six

An elevated numeral refers to footnote at bottom of page.

Quadruple space

[1] Dave Smith, ''Casting a Light on Rasputin's Shadow,'' Los Angeles Times 9 June 1977, pt. 4: 1.

Single space

For proper footnote format, *see Fig 7-2, p. 125.*

Spray 2

decades of being judged a demoniacal libertine, Rasputin now deserves to be viewed from another point of view—as a man who was intensely religious, who passionately desired peace, and who was deeply devoted to his family and friends.

Who was this so-called horror incarnate, this man named Rasputin? It is said that on the night of January 23, 1871, a great meteor seared a flaming path across the skies of Western Siberia, hurtled in an arc over the little village of Pokrovskoye and, at the very moment that the meteor burned out, a seven-pound boy was born to Anna Egorovina, the wife of Efim Akovlevich, a Russian farmer. The couple named the boy, their second son, Grigori Efimovich Rasputin.

What was this second son, this Rasputin, really like? "Supporters called him a spiritual leader and claimed he had healing powers; detractors called him a satyr and said his depraved faithful were merely in awe of his sexual endowments."[2] By the time he was lured to his death in the basement of a St. Petersburg palace in 1916, he had aroused such intensities of

[2] Smith 10.

Spray 3

hatred and loyalty that the facts of his early life had already become blurred and sensationalized. Was it true that at sixteen he was already known in his part of Siberia as an insatiable lecher whom peasant girls found irresistible? Did he really have gifts of second sight and prophecy that cast a glow of religious mysticism around him? Did he disappear from his home for long intervals, wandering about Russia and even to the Holy Land as a starets, a pilgrim of God, who was simultaneously a drunkard and an insatiable womanizer? Was he really a member of the secret group known as the Khlysts, outlawed fanatics who held frenzied rites in torch-lit forest glades that ended with wild, naked dancing and savage sexual orgies?[3] In these suppositions—all part of the legend before Rasputin died—there is probably a kernel of truth. Nevertheless, this remarkable man also had another side, which has been entirely overlooked.

To begin with, Rasputin was a man of intense religious feelings. His love for Christianity bordered

[3] E. M. Halliday, "Rasputin Reconsidered," Horizon 8.4 (1967): 83.

Long quotations are introduced by a colon, double-spaced, and indented 10 spaces. Double-space before and after the long quotation.

Spray 4

on an exuberant devotion. Maria Rasputin writes of her father's simple peasant faith:

> Entering his fourteenth year, my father passed into a new phase, his interest, which soon blossomed into a preoccupation, with religion. Although he had not learned to read or write, skills he did not acquire until his later years in St. Petersburg, he possessed a remarkable memory and could quote whole passages of the Bible from having heard them read but once.[4]

Rasputin, moreover, taught a lofty, sublime sort of Christianity at a time when numerous Russian politicians were becoming suspicious of the Christian religion. Yet his teaching, made all the more simple by his innate ability to explain abstruse theological concepts in plain, comprehensible terms, was understood by even the most common plowman. Consequently, as Christian Orthodoxy waned among those in power, Rasputin was sought out more and more by the ordinary

[4] Maria Rasputin and Patte Barham, Rasputin: The Man Behind the Myth (Englewood Cliffs: Prentice, 1977) 15.

Spray 5

man in the street.[5]

When Rasputin moved to St. Petersburg, he could often be found breakfasting with women followers and talking about God and the ''Mysterious resurrection.'' Suddenly, he would begin to hum softly to himself. Soon the voices around him would join in, swelling to a loud chorus. Then he would leap from his seat and dance around the room.[6] This religious demonstration was accepted as sincere by the Russian peasants, with whom dance had remained a rite of primitive religious activity, assuming the character of prayer.[7]

But a vital religion was not the only positive force in the life of Rasputin. He also expressed a passionate desire for peace and political harmony in Russia. For instance, he was deeply concerned about the Russian underdog. He had vague notions of turning over the landowners' land to the peasants, and the

[5] M. Rasputin 130.

[6] René Fülöp-Miller, Rasputin: The Holy Devil (New York: Garden City Pub., 1927) 268.

[7] Fülöp-Miller 267.

Spray 6

landowners' mansions to the educational system. He was genuinely concerned about the treatment of Jews and other minorities. His concern about the poor people caused many to liken him. . . .

"Works Cited" appears on a separate page.

Spray 7

Works Cited

Fülöp-Miller, René. Rasputin: The Holy Devil. New York: Garden City Pub., 1927.

Halliday, E. M. "Rasputin Reconsidered." Horizon 8.4 (1967): 81-87.

Massie, Robert K. Nicholas and Alexandra. New York: Atheneum, 1972.

Pares, Bernard. The Fall of the Russian Monarchy. New York: Knopf, 1939.

Rasputin, Maria, and Patte Barham. Rasputin: The Man Behind the Myth. Englewood Cliffs: Prentice, 1977.

Smith, Dave. "Casting a Light on Rasputin's Shadow." Los Angeles Times 9 June 1977, pt. 4: 1, 10, 11.

Checklist For Preparing the Final Draft

Subject

1. My subject meets the criteria of the assignment.
2. I have found enough sources to prove my thesis.
3. My title reveals my subject.

Sources

4. I have evaluated each source adequately.
5. I have summarized, paraphrased, or quoted properly to avoid plagiarism.
6. All assertions not my own are documented.

Organization

7. My thesis predicts and controls my paper.
8. My paper shows an organized progression of thought (it follows the outline/abstract).

Writing

9. My opening paragraph is effective.
10. My writing is coherent.
11. I have avoided the passive voice whenever possible.
12. I have used concrete language.
13. I have been concise.
14. Spelling, punctuation, and other mechanical problems have been eliminated.
15. I have deleted all slang, contractions, and clichés.
16. I have checked my diction to assure that my words reflect precisely what I want to say.

Form

17. The visual form of the paper adheres to the style sheet (MLA/APA) recommended for my subject.
18. All documentation is accurate and consistent with the appropriate style sheet.
19. All quotations have been integrated into the text correctly and smoothly.
20. I have given my paper a final proofreading.

APPENDIX*

General and Specialized References

A **A list of general references**

B **A list of specialized references**

**This appendix was prepared by Marshall E. Nunn, Reference Librarian, Glendale Community College, Glendale, CA.*

A

A list of general references

In the library, information on a topic is likely to be scattered throughout numerous books, magazines, journals, and newspapers, most of which are indexed by general references. Increasingly, this information is available in three non-printed versions: microfiche, on-line, and CD-ROM. Some of these references alphabetically index by author and subject the contents of magazines, journals, and newspapers; others similarly index the titles and contents of available books. The experienced researcher, therefore, usually begins a search for information by consulting the general references.

This section will systematically list the common general references and give a brief description of the information they provide. General references index information available on a variety of subjects; specialized references, which we will cover later, index information on specific subjects.

A-1 Books that list other books

The best efforts of ambitious biliographers cannot produce an exhaustive list of all books in print. Nevertheless, many important references catalog the publication of books. The following are the prime sources for information about existing books:

a. Books currently in print

Books in Print. 7 vols. New York: Bowker, 1948–present. Published annually in October and updated by annual supplements in April.

Books in Print Supplement. 2 vols. New York: Bowker, 1975–present. Published annually about six months after the yearly *Books in Print* volumes.

Books in Print Online. Updated monthly. Available from Dialog Information Services, Inc. or Bibliographic Retrieval Services, Inc. Contains records for titles that are in-print, forthcoming, out-of-print, or out-of-stock.

Books in Print on Microfiche. Updated quarterly. Contains information on forthcoming books also.

Books in Print Puls. Accesses *Books in Print* database of over 770,000 titles from a single CD-ROM disc. Updated quarterly.

Paperbound Books in Print. 3 vols. New York: Bowker, 1955–present. Published biannually in the spring and fall.

Publishers' Trade List Annual. 4 vols. New York: Bowker, 1873–present. A compilation of yearly catalogs from almost all important publishers, arranged alphabetically by the publisher's name.

Subject Guide to Books in Print. 4 vols. New York: Bowker, 1957–present. Published annually and simultaneously with *Books in Print.* A companion volume to the three titles listed above.

Subject Guide to Books in Print on Microfiche. Updated quarterly. Includes information on in-print and forthcoming titles.

b. Bibliographies

Bibliographic Index. New York: Wilson, 1937–present. A subject list of bibliographies in English and foreign languages, published in paper issues in April and August and in an annual bound volume in December. Also available on CD-ROM and WILSONDISC Demonstration Discs and on on-line through WILSONLINE or WILSEARCH.

Cumulative Book Index. New York: Wilson, 1898–present. The *CBI*, an international bibliography of all books published anywhere in the world in English, is published each month, except August, in paper issues; there is also an annual bound cumulative volume. Also available on on-line through WILSONLINE or on CD-ROM through WILSONDISC.

The catalogs of national libraries come closer to achieving bibliographical universality than do any other listings. The most pertinent sources for the purposes of most students are:

National Union Catalog, Pre-1956 Imprints. A Cumulative Author List Representing Library of Congress Printed Cards and Titles Reported by Other American Libraries, 685 vols. London: Mansell, 1968–80.

———. *Supplement.* Vols. 686–754. London: Mansell, 1980–81. Reports from contributing libraries received to Aug. 1977 and Library of Congress cards received to Aug. 1979 are included.

National Union Catalog, 1956 Through 1967. A Cumulative Author List Representing Library of Congress Printed Cards and Titles Reported by Other American Libraries. 125 vols. Totowa, N.J.: Rowman and Littlefield, 1970–72.

National Union Catalog. Books. Jan. 1983–present. Washington, D.C.: U.S. Library of Congress, 1983–present. Monthly. Published in microfiche format.

National Union Catalog Cumulative Author List, 1968–72. 128 vols. Ann Arbor, Mich.: J.W. Edwards, 1973.

National Union Catalog, 1973–1977. 150 vols. Totowa, N.J.: Rowman and Littlefield, 1978.

For information on the existence of incunabula—books published before 1500—see:

Goff, Frederick R. *Incunabula in American Libraries: A Third Census of Fifteenth-Century Books Recorded in North American Collections.* New York: Bibliographical Soc. of America, 1964. Locates close to 50,000 copies of incunabula in America.

———. A supplement. New York: Bibliographical Society of America, 1972.

Lower-division students, although not likely to do research based on incunabula, should know that catalogs exist for them.

c. Book industry journals

Publishers Weekly. New York: Bowker, 1872–present. Weekly record of all books published in the United States. Semi-annual issues announce books scheduled for publication.

d. Books about book reviews

Book Review Digest. New York: Wilson, 1905–present. Lists reviews and prints digests of reviews from 81 American, Canadian, and English periodicals. Since April 1983 is available on WILSONLINE database.

Book Review Index. Detroit: Gale, 1965–present. Lists reviews from many more periodicals than *Book Review Digest*, but does not print excerpts of reviews. Available on-line through DIALOG Information Services, Inc.

A-2 Books about periodicals and newspapers

Since its beginning in the eighteenth century, periodical literature—whether published weekly, monthly, seasonally, in serial form, or simply on a random basis—has become increasingly important for scholarly research, especially in any field where up-to-date knowledge is important. Millions of articles are published annually in periodicals, making a complete indexing of them nearly impossible. However, the following books about periodicals are especially useful:

a. Periodical and newspaper directories

Ayer Directory of Publications. Philadelphia: Ayer, 1880–1982. An annual list of newspapers and periodicals published in the United States. The directory is organized by states and cities, and contains indexes.

The IMS . . . Ayer Directory of Publications, 1983–86. Fort Washington, PA: IMS Press, 1980–86. Published annually. Superseded *Ayer Directory of Publications*.

Gale Directory of Publications (formerly *Ayer Directory of Publications*). *An Annual Guide to Newspapers, Magazines, Journals, and Related Publications*, 2 vols. Detroit: Gale Research Co., 1987–present. Supersedes *Ayer Directory of Publications* and *IMS . . . Ayer Directory of Publications*.

Editor and Publisher International Yearbook. New York: Editor and Publisher, 1921–present. Provides information on newspapers, advertising agencies, syndicates, and other aspects of journalism in the United States, Canada, and other countries.

Standard Periodical Directory. 10th ed. 1987. New York: Oxbridge, 1982. Issued biannually, this directory is an exhaustive list of periodicals published in the United States and Canada; arranged by subjects.

Ulrich's International Periodicals Directory. 3 vols. New York: Bowker, 1932–present. Published biannually. As of 1988–89 ed. includes *Irregular Serials and Annuals*, formerly published separately. Supplemented by *Ulrich's Quarterly*, which provides continuous, up-to-date information on new titles, title changes, and cessations. *Ulrich's Plus* is a comprehensive periodical database on a compact disc; it includes information from *Ulrich's International Periodicals Directory, Irregular Serials and Annuals*, and Bowker's *International Serials Database Update*.

b. Union lists of periodicals and newspapers

Union lists catalog and record the collection of periodical and newspaper titles available in various libraries. The following are among the most prominent union lists:

American Newspapers, 1821–1936: A Union List of Files Available in the United States and Canada. New York: Wilson, 1937. Catalogs files of newspapers in nearly 6,000 libraries and private locations.

Brigham, Clarence S. *History and Bibliography of American Newspapers, 1690–1820*, 2 vols. Worcester: American Antiquarian Soc., 1947. The best list for anyone trying to find articles in old newspapers.

New Serial Titles: A Union List of Serials Commencing Publication after Dec. 31, 1949. Washington: U.S. Library of Congress, 1953–present. Keeps track of periodicals published after 1949. Monthly, with annual cumulations.

New Serial Titles, 1950–1970 Cumulative, 4 vols. New York: Bowker, 1973.

New Serial Titles, 1950–1970, Subject Guide, 2 vols. New York: Bowker, 1975.

Union List of Serials in Libraries of the United States and Canada. 3d ed., 5 vols. New York: Wilson, 1965. First published in 1927, this list does an extraordinarily thorough job of locating files of periodicals in nearly a thousand libraries. It is supplemented by *New Serial Titles*, listed above.

c. Indexes of periodicals and newspapers

An index lists topics of magazine and newspaper articles alphabetically, giving each article's title and page number. William Poole, working with a group of dedicated librarians, compiled the first American index in 1802. His index is still in use, along with the following:

Index to U.S. Government Periodicals. Chicago: Infodata International, Inc., 1974–present. An index to 185 U.S. Government periodicals. Published quarterly. Since 1986 available on-line from Bibliographic Retrieval Services, Inc. and from WILSONLINE Information System.

Index to the Times, 1906–72. London: The Times, 1907–73. Superseded by *The Times Index.*

The Times Index, 1973–present. Reading, Eng.: Newspaper Archive Developments, 1973–present. Monthly, with annual cumulations. Supersedes *Index to the Times.*

Magazine Index. Belmont, Calif.: Information Access Corp., 1976–present. Indexes about 435 popular periodicals on microfilm. It is cumulated and updated monthly. The same database is available on compact disc on *Magazine Index Plus*, which also indexes *The New York Times.*

National Newspaper Index. Belmont, Calif.: Information Access Corp., 1979–present. An index to the *New York Times, Wall Street Journal, Christian Science Monitor, Washington Post,* and *Los Angeles Times* produced on microfilm and updated monthly. Also available on CD-ROM database.

News Bank Index. New Canaan: 1982–present. An index to newspapers from over 100 cities in the United States. Articles on current topics of interest to students and other researchers are reproduced on microfiche each month, accompanied by a monthly printed index.

New York Times Index. New York: The Times, 1913–present. A semimonthly and annual index to the daily issues of the *New York Times.*

Poole's Index to Periodical Literature, 1802–1907, 7 vols. Boston: Houghton, 1882–1907. This pioneer work indexes close to 600,000 articles in American and English periodicals. Contains a subject index only.

Readers' Guide to Periodical Literature, 1900–present. New York: Wilson, 1905–present. Published semi-monthly (monthly in July and August) with quarterly and annual cumulations, this is by far the most popular periodical index, and has been widely used to research sources for thousands of freshman and graduate papers. Contains an author, subject, and title index to about 174 notable magazines in numerous fields.

Social Sciences and Humanities Index. New York: Wilson, 1965–present. Replaced *International Index.* New York: Wilson, 1907–1965. Since 1974, published separately as *Social Sciences Index* and *Humanities Index.* These two indexes are excellent guides to essays in scholarly journals such as *The New England Quarterly* or *Political Science Quarterly*; they both index articles by subject and author.

On-line and CD-ROM Access of Wilson Indexes: The H. W. Wilson Company, publishers of *The Readers' Guide to Periodical Literature, General Science Index, Humanities Index, Social Sciences Index* and other periodical indexes, has announced an on-line and CD-ROM access to its subject indexes. This access will provide the researcher with the ability to search and retrieve data quickly from these valuable index databases.

A-3 Books about general knowledge: encyclopedias

The encyclopedia is the czar of general knowledge books, and a good place to begin research on almost any topic. While they seldom treat a topic in minute detail, encyclopedias are usually factual and current. Among the best are:

Academic American Encyclopedia. 21 vols. Danbury: Grolier, 1988. This new entry in the encyclopedia field emphasizes brevity and clearness in short articles, as well as current coverage, over the long, detailed, and scholarly articles found in its well-established competitors. It contains more than 16,000 illustrations and is available on-line, on video-disc, and on CD-ROM.

Collier's Encyclopedia. 24 vols. New York: Macmillan, 1988. Emphasizes modern subjects, but also contains information that supplements high school and college courses. Aims at covering every major area in simplified terms. Includes an index volume. Accompanied by a *Year Book*.

Concise Columbia Encyclopedia. New York: Columbia UP, 1983. An excellent one-volume encyclopedia.

Encyclopaedia Britannica. 15th ed. 32 vols. Chicago: Encyclopaedia Britannica, 1988. The latest and most up-to-date of the multivolume general encyclopedias. Published originally in England, it retains a British flavor. It is the oldest and most distinguished of the encyclopedias, emphasizing both old and new areas of knowledge. The newest edition comes with elaborate index volumes that synopsize information on various topics. Supplemented by the *Britannica Book of the Year*.

Encyclopedia Americana. 30 vols. Danbury: Grolier, 1988. A scholarly encyclopedia consisting mainly of short entries, with complex subjects treated in longer articles. Excellent coverage of science and technology. Includes an index volume. Accompanied by *Americana Annual* volumes.

The Lincoln Library of Essential Information. 2 vols. Buffalo, N.Y.: Frontier Press, 1974–present. Revised with every printing to remain current. Divided into twelve areas of knowledge that are subdivided into sections. Contains numerous charts, graphs, and tables. Includes an index.

The Random House Encyclopedia. New rev. ed. New York: Random, 1983. The emphasis is on color illustrations in this one-volume encyclopedia.

A-4 Books about words: dictionaries

Dictionaries were originally invented to list equivalent words in two languages, as an aid in translating from one language to another. Sumerian clay tablets listed Sumerian words beside their Semitic-Assyrian equivalents. By the seventeenth century, *dictionary* had come to mean a book that explained the etymology, pronunciation, meaning, and correct usage of words. Nathan Bailey's *Universal Etymological English Dictionary*, published in 1721, was the first comprehensive dictionary in English.

Modern dictionaries provide information about the meaning, derivation, spelling, and syllabication of words, and about linguistic study, synonyms, antonyms, rhymes, slang, colloquialisms, dialect, and usage. Unabridged dictionaries contain complete information about words; abridged dictionaries condense their information so as to be more portable.

a. General dictionaries

The American Encyclopedic Dictionary. Comp. by the Oxford University Press. Topsfield, MA: Salem House, 1987.

The American Heritage Dictionary. Ed. William Morris. 2nd college ed. Boston: Houghton, 1982. The distinguishing feature of this dictionary is that it was written in conjunction with a usage panel and a long list of consultants in specialized areas. It is greatly praised for its excellent photography and illustrations.

The New Lexicon Webster's Dictionary of the English Language. Deluxe Encyclopedic ed. New York: Lexicon Publishers, 1987.

9,000 Words: A Supplement to Webster's Third New International Dictionary. Springfield, MA: Merriam, 1983.

Oxford English Dictionary. 13 vols. Oxford: Clarendon, 1888–1933. A monumental work that presents the historical development of each word in the English language since 1150, illustrating correct usage with varied quotations. An updated version has been in preparation since 1972.

———. A Supplement to the *Oxford English Dictionary*, 4 vols. Ed. R. W. Burchfield. Oxford: Clarendon, 1972–86.

The Random House Dictionary of the English Language. 2nd, Unabridged ed. Stuart Berg Flexner, ed.-in-chief. New York: Random, 1987.

12,000 Words: A Supplement to Webster's Third New International Dictionary. Springfield, MA: Merriam, 1983.

Webster's New Universal Unabridged Dictionary. 2nd ed., deluxe. New York: Simon, 1983.

Webster's Ninth New Collegiate Dictionary. Springfield, MA: Merriam, 1983.

Webster's Third New International Dictionary of the English Language. 3d ed. Springfield, MA: Merriam, 1961.

b. Specialized dictionaries

Cassidy, Frederic G., ed. *Dictionary of American Regional English*. Cambridge, MA: Belknap Press, 1985– The first volume, A–C, in this landmark set has been published.

Chapman, Robert L., ed. *New Dictionary of American Slang*. New York: Harper, 1986. Based on *The Dictionary of American Slang*, by Wentworth and Flexner.

Craigie, William A., and James R. Hulbert. *Dictionary of American English on Historical Principles*. 4 vols. Chicago: U of Chicago P. 1936–44. A valuable work for anyone interested in how English developed during Colonial times. Indicates which words originated in America and which in other English-speaking countries. Excludes dialects and slang.

Partridge, Eric. *Dictionary of Slang and Unconventional English*. Ed. by Paul Beale. 8th ed. New York: Macmillan, 1984.

Wentworth, Harold, and Stuart B. Flexner. *Dictionary of American Slang*. 2nd supplemented ed. New York: Crowell, 1975. A comprehensive listing of current American slang, including taboo words and expressions.

c. Dictionaries of synonyms and antonyms

Dictionaries of synonyms and antonyms list the equivalents and opposites of words. Among the best-known are the following:

Chambers Twentieth Century Thesaurus: A Comprehensive Word-Finding Dictionary. Ed. by C. M. Schwartz *et al*. New York: Cambridge University Press, 1987.

Laird, Charlton. *Webster's New World Thesaurus*. Updated by William D. Lutz. New York: Simon, 1985.

Landau, Sidney, ed. *The Doubleday Roget's Thesaurus in Dictionary Form*. Rev. ed. New York: Doubleday, 1987.

The Random House Thesaurus. Ed. by Jess Stein and Stuart Berg Flexner. New York: Random, 1984.

Roget's Thesaurus of English Words and Phrases. New ed. prepared by Susan M. Lloyd. London: Longman, 1982.

Roget's II: The New Thesaurus, by the editors of the American Heritage Dictionary. Boston: Houghton, 1980.

A-5 Books about places

Reference books on places come in two forms: atlases and gazetteers.

a. Atlases

An atlas is a bound collection of maps, sometimes amplified by charts, tables, and plates, that provide information about the people, culture, and economy of the countries covered. Among the most comprehensive and useful atlases are the following:

American Map Corporation. *The Great World Atlas*. 1st ed. New York: American Map Corporation, 1986.

Britannica Atlas/Encyclopaedia Britannica, Inc. Chicago: Encyclopaedia Britannica, 1987.

Hammond Gold Medallion World Atlas. Maplewood, N.J.: Hammond, Inc., 1987.

The Harper Atlas of World History. Ed. by Pierre Vidal/Naquet. New York: Harper, 1987.

Maps on File. Ed. Lester A. Sobel. New York: Facts on File, 1981. A looseleaf service with annual supplements.

National Geographic Society. Cartographic Division. *National Geographic Atlas of Our Universe*. Rev. ed. Roy A. Gallant. Washington: National Geographic Soc., 1986.

Prentice-Hall University Atlas. Ed. by Harold Fullard, *et al.* Englewood Cliffs, N.J.: Prentice-Hall, 1984.

Rand McNally and Company. *Rand McNally Commercial Atlas and Marketing Guide*. New York: Rand, 1876–present. Annual.

Rand McNally and Company. *Rand McNally Cosmopolitan World Atlas*. Rev. ed. Chicago: Rand, 1987.

Times Atlas of the World. 7th rev. ed. New York: Times Books, 1985.

b. Gazetteers

A gazetteer is a geographical dictionary or index that gives basic information about the most important regions, cities, and natural features of the countries of the world. The pronunciation and even syllabication of names are often included with this information. A gazetteer is consulted when a researcher wants information about the legal or political status of a country, its location, and its most important features. The best general gazetteers are:

Goodal, Brian. *Facts on File Dictionary of Human Geography*. New York: Facts on File, 1987.

Munro, David, ed. *Chambers World Gazetteer; An A–Z of Geographical Information*. New York: Cambridge University Press, 1988.

Paxton, John. *The Statesman's Yearbook World Gazetteer.* 3d ed. New York: St. Martin, 1986.

Small, Ronald J. *A Modern Dictionary of Geography*. London: Arnold, 1986.

Webster's New Geographical Dictionary. Springfield: Merriam, 1984.

A-6 Books about people

Biographical reference books are classifiable under four primary headings: (a) general biography of deceased persons; (b) general biography of living persons; (c) national biography of deceased persons; and (d) national biography of living persons.

a. General biography of deceased persons

Chambers Biographical Dictionary. Ed. by J. O. Thorne and T. C. Calocott. New York: Cambridge University Press, 1986.

Encyclopedia of World Biography. 20th Century Supplement. Vol. 13: A–F. David Eggenberger, ed.-in-chief. Palatine, IL: Jack Heraty & Associates, 1987. A supplemental volume to *The McGraw-Hill Encyclopedia of World Biography*.

The McGraw-Hill Encyclopedia of World Biography. 12 vols. New York: McGraw, 1973. Geared to high school and college students, this work is a compilation of 5,000 biographies of individuals famous throughout history. Each entry includes a bibliography. An index is also provided.

New Century Cyclopedia of Names. Rev. ed. 3 vols. New York: Appleton, 1954. Identifies all kinds of important proper names, including the names of persons, places, events, and characters from literature and opera.

Slocum, Robert B. *Biographical Dictionaries and Related Works.* 2 vols. Detroit: Gale, 1986. This work lists all major biographical works—over 16,000 titles. An excellent place to begin finding biographies. International in scope.

Webster's Biographical Dictionary. Springfield, MA: Merriam, 1980. A dictionary of the names of noteworthy persons, with pronunciation and concise biographies. Covers heads of state and other high officials.

b. General biography of living persons

Biographical Books, 1876–1949. New York: Bowker, 1983. A companion volume to *Biographical Books, 1950–1980*.

Biographical Books, 1950–1980. New York: Bowker, 1980.

Biography and Genealogy Master Index. 8 vols. 2nd ed. Detroit: Gale, 1980.

———, 1981–82 supplement. 3 vols. Detroit: Gale, 1982.

———, 1983 supplement. 2 vols. Detroit: Gale, 1983.

———, 1984 supplement. Detroit: Gale, 1984.

Current Biography. vol. 1–present. New York: Wilson, 1940–present. Monthly, with annual cumulative volume.

International Who's Who. London: Europa, 1935–present. Issued annually. Provides sketches of important people all over the world.

New York Times Biographical Service; A Compilation of Current Biographical Information of General Interest. vol. 1–present. New York: Times, 1970–present. Monthly, in a looseleaf format.

Who's Who in the World. 8th ed. Chicago: Marquis, 1986.

c. National biography of deceased persons (American and British)

Appleton's Cyclopedia of American Biography. 7 vols. New York: Appleton, 1887–1900. Contains full-length articles, often illustrated with portraits and autographs of the biographee. Includes people from Mexico and South America.

Concise Dictionary of American Biography. 3d ed., complete to 1960. New York: Scribner's, 1980. A one-volume edition of the large set.

Dictionary of American Biography. 21 vols. New York: Scribner's, 1928–37. A 1944–73 supplement in 3 vols. This is considered the most scholarly of all American biographical dictionaries. An abbreviated edition is available which provides in one volume all the essential facts contained in the larger work.

Dictionary of American Biography. Supplements. New York: Scribner's, 1944–present.

Dictionary of National Biography. 22 vols. London: Smith, Elder, 1908–09. Supplements 1–7, 7 vols. London: Smither, 1912–71. Condensed edition: *The Concise Dictionary of National Biography from the Beginnings to 1950.* 2 vols. London: Oxford UP, 1948–61. The large edition provides rounded-out sketches of notable inhabitants (now deceased) of Great Britain and the colonies from the earliest historical period to contemporary times. The small edition contains abstracts of the large edition.

Dictionary of National Biography. Supplements. New York: Macmillan, 1912–present.

The Dictionary of National Biography. The Concise Dictionary. 2 vols. London: Oxford UP, 1966–82.

Notable American Women, 1607–1950: A Biographical Dictionary. Ed. Edward T. James. Cambridge: Belknap Press of Harvard University, 1971. One of the best scholarly Biographies to focus on the work of the prominent women in America.

Notable American Women—The Modern Period: A Biographical Dictionary. Ed. Barbara Sicherman *et al.* Cambridge: Belknap Press of Harvard University, 1980.

Webster's American Biographies. Charles Van Doren, ed. Robert McHenry, associate ed. Springfield, MA: Merriam, 1975.

Who Was Who. 1897/1915–   . New York: St. Martin's, 1920–present. A companion volume to *Who's Who.*

Who Was Who in America. 1897/1942–   . Chicago: Marquis, 1943–present. A companion volume of *Who's Who in America.*

d. National biography of living persons (American and British)

National Cyclopaedia of American Biography. 63 vols. New York: White, 1892–1984. A monumental work that presents a complete political, social, commercial, and industrial history in the form of sketches of individuals, deceased and living, who helped shape America.

Who's Who. London: Black, 1849–present. Annual. Contains excellent biographical sketches of prominent people living in Great Britain and its commonwealth.

Who's Who in America. Chicago: Marquis, 1899–present. Editions come out biennially. Identifies people of special prominence in all lines of work. Supplemented by *Who's Who in the East, Who's Who in the Midwest, Who's Who in the South and Southwest,* and *Who's Who in the West*—all issued by the Marquis Company.

Who's Who of American Women. Chicago: Marquis, 1958–present. Biennial. A dictionary identifying American women who have made a name for themselves in various fields.

The Marquis *Who's Who* database is available on-line through DIALOG Information Services, Inc.

Many countries and professions now publish "Who's Who" rosters. Examples are:

Who's Who in Australia
Who's Who in China
Who's Who in France
Who's Who in Germany
Who's Who in Italy
Who's Who in the Arab World
Who's Who in the Soviet Union

Who's Who in American Art
Who's Who in American Politics
Who's Who in Engineering
Who's Who in Finance and Industry
Who's Who in Government
Who's Who in Labor
Who's Who in Soviet Social Sciences, Humanities, Art and Government

Ask your librarian about other areas in which a "Who's Who" roster is published. There are too many to include here.

e. Indexes to biographical material

Bio-base; A Periodic Cumulative Master Index on Microfiche to Sketches Found in About 500 Current and Historical Biographical Dictionaries. 1984. Master Cumulation. Detroit: Gale, 1984. Microfiche.

Biography Almanac: A Comprehensive Reference Guide to More Than 24,000 Famous and Infamous Newsmakers from Biblical Times to the Present. Ed. Susan L. Statler. 3 vols. 3d ed. Detroit: Gale, 1987. Supplements are issued between editions.

Biography Index. New York: Wilson, 1947–present. Issued quarterly with annual and triennial cumulations. This work is a guide to articles and books written about all kinds of persons, living and dead. Also available on-line through WILSONLINE and on CD-ROM through WILSON-DISC.

New York Times Obituaries Index, 1858–1968. New York: Times, 1970.

New York Times Obituaries Index, 1969–1978. New York: Times, 1980.

A-7 Books about government publications

The work of government bureaucracy is reflected in government publications—in speeches, annual reports, transcripts of hearings, statistical charts, regulations, and research results. Government publications—issued at public expense by thousands of federal, state, and local agencies—are available to the general public. The United States Government Printing Office (GPO), an independent body of the legislative branch of government, is the chief government printer. Distribution of materials is supervised by the Superintendent of Public Documents, from whom government publications may be ordered. The most important references that list government publications are:

Ames, John G. *Comprehensive Index to the Publications of the United States Government, 1881–1893.* 2 vols. Washington: GPO, 1905. This work will help a researcher locate government information by subject or title. Covers a decade of post-Civil War times.

Poore, Benjamin P. *A Descriptive Catalogue of the Government Publications of the United States, September 5, 1774–March 4, 1881.* Washington: GPO, 1885. A 1,392-page compilation, invaluable to the student of early U.S. history.

U.S. Superintendent of Documents. *Catalog of the Public Documents of Congress and of All Departments of the Government of the United States for the Period March 4, 1893–December 31, 1940.* 25 vols. Washington: GPO, 1896–1945. A comprehensive summary of materials published before 1945.

———. *Monthly Catalog of United States Government Publications.* Washington: GPO, 1895–present. A monthly catalog, arranged by departments, that provides up-to-date listings of publications from all governmental agencies. Includes subject indexes. Also available on-line through WILSONLINE Information System.

———. *U.S. Government Books; Publications for Sale by the U.S. Government Printing Office.* Washington: GPO, 1982–present. Published quarterly.

A catalog of almost 1,000 popular government publications arranged by subject. Replaces the GPO's *Price Lists*.

In addition to these catalogs, the GPO offers a subscription service on microfiche titled *Publications Reference File*. The *PRF* lists all publications and subscriptions currently for sale by the GPO. The *PRF* is also available on-line through DIALOG Information Retrieval Service.

Several guides exist that orient the novice to the vast number of government publications. Among the best are the following:

Andriot, John L., ed. *Guide to U.S. Government Publications*. 1986 ed. McLean, VA: Documents Index, 1986.

D'Aleo, Richard J. *FEDfind: Your Key to Finding Federal Government Information*. 2nd ed. Springfield, VA: ICUC Press, 1986.

Directory of Government Document Collections & Librarians. 4th ed. Barbara Kile and Audrey Taylor, eds. Bethesda, MD: Congressional Information Service, 1984.

Government Reference Books. Littleton, CO: Libraries Unlimited, 1970–present. Biennial.

Lester, Daniel W. and Marilyn A. Lester. 5 vols. *Checklist of United States Public Documents*, 1789–1976. Arlington, VA: U.S. Historical Documents Inst., 1978.

Morehead, Joe. *Introduction to United States Public Documents*. 3d ed. Littleton, CO: Libraries Unlimited, 1983.

Schwarzkopf, Le Roy C. *Government Reference Serials*. Littleton, CO: Libraries Unlimited, 1988.

Schwarzkopf, Le Roy C. *Guide to Popular U.S. Government Publications*. Littleton, CO: Libraries Unlimited, 1986.

Sears, Jean L. and Marilyn K. Moody. *Using Government Publications*. 2 vols. Phoenix, AZ: Oryx Press, 1985–86.

Foreign countries have their own government printing offices, catalogs, and indexes.

A-8 Books about nonbooks

In recent years nonbooks have become a necessary and distinctive part of library collections. Materials stored on microform, film, video, and sound recordings are often valuable to researchers.

a. General guides

Educators Guide. Series. Randolph: Educators Progress Service. Includes guides to free films, filmstrips, and audio and video materials.

Fisher, Kim N. *On the Screen: A Film, Television, and Video Research Guide*. Littleton, CO: Libraries Unlimited, 1986.

Media Review Digest. Ann Arbor: Pierian, 1973–present. An annual guide to reviews and descriptions of nonbook material.

The Video Source Book. Syosset: National Video Clearinghouse, 1979–present. Annual.

b. Indexes of microforms

Dissertation Abstracts International. Ann Arbor: Xerox University Microfilms, 1969–present. Issued monthly, this index lists and provides copies of dissertations produced in all major American universities.

Dodson, Susanne. *Microform Research Collections.* 2nd ed. Westport: Meckler, 1984.

Guide to Microforms in Print: Author, Title. Westport: Meckler, 1978–present. Annual. An annual supplement is published separately.

Newspapers in Microform. Catalog. Ann Arbor: University Microfilm International. Annual.

Niles, Ann, ed. *Index to Microform Collections.* 2 vols. Westport: Meckler, 1984–87.

Princeton Microform Guide. Princeton: Princeton Microfilm. Biennial. A catalog.

The Resource Book . . . Periodicals on Microfiche, Newspapers in Microform . . . . Ann Arbor: University Microfilms International. Revised annually. A catalog.

Serials in Microform. Ann Arbor: University Microfilms International. Revised annually.

U.S. Library of Congress. Catalog Publications Division. *Newspapers in Microform, 1948–1972.* Washington, 1973.

U.S. Library of Congress. Catalog Publications Division. *Newspapers in Microform.* Washington, 1975–present. Annual.

c. Guides to films

The American Film Institute Catalog of Motion Pictures: Feature Films, 1921–1930. 2 vols. Ed. Kenneth W. Munden. New York: Bowker, 1971.

The American Film Institute Catalog of Motion Pictures: Feature Films, 1961–1970. 2 vols. Ed. Richard Krafsur. New York: Bowker, 1976.

American Folklore Films and Videotapes: A Catalog. Comp. Center for Southern Folklore. 2nd ed. New York: Bowker, 1976.

Cowie, Peter, ed. *International Film Guide.* New York: Zoetrope, 1987.

Educational Film/Video Locator of the University Film Centers and R.R. Bowker. 3d ed. New York: Bowker, 1986.

The Film Catalog: A List of Holdings in the Museum of Modern Art. Jon Gartenberg with others, eds. Boston: G.K. Hall, 1985.

Film Programmer's Guide to 16 mm. Rentals. Ed. Kathleen Weaver. 3d ed. Albany: Reel Research, 1980.

Limbacher, James L. *Feature Films on 8 mm., 16 mm., and Videotape: A Directory of Feature Films Available for Rental, Sale, and Lease in the United States and Canada*. 8th ed. New York: Bowker, 1985.

Media Referral Service. *The Film File, 1984–85*. 4th ed. Minneapolis: Media Referral Service, 1984. A reference and selection guide to over 20,000 films and videocassettes available from over 100 U.S. and Canadian producers and distributors.

National Union Catalog. *Audiovisual Materials.* Washington: U.S. Library of Congress. Microfiche.

Scheuer, Steven H., ed. *The Complete Guide to Videocassette Movies*. New York: Holt, 1987.

U.S. Library of Congress. *Library of Congress Catalog—Motion Pictures and Filmstrips, 1953–1957, 1958–1962, 1963–1967, 1968–1972*. Ann Arbor: Edwards, 1958–1973. Superseded by *Films and Other Materials for Projection*. Washington, 1974–79.

Film catalogs are available from many colleges and universities, such as the following:

Indiana University
Kent State University
Pennsylvania State University
UCLA
University of Illinois
University of Iowa
University of Minnesota
University of Southern California

d. Guides to sound recordings: music

American Music Recordings: A Discography of 20th Century U.S. Composers. Ed. Carol J. Oja. New York: Inst. for Studies in American Music, Brooklyn College, City University of New York, 1982.

Bibliography of Discographies. 2 vols. Comp. by Gerald D. Gibson [*et al.*] New York: Bowker, 1977–81.

Cohn, Arthur. *Recorded Classical Music: A Critical Guide to Compositions and Performances*. New York: Schirmer, 1981.

Greenfield, Edward [*et al.*] *The Complete Penguin Stereo Record and Cassette Guide*. New York: Penguin, 1984.

———. *The Penguin Guide to Compact Discs, Cassettes, and LPs*. New York: Viking Penguin, 1986.

Grimes, Janet G., ed. *CD Review Digest Annual*. 3 vols. Voorheesville: Peri Press, 1987. Contents: vol. 1, 1983–84. Vol. 2, 1985. Vol. 3, 1987.

Harris, Steve. *Film, Television, & Stage Music on Phonograph Records: A Discography*. Jefferson: McFarland, 1987.

Rodgers and Hammerstein Archives of Recorded Sound. *Dictionary Catalog of the Rodgers and Hammerstein Archives of Recorded Sound.* 15 vols. Boston: Hall, 1981.

Rust, Brian. *The American Record Label Book: From the Mid-19th Century Through 1942.* New York: Da Capo, 1983.

Schwann Compact Disc Catalog. Boston: Schwann, 1985–present. Monthly. The *Schwann Super Catalog* is published quarterly.

Schwann-1 Record & Tape Guide. Boston: Schwann, 1949–present. Monthly.

Tudor, Dean. *Popular Music: An Annotated Guide to Recordings.* Littleton, CO: Libraries Unlimited, 1984.

U.S. Library of Congress. *Library of Congress Catalog—Music ad Phonorecords, 1953–72.* Washington: Library of Congress, 1953–1972. Superseded by: National Union Catalog. *Music, Books on Music, and Sound Recordings.* Washington: Library of Congress, 1973–present. Semiannual.

e. Guides to sound recordings: speeches, readings, and oral history

Columbia University. Oral History Research Office. *The Oral History Collection of Columbia University.* Ed. Elizabeth Mason and Louis M. Starr. New York, 1979.

Dictionary of Oral History Programs in the United States. Ed. Patsy A. Cook. Sanford, NC: Microfilming Corp. of America, 1982.

Havlice, Patricia. *Oral History: A Reference Guide & Bibliography.* Jefferson: McFarland, 1985.

Hoffman, Herbert H. and Rita L. Hoffman. *International Index to Recorded Poetry.* New York: Wilson, 1984.

On Cassette 1988–89: A Comprehensive Bibliography of Spoken Word Audiocassettes. New York: Bowker, 1988.

Rust, Brian. *Discography of Historical Records on Cylinders and 78s.* Westport: Greenwood, 1979.

U.S. Library of Congress. Poetry Office. *Literary Recordings: A Checklist of the Archive of Recorded Poetry and Literature in the Library of Congress.* Rev., enl. ed. Washington: Government Printing Office, 1981.

B

A list of specialized references

A specialized reference classifies and indexes information about a specific subject. Depending on the complexity of your topic, you may or may not have to consult a specialized reference. Numerous such references exist, covering virtually all subjects. A complete listing of all the specialized references on popular subjects such as history and literature, for instance, would easily fill an entire book.

Specialized references are listed here in alphabetical order by subject, and are restricted to those most likely to be useful in student research.

B-1 Art

American Art Directory. New York: Bowker, 1952–present. Revised biennially. Gives information about museums and other art organizations in the United States and Canada.

Art Books, 1876–1949. New York: Bowker, 1981. A bibliography of more than 20,000 books in the fine and applied arts.

Art Books, 1950–1979. New York: Bowker, 1980. A bibliography of more than 36,000 books on the visual arts.

Art Books, 1980–1984. New York: Bowker, 1985.

Art Index. New York: Wilson, 1929–present. Provides an index to archeology, architecture, history of art, fine arts, industrial design, interior decorating, landscape design, photography, and other subjects connected with art. Also available on-line from WILSONLINE and on CD-ROM from WILSONDISC.

Bunting, Christine, ed. *Reference Tools for Fine Arts Visual Resources Collections.* Tucson: Arts Libraries Society of North America, 1984.

Contemporary Artists. 2nd ed. Ed. by Muriel Emanuel [*et al.*] Chicago: St. Martin, 1983.

Encyclopedia of World Art. 15 vols. New York: McGraw, 1959–68. Supplement. New York: McGraw, 1983–present. 2 supplementary vols. have been published.

Fine and Applied Arts Terms Index. Ed. Laurence Urdang. Detroit: Gale, 1983.

Kleinbauer, W. Eugene and Thomas P. Slavens. *Research Guide to the History of Western Art.* Chicago: American Library Assn., 1982.

Larousse Dictionary of Painters. New York: Larousse, 1981.

Macmillan Encyclopedia of Architects. Ed. in chief, Adolph K. Placzek. 4 vols. New York: Free Press, 1982.

Marks, Claude. *World Artists, 1950–1980.* New York: Wilson, 1984.

Osborne, Harold, ed. *The Oxford Companion to Art.* Oxford: Clarendon, 1970. An excellent source for the student who wants to become familiar with the fundamentals of art and art history.

Oxford Companion to Twentieth Century Art. Ed. Harold Osborne. Oxford: Oxford UP, 1981.

The Pelican History of Art. East Rutherford: Penguin, 1953–present. In progress. When completed, this 50-volume expansive work will cover all aspects of art—ancient, medieval, and modern. Includes architecture.

Petteys, Chris [*et al.*] *Dictionary of Women Artists; An International Dictionary of Women Artists Born Before 1900*. Boston: Hall, 1985.

Pollard, Elizabeth B. *Visual Arts Research: A Handbook*. Westport: Greenwood, 1986.

Print Index: A Guide to Reproductions. Comp. Pamela J. Parry and Kathe Chipman. Westport: Greenwood, 1983.

The Random House Library of Painting and Sculpture. Gen. ed. David Piper. 4 vols. New York: Random, 1981.

Shipley, Lloyd W., comp. *Information Resources in the Arts; A Directory*. Washington: GPO, 1986.

Who's Who in American Art. New York: Bowker, 1936/37–present.

ART JOURNALS

Art in America
Art International
Artforum
Communication Arts Magazine
Studio International

B-2 Business and economics

AMA Management Handbook. William K. Fallo, ed. New York: American Management Assn., 1983.

An Atlas of the U.S. Economic Growth 1967–2000. Washington: National Planning Assoc. Data Services, 1985.

Avneyon, Eitan A. *Dictionary of Finance*. New York: Macmillan, 1987.

Buell, Victor P., ed. *Handbook of Modern Marketing*. 2nd ed. New York: McGraw-Hill, 1986.

Business Periodicals Index. New York: Wilson, 1959–present. Also available on-line from WILSONLINE and on CD-ROM from WILSONDISC.

Currier, Chet. *The Investor's Encyclopedia*. New York: Franklin Watts, 1985.

Daniells, Lorna M. *Business Information Sources*. Rev. ed. Berkeley: Univ. of Calif., 1985.

Downes, John and Jordan E. Goodman. *Barron's Finance and Investment Handbook*. 2nd ed. New York: Barron's, 1987.

Dun and Bradstreet Corp. *Dun's Online Databases* provide a wealth of business and economic information.

Economic Handbook of the World. Ed. Arthur S. Banks *et al*. New York: McGraw-Hill, 1981.

Encyclopedia of American Economic History: Studies of the Principal Movements and Ideas. Ed. Glenn Porter. 3 vols. New York: Scribner's, 1980.

Encyclopedia of Banking and Finance. Ed. F. K. Garcia. 8th ed. Boston: Bankers Publishing, 1983.

Encyclopedia of Business Information Sources. 7th ed. Ed. by James Woy *et al*. Detroit: Gale, 1988.

Estes, Ralph. *Dictionary of Accounting*. 2nd ed. Cambridge, MA: MIT Press, 1985.

Fink, Mary M., ed. *Biographical Dictionary of American Labor*. Westport: Greenwood, 1984.

Friedman, Jack P. *Dictionary of Business Terms*. Woodbury: Barron's, 1987.

International Marketing Handbook. 3 vols. 3d ed. Detroit: Gale, 1988.

Johannsen, Hano and G. Terry Page. *International Dictionary of Management*. 3d ed. New York: Nichols, 1986.

Miller, Richard B. *Bankers Almanac*. Boston: Bankers Publishing, 1985–present. Annual.

Miller, William J. *Encyclopedia of International Commerce*. Centreville: Cornell Maritime Press, 1985.

Moody's Handbook of Common Stocks. New York: Moody's, 1965–present.

The New Palgrave: A Dictionary of Economics. 4 vols. John Eatwell [*et al.*], eds. New York: Stockton Press, 1987.

Ostrow, Rona. *The Dictionary of Retailing*. New York: Fairchild, 1985.

Pearce, David W., ed. *The MIT Dictionary of Modern Economics*. 3d ed. Cambridge, MA: MIT Press, 1986.

Roberts, Harold S. *Roberts' Dictionary of Industrial Relations*. 3d ed. Washington: Bureau of National Affairs, 1986.

Rosenberg, Jerry M. *Dictionary of Banking and Financial Services*. 2nd ed. New York: Wiley, 1985.

———. *Dictionary of Business and Management*. 2nd ed. New York: Wiley, 1983.

Standard & Poor's Register of Corporations, Directors, and Executives. New York: Standard & Poor's, 1975–present.

Thomas Register of American Manufacturers and *Thomas Register Catalog File*. New York: Thomas, 1905–present.

Thomsett, Michael C., comp. *Investment and Securities Dictionary*. Jefferson: McFarland, 1986.

U.S. Bureau of Labor Statistics. *Handbook of Labor Statistics*. Washington: GPO, 1926–present.

University Microfilm, Inc. *ABI/INFORM*. On disc, provides abstracts of articles from nearly 700 business journals, updated bimonthly.

Valentine, Stuart. *International Dictionary of the Securities Industries*. New York: Nichols, 1985.

BUSINESS AND ECONOMICS JOURNALS AND NEWSPAPERS

Administrative Management
American Economic Review
Barron's National Business and Financial Weekly
Business Month
Business Week
Forbes
Fortune
Harvard Business Review
Los Angeles Business Journal
Monthly Labor Review
Nation's Business
Wall Street Journal

B-3 Dance

American Dance Directory. New York: Assoc. of American Dance Companies, 1980–present.

Bibliographic Guide to Dance. Boston: Hall, 1975–present.

Clarke, Mary and Clement Crisp. *The Ballet Goer's Guide*. London: Michael Joseph, 1981.

Forbes, Fred R. *Dance: An Annotated Bibliography, 1965–1982*. New York: Garland, 1986.

Grant, Gail. *Technical Manual and Dictionary of Classical Ballet*. 3d rev. ed. New York: Dover, 1982.

Kerensky, Oleg. *The Guiness Guide to Ballet*. Enfield: Guiness, 1981.

Koegler, Horst. *The Concise Oxford Dictionary of Ballet*. 2nd ed. New York: Oxford UP, 1982.

The Lively Arts Information Directory. 2nd ed. Ed. by Steven R. Wasserman and Jacqueline W. O'Brien. Detroit: Gale, 1985.

Mara, Thalia. *The Language of Ballet: A Dictionary*. Princeton: Princeton Book Company, 1987.

DANCE JOURNALS

Ballet News
Ballet Review
Dance Magazine
Dance Research Journal

B-4 Ecology

This term encompasses energy, environmental, and conservation issues.

Berger, Melvin. *Hazardous Substances: A Reference*. Hillside: Enslow, 1986.

Brink, Michael. *Solar Energy Sourcebook*. Englewood Cliffs: Prentice-Hall, 1985.

California Environmental Directory: A Guide to Organizations and Resources. Claremont: California Institute of Public Affairs, 1977–present.

Conservation Directory. Washington: National Wildlife Federation, 1966–present. Annual.

Cuff, David J. and William J. Young. *The United States Energy Atlas*. 2nd ed. New York: Macmillan, 1986.

Energy Statistics Yearbook. New York: United Nations, 1979–present.

Environment Abstracts. New York: Environment Information Center, 1971–present.

Environment Abstracts Annual. New York: Environment Information Center, 1980–present.

Environment Index. New York: Environment Information Center, 1971–present.

Frick, G. William and Thomas F. P. Sullivan. *Environmental Glossary*. 4th ed. Rockville: Government Institutes, 1986.

Handbook of Air Pollution Analysis. 2nd ed. Roy M. Harrison and Roger Perry, eds. New York: Chapman and Hall/Methuen, 1986.

Loftness, Robert L. *Energy Handbook*. 2nd ed. New York: Van Nostrand, 1984.

Pollution Abstracts. Bethesda: Cambridge Scientific Abstracts, 1970–present. Bimonthly. Available also as a computerized database.

Romer, Robert H. *Energy: Facts and Figures*. Amherst: Spring Street Press, 1985.

Sax, N. Irving. *Dangerous Properties of Industrial Materials*. 6th ed. New York: Van Nostrand Reinhold, 1984.

Schultz, Marilyn S. and Vivian L. Kasen. *Encyclopedia of Community Planning and Environmental Protection*. New York: Facts on File, 1983.

Solar Index. Denver: Solar Index, Inc., 1981–present. A periodical index.

SYNERJY: A Directory of Energy Alternatives. New York: SYNERJY, 1974–present. Semiannual; July issues are cumulative for one year.

World Directory of Energy Information. Comp. Cambridge Information and Research Services; ed. Christopher Swain and Andrew Buckley. New York: Facts on File, 1981–present.

ECOLOGY JOURNALS

Conservationist
Environment
Environmental Ethics
International Wildlife
Sierra: The Sierra Club Bulletin
Solar Energy

B-5 Education

American Council on Higher Education. *Fact Book on Higher Education*. Washington, 1959–present.

Barrow, Robin and Geoffrey Milburn. *A Critical Dictionary of Educational Concepts*. New York: St. Martin, 1986.

Bibliographic Guide to Education. Boston: Hall, 1978–present. Published annually.

The College Blue Book. New York: Macmillan, 1923–present.

Current Index to Journals in Education. Phoenix: Oryx, 1969–present.

Dejnozka, Edward L. and David E. Kapel. *American Educator's Encyclopedia*. Westport: Greenwood, 1982.

Directory of American Scholars: A Bibliographical Directory. New York: Bowker, 1942–present.

Education Index. New York: Wilson, 1929–present. Also available on-line through WILSONLINE and on CD-ROM through WILSONDISC.

Education Literature, 1907–1932. 12 vols. New York: Garland, 1979.

Educational Media and Technology Yearbook. Littleton, CO: Libraries Unlimited, 1985–present. Formerly titled *Educational Media Yearbook*.

Encyclopedia of Educational Research. 5th ed. 4 vols. New York: Free Press, 1982.

EPIE Institute. *T.E.S.S., The Educational Software Selector*. New York: Teachers College Press, 1984–present.

Hawes, Gene R. *Concise Dictionary of Education*. New York: Van Nostrand Reinhold, 1982.

The International Encyclopedia of Education: Research and Studies. 10 vols. Torsten Husen and T. Neville Postlethwaite, eds. Elmsford: Pergamon Press, 1985.

Quay, Richard H. *Research in Higher Education: A Guide to Source Bibliographies*. 2nd ed. Phoenix: Oryx, 1985.

The Teacher's Almanac, 1986–1987. Sherwood Harris and Lorna B. Harris, eds. New York: Facts on File, 1986.

The World of Learning. London: Europa, 1948–present. Annual.

EDUCATION JOURNALS

American Educational Research Journal
American Journal of Education
Change
Chronicle of Higher Education
Education Computer News
Harvard Education Review
Journal of Higher Education
Phi Delta Kappan

B-6 Ethnic studies

a. General

Allen, James P. and Eugene J. Turner. *We the People: An Atlas of America's Ethnic Diversity.* New York: Macmillan, 1988.

Cashmore, E. Ellis. *Dictionary of Race and Ethnic Relations.* London: Routledge & K. Paul, 1984.

Ethnic Information Sources of the United States. 2 vols. 2nd ed. Ed. by Paul Wasserman and Alice E. Kennington. Detroit: Gale, 1983.

Harvard Encyclopedia of American Ethnic Groups. Cambridge: Belknap Press of Harvard University, 1980.

Kirloch, Graham C. *Race and Ethnic Relations; An Annotated Bibliography.* New York: Garland, 1984.

ETHNIC STUDIES (GENERAL) JOURNALS

Ethnic and Racial Studies
Ethnic Forum
Journal of Ethnic Studies

b. American Indian studies

Brumble, H. David, III. *An Annotated Bibliography of American Indian and Eskimo Autobiographies.* Lincoln: U of Nebraska P, 1981.

Dockstader, Frederick J. *Great North American Indians: Profiles in Life and Leadership.* New York: Van Nostrand, 1977.

Frazier, Gregory W. *The American Indian Index: A Directory of Indian Country, USA.* Randolph J. Punley, ed. Denver: Arrowstar, 1988.

Hirschfelder, Arlene B., *et al. Guide to Research on North American Indians.* Chicago: American Library Assn., 1983.

Klein, Barry T. *Reference Encyclopedia of the American Indian.* 2 vols. 4th ed. New York: Todd, 1986.

Waldman, Carl. *Atlas of the North American Indian.* New York: Facts on File, 1985.

AMERICAN INDIAN JOURNALS

Akwesasne Notes
American Indian Culture and Research Journal
American Indian Quarterly

c. *Asian American studies*

Kim, Hyung-Chan. *Dictionary of Asian American History.* New York: Greenwood, 1986.

Kitano, Harry H. and Roger Daniels. *Asian Americans: The Emerging Minority.* Englewood Cliffs: Prentice, 1988.

ASIAN AMERICAN JOURNALS

Amerasia Journal
Asiam
East Wind
Rice

d. *Black American studies*

Bibliographic Guide to Black Studies. Boston: Hall, 1975–present.

Black Immigration and Ethnicity in the United States; An Annotated Bibliography. Center for Afroamerican and African Studies, Univ. of Michigan. Westport: Greenwood, 1985.

The Black Resource Guide. 1986 ed. R. Benjamin Johnson and Jacqueline L. Johnson, comps. Washington, 1986.

David, Nathaniel, comp. and ed. *Afro-American Reference; An Annotated Bibliography of Selected Resources.* Westport: Greenwood, 1985.

In Black and White: A Guide to Magazine Articles, Newspaper Articles, and Books Concerning More than 15,000 Black Individuals and Groups. 3d ed. 2 vols. Ed. Mary M. Spradling. Detroit: Gale, 1980. *Supplement.* Detroit: Gale, 1985.

Index to Periodical Articles By and About Blacks. Boston: Hall, 1950–present.

National Urban League, Inc. *The State of Black America.* New York, 1976–present. Annual.

Ploski, Harry A. and James Williams, comps. and eds. *The Negro Almanac: A Reference Work on the Afro-American.* 4th ed. New York: Wiley, 1983.

Stevenson, Rosemary, comp. *Index to Afro-American Reference Sources.* Westport: Greenwood, 1988.

Who's Who Among Black Americans. Lake Forest: Educational Communications, 1976–present.

BLACK AMERICAN JOURNALS

Ebony
Journal of Black Studies
Journal of Negro History
Phylon

e. Hispanic American studies

Chicano Literature: A Reference Guide. Julio A. Martinez and Francisco A. Lomeli, eds. Westport: Greenwood, 1985.

Foster, David W., ed. *Sourcebook of Hispanic Culture in the United States.* Chicago: American Library Assn., 1983.

Hispanic American Periodicals Index. Los Angeles: UCLA Latin American Center Publications, 1974–present.

Hispanic Policy Development Project. *The Hispanic Almanac.* New York, 1984.

Hispanics in the United States: A New Social Agenda. Ed. Pastora San Juan Cafferty and William McCready. New Brunswick: Transaction, 1984.

Meier, Matt S. and Feliciano Rivera. *Dictionary of Mexican American History.* Westport: Greenwood, 1981.

HISPANIC AMERICAN JOURNALS

Aztlan
Hispanic: The Magazine of the Contemporary Hispanic
Hispanic Link Weekly Report
Nuestro: The Magazine for Latinos

B-7 High technology

This term encompasses the dynamic and fast-changing areas of computers, computer aided design and manufacture, electronics, robotics, and artificial intelligence.

Advances in Automation and Robotics: Theory and Application. Ed. George N. Sardis. Greenwich: JAI, 1985–present.

Amos, S. W. *Dictionary of Electronics.* 2nd ed. Stoneham: Butterworth, 1987.

Bowker Complete Sourcebook of Personal Computing. New York: Bowker, 1984–present.

Computer Literature Index. Phoenix: Applied Computer Research, 1971–present.

Conners, Martin. *Computers and Computing Information Resources Directory.* 1st ed. Detroit: Gale, 1987.

———. *Supplement.* Detroit: Gale, 1987.

Downing, Douglas and Michael Covington. *Dictionary of Computer Terms.* Woodbury: Barron's, 1986.

Edmunds, Robert A. *The Prentice-Hall Encyclopedia of Information Technology.* Englewood Cliffs: Prentice, 1987.

Encyclopedia of Artificial Intelligence. 2 vols. Stuart C. Shapiro, ed.-in-chief [*et al.*] New York: Wiley, 1987.

Encyclopedia of Information Systems and Services, 1988. 3 vols. 8th ed. Ed. by Amy Lucas and Annette Novallo. Detroit: Gale, 1988.

———. *New Information Systems and Services.* A supplement to the encyclopedia listed above.

Humphrey, Susanne M. and Biagio, J. Melloni. *Databases: A Primer for Retrieving Information by Computer.* Englewood Cliffs: Prentice, 1986.

Hunt, V. Daniel. *Artificial Intelligence & Expert Systems Sourcebook.* New York: Chapman & Hall, 1986.

———. *Robotics Sourcebook.* New York: Elsevier, 1988.

Longley, Dennis and Michael Shain. *Dictionary of Information Technology.* 2nd ed. New York: Oxford, 1986.

McGraw-Hill Personal Computer Programming Encyclopedia: Languages and Operating Systems. William J. Birnes, ed. [and] Nancy Hayfield. New York: McGraw, 1985.

The MS-DOS Encyclopedia. Ray Duncan, General Ed. Redmond: Microsoft, 1988.

Nof, Shimon Y. *Handbook of Industrial Robotics.* New York: Wiley, 1985.

The Software Encyclopedia 1988. 2 vols. New York: Bowker, 1988.

Waldman, Harry. *Dictionary of Robotics.* New York: McGraw, 1985.

HIGH TECHNOLOGY JOURNALS

A+
Abacus
Artificial Intelligence
Byte
Computers and People
Datamation
Macworld
PC Magazine
Robotics World
Software News
Technology Review

B-8 History

a. World history

Boorstin, Daniel J. *The Discoverers: A History of Man's Search to Know His World and Himself.* New York: Random, 1983.

Cambridge Ancient History. 3d ed. London: Cambridge UP, 1970–present.

Cambridge Mediaeval History. Planned by J. B. Bury; ed. H. M. Gwatkin and J. P. Whitney. 2nd ed. Cambridge: Cambridge UP, 1975–present.

Durant, Will and Ariel. *The Story of Civilization.* 11 vols. New York: Simon, 1935–1975. A monumental work of enduring worth, written in an extremely readable style.

Embree, Ainslie T. *Encyclopedia of Asian History.* 4 vols. New York: Macmillan, 1988.

Everyman's Dictionary of Dates. 7th ed. Rev. by Audrey Butler. London: Dent, 1985.

Garraty, John and Peter Gay, eds. *The Columbia History of the World.* New York: Dorset, 1981.

The Harper Atlas of World History. Ed: Pierre Vidal-Naquet. New York: Harper, 1987.

Historical Abstracts, Parts A & B. Santa Barbara: ABC-Clio, 1955–present. Quarterly. Available on-line from DIALOG.

McEvedy, Colin. *The Macmillan World History Factfinder.* New York: Macmillan, 1985.

The New Cambridge Modern History. 14 vols. Cambridge: Cambridge UP, 1957–79.

Ritter, Harry. *Dictionary of Concepts in History.* Westport: Greenwood, 1986.

Strayer, Joseph R., ed. *Dictionary of the Middle Ages.* New York: Scribner's, 1982–present. A projected 12-vol. set of monumental proportions.

WORLD HISTORY JOURNALS

Current History
History Today
Journal of Modern History
Journal of the History of Ideas

b. American history

Album of American History. Rev. ed. 3 vols. New York: Scribner's, 1969. *Supplement I, 1968–1982.* New York: Scribner's, 1985.

America: History and Life. Part A: Article Abstracts and Citations. Santa Barbara: ABC-Clio, 1964–present. Published 3 times a year. Also available on-line from DIALOG.

American History: A Bibliographic Review. Westport: Meckler, 1985–present. Annual.

The Annals of America. 2 vols. Chicago: Encyclopaedia Britannica, 1968–74.

Atlas of American History. 2d rev. ed. New York: Scribner's, 1984.

Carruth, Gordon, *Encyclopedia of American Facts & Dates.* 8th ed. New York: Harper, 1987.

Commager, Henry S. *Documents of American History.* 9th ed. 2 vols. Englewood Cliffs: Prentice, 1974. A collection of the most famous documents relating to American history from 1492 to contemporary times.

Dictionary of American History. Rev. ed. 8 vols. New York: Scribner's, 1976.

Encyclopedia of American History. 6th ed. Ed. Richard B. Morris. New York: Harper, 1982.

Historical Times Illustrated Encyclopedia of the Civil War. Patricia L. Faust [*et al.*], eds. New York: Harper, 1986.

Kane, Joseph N. *Facts About the Presidents.* 4th ed. New York: Wilson, 1981. *Supplement.* New York: Wilson, 1985.

———. *Famous First Facts.* 4th ed. New York: Wilson, 1981.

The Presidents: A Reference History. Ed. Henry F. Graff. New York: Scribner's, 1984.

Whitman, Alden, ed. *American Reformers.* New York: Wilson, 1985.

Women in American History: A Bibliography. Vol. 2: Jessica Brown and Susan Kinnell, eds. Santa Barbara: ABC-Clio, 1985. Survey of periodical literature, 1976–1983.

AMERICAN HISTORY JOURNALS

American Heritage
American Historical Review
American History Illustrated
Journal of American History

B-9 Literature

a. General

Abstracts of English Studies. Calgary: Univ. of Calgary Press, 1958–present.

Bartlett, John. *Familiar Quotations.* 15th ed. Ed. Emily M. Beck. Boston: Little, 1980.

Beacham, Walton, ed. *Research Guide to Biography and Criticism: Drama.* Washington: Beacham, 1986.

———. Research Guide to Biography and Criticism: Literature. 2 vols. Washington: Beacham, 1985.

Benet's Reader's Encyclopedia. 3d ed. New York: Harper, 1987.

B

Contemporary Authors: The International Bio-Bibliographical Guide to Current Authors and Their Works. Detroit: Gale, 1962–present.

Contemporary Literary Criticism. Detroit: Gale, 1973–present.

Contemporary Poets. 4th ed. James Vinson and D. L. Kirkpatrick, eds. New York: St. Martin's, 1985.

Dictionary of Literary Biography. Editorial director, Matthew J. Bruccoli. Detroit: Gale, 1978–present.

Encyclopedia of World Literature in the 20th Century. 2nd rev. ed. 5 vols. Ed. Leonard G. Klein. Detroit: Gale, 1981–84.

Essay and General Literature Index. New York: Wilson, 1934–present. Also available on-line from WILSONLINE.

European Writers. Ed. by George Stade [*et al.*] New York: Scribner's, 1983–present. 7 vols. have been published.

Fowler, Roger, ed. *A Dictionary of Modern Critical Terms.* Rev. ed. New York: Routledge & K. Paul, 1987.

Good Reading: A Guide for Serious Readers. 22nd ed. Arthur Waldhorn [*et al.*], eds. New York: Bowker, 1985.

Granger's Index to Poetry. 8th rev. ed. New York: Columbia UP, 1986.

Griffith, Benjamin W. *A Pocket Guide to Literature and Language Terms.* New York: Barron's, 1986.

Holman, C. Hugh. *A Handbook to Literature.* 5th ed. New York: Macmillan, 1986.

Kirkpatrick D. L. *Contemporary Dramatists.* 4th ed. Chicago: St. James. 1988.

———. *Contemporary Novelists.* 4th ed. New York: St. Martin's, 1986.

Kuntz, Joseph M. and Nancy C. Martinez. *Poetry Explication: A Checklist of Interpretation Since 1925 of British and American Poems, Past and Present.* Boston: Hall, 1980.

McGraw-Hill Encyclopedia of World Drama: An International Reference Work in 5 Volumes. Ed. in chief, Stanley Hochman. 2nd ed. 5 vols. New York: McGraw, 1984.

Major Modern Dramatists. 2 vols. Blandine M. Rickert [*et al.*], comps. and eds. New York: Ungar, 1984–86.

Modern Language Association of America. *MLA International Bibliography of Books and Articles on the Modern Languages and Literatures.* New York: 1921–present. Available (since 1981) on CD-ROM through WILSON-DISC Information System.

The Oxford Companion to the Theatre. 4th ed. Ed. Phyllis Hartnoll. Fair Lawn: Oxford UP, 1984.

Patterson, Margaret C. *Literary Research Guide.* 2nd ed. New York: Modern Language Assoc., 1983.

Salem, James M. *Drury's Guide to the Best Plays.* 4th ed. Metuchen: Scarecrow, 1987.

Seymour-Smith, Martin. *The New Guide to Modern World Literature.* 3d ed. New York: Peter Bedrich, 1985.

Short Story Criticism, Excerpts from Criticism of the Works of Short Fiction Writers. Detroit: Gale, 1988–present.

Todd, Janet, ed. *A Dictionary of British and American Women Writers, 1660–1800.* Totowa: Rowman & Littlefield, 1985.

Wakeman, John, ed. *World Authors: 1950–1970.* New York: Wilson, 1975.

Walker, Warren S. *Twentieth Century Short Story Explication.* 3d ed. Hamden: Shoe String Press, 1977.

———. *Supplements.* Hamden: Shoe String Press, 1980–present.

b. American literature

American Literary Scholarship: An Annual. Durham, N.C.: Duke UP, 1963–present.

American Women Writers: A Critical Reference Guide from Colonial Times to the Present. Ed. Lina Mainiero. 4 vols. New York: Ungar, 1979–82.

Annals of American Literature, 1602–1983. Richard M. Ludwig and Clifford A. Nault, Jr., eds. New York: Oxford, 1986.

Bibliography of American Literature. Comp. Jacob Blanck for the Bibliographical Society of America. New Haven: Yale UP, 1955–

The Cambridge Handbook of American Literature. Jack Salzman, ed. New York: Cambridge, 1986.

Columbia Literary History of the United States. New York: Columbia, 1988.

Gerhardstein, Virginia B. *Dickinson's American Historical Fiction.* 5th ed. Metuchen: Scarecrow, 1986.

Hart, James D. *The Oxford Companion to American Literature.* 5th ed. New York: Oxford UP, 1983.

Kirkpatrick, D. L., ed. *Reference Guide to American Literature.* 2nd ed. Chicago: St. James, 1987.

Literary History of the United States. Ed. Robert E. Spiller, *et al.* 4th ed., rev. 2 vols. New York: Macmillan, 1974.

Modern American Literature. Comp. and ed. Dorothy Nyren *et al.* 4th ed. 4 vols. New York: Ungar, 1969–76.

Rogal, Samuel J. *A Chronological Outline of American Literature.* Westport: Greenwood, 1987.

c. British literature

Andrews, John F., ed. *William Shakespeare: His World, His Work, His Influence.* 3 vols. New York: Scribner's, 1985.

Annals of English Literature, 1475–1950: The Principal Publications of Each Year. 2nd ed. Oxford: Clarendon, 1961.

Battestin, Martin C., ed. *British Novelists, 1660–1800.* 2 vols. Detroit: Gale, 1985.

British Writers. Gen. ed. Ian Scott-Kilvert. 8 vols. New York: Scribner's, 1979–1983.

The Cambridge Guide to English Literature. Comp. Michael Stapleton. Cambridge: Cambridge UP, 1983.

Cambridge History of English Literature. 15 vols. Cambridge: Cambridge UP, 1919–30. Considered the most authoritative history of English literature. The volumes represent a collaboration by specialists, and cover all aspects of English literary history from its beginnings to the twentieth century. The work is updated by: Sampson, George. *Concise Cambridge History of English Literature.* 3d ed. Cambridge: Cambridge UP, 1970.

English Novel Explication. Supplement. Hamden: Shoe String Press, 1976–present. Supplements *English Novel Explication: Criticism to 1972.* Comp. Helen H. Palmer and Anne J. Dyson.

Gillie, Christopher. *A Companion to British Literature.* Detroit: Gale, 1980.

Modern British Literature. Comp. and ed. Ruth Z. Templeton *et al.* 5 vols. New York: Ungar, 1966–85. A part of the Library of Literary Criticism series.

The New Cambridge Bibliography of English Literature. Margaret Dabble, ed. 5th ed. New York: Oxford, 1985.

Oxford History of English Literature. Oxford: Clarendon, 1945–present.

Todd, Janet, ed. *A Dictionary of British and American Women Writers, 1660–1800.* Totowa: Rowman and Littlefield, 1985.

LITERATURE JOURNALS

American Literature
Journal of Modern Literature
Modern Fiction Studies
PMLA
Speculum
World Literature Today

B-10 Music

Baker's Biographical Dictionary of Musicians. 7th ed. Rev. by Nicolas Slonimsky. New York: Schirmer/Macmillan, 1984.

Bordman, Gerald, *American Musical Theatre: A Chronicle.* Expanded ed. New York: Oxford UP, 1986.

Bull, Storm. *Index to Biographies of Contemporary Composers.* 3 vols. Metuchen: Scarecrow, 1964–87.

Clifford, Mike. *The Harmony Illustrated Encyclopedia of Rock.* 5th ed. New York: Harmony/Crown, 1986.

Cohen, Aaron I. *International Encyclopedia of Women Composers.* New York: Bowker, 1981.

The Definitive Kobbe's Opera Book. Ed., rev. and updated by The Earl of Harewood. New York: Putnam's, 1987.

Ewen, David, comp. and ed. *Great Composers: 1300–1900.* New York: Wilson, 1983.

Gangwere, Blanche. *Music History from the Late Roman Thru the Gothic Periods, 313–1425: A Documented Chronology.* Westport: Greenwood, 1986.

Griffiths, Paul. *The Thames and Hudson Encyclopedia of 20th-Century Music.* London: Thames and Hudson, 1986.

International Who's Who in Music and Musicians' Directory. Cambridge, Eng.: Melrose, 1975–present.

Music Index. Detroit: Information Coordinators, Inc., 1949–present. An important periodical index.

Musical America. *International Directory of the Performing Arts.* New York: 1960–present. Annual.

The New Grove Dictionary of American Music. 4 vols. H. Wiley Hitchcock and Stanley Sadie, eds. New York: Grove's Dictionaries of Music, 1986.

The New Grove Dictionary of Music and Musicians. Ed. Stanley Sadie. 20 vols. London: Macmillan, 1980. A comprehensive reference source on all aspects of music since 1450.

The New Grove Dictionary of Musical Instruments. 3 vols. Stanley Sadie, ed. New York: Grove's Dictionaries of Music, 1984.

New Oxford History of Music. Ed. J. A. Westrup *et al.* 10 vols. New York: Oxford UP, 1954–present.

Popular Music: An Annotated Index to American Popular Songs. Ed. Nat Shapiro and Bruce Pollock. Detroit: Gale, 1964–present.

Pruett, James W. and Thomas P. Slavens. *Research Guide to Musicology.* Chicago: American Library Assn, 1985.

Randel, Don M., ed. *The New Harvard Dictionary of Music.* Cambridge, MA: Harvard, 1986.

Shapiro, Nat. *Popular Music, 1920–1979: A Revised Cumulation.* Detroit: Gale, 1985.

———. *Popular Music, 1980–1984.* Detroit: Gale, 1986.

Slonimsky, Nicholas. *Supplement to Music Since 1900.* New York: Scribner's, 1986.

Taylor, Paul. *Popular Music Since 1955: A Critical Guide to the Literature.* Boston: Hall, 1985.

Thompson, Oscar, ed. *The International Cyclopedia of Music and Musicians.* 11th ed. New York: Dodd, Mead, 1985.

Who's Who in American Music: Classical. 2nd ed. Ed. by Jaques Cattell Press, 1985.

MUSIC JOURNALS

High Fidelity
Musical America
Musical Quarterly
Opera News

B-11 Mythology/Classics

Brewer's Dictionary of Phrase and Fable. Centenary ed. New York: Harper, 1981.

Bulfinch's Mythology. 2nd rev. ed. New York: Crowell, 1970.

Campbell, Joseph. *Historical Atlas of World Mythology.* Vol. 1- New York: Van der Marck, 1988–present.

Civilization of the Ancient Mediterranean: Greece and Rome. Ed. by Michael Grant and Rachel Kitzinger. 3 vols. New York: Scribner's, 1988.

Frazer, Sir James. *The Golden Bough.* 13 vols. New York: St. Martin's, 1960.

Grant, Michael. *Greek and Latin Authors: 800 B.C.–A.D. 1000.* New York: Wilson, 1980.

———. *A Guide to the Ancient World: A Dictionary of Classical Place Names.* New York: Wilson, 1986.

———. *The Roman Emperors: A Biographical Guide to the Rulers of Imperial Rome, 31 B.C.–A.D. 476.* New York: Scribner's, 1985.

Halton, Thomas P. and Stella O'Leary. *Classical Scholarship: An Annotated Bibliography.* White Plains: Kraus, 1986.

Hamilton, Edith. *Mythology.* Boston: Little, 1942.

New Larousse Encyclopedia of Mythology. Introd. by Robert Graves. New York: Crescent, 1987.

The Oxford Classical Dictionary. 2nd ed. Ed. N. G. Hammond and H. H. Scullard. Oxford: Oxford UP, 1970.

South, Malcolm, ed. *Mythical and Fabulous Creatures: A Sourcebook and Research Guide.* Westport: Greenwood, 1987.

Walker, Barbara G. *The Woman's Encyclopedia of Myths and Secrets.* New York: Harper, 1983.

MYTHOLOGY/CLASSICS JOURNALS

Classical Bulletin

Classical Journal
Classical Quarterly
Greece and Rome

B-12 Philosophy

Bynagle, Hans E. *Philosophy; A Guide to the Reference Literature.* Littleton, CO: Libraries Unlimited, 1986.

Copleston, Frederick. *History of Philosophy.* 9 vols. Westminster: Newman Bookshop, 1946–75.

The Encyclopedia of Philosophy. Ed. in chief: Paul Edwards. 8 vols. in 4. Rpt. New York: Macmillan, 1972.

Gregory, Richard L., ed. *The Oxford Companion to the Mind.* New York: Oxford, 1987.

The Handbook of Western Philosophy. Ed. by G. H. R. Parkinson, New York: Macmillan, 1988.

Handbook of World Philosophy: Contemporary Developments Since 1945. Westport: Greenwood, 1980.

International Directory of Philosophy and Philosophers, 1986–89. 6th ed. Ramona Cormier and Richard H. Lineback, eds. Bowling Green: Philosophy Documentation Center, 1986.

Lacey, A. R. *A Dictionary of Philosophy.* 2nd ed. New York: Routledge & K. Paul, 1986.

Philosopher's Index: An International Index to Philosophical Periodicals. Bowling Green: Bowling Green University, 1967–present. Also available online through DIALOG.

Tice, Terrence N. and Thomas P. Slavens. *Research Guide to Philosophy.* Chicago: American Library Assn., 1983.

World Philosophy: Essay-Reviews of 225 Major Works. Ed. Frank N. Magill. 5 vols. Englewood Cliffs: Salem, 1982.

PHILOSOPHY JOURNALS

American Philosophical Quarterly
International Philosophical Quarterly
Journal of Philosophy
Mind

B-13 Psychology

American Psychiatric Association. *The American Psychiatric Association's Glossary.* Washington, 1984.

Annual Review of Psychology. Palo Alto: Annual Reviews, 1950–present.

Child Development Abstracts and Bibliography. Chicago: U of Chicago P., 1927–present.

Concise Encylopedia of Psychology. Raymond J. Corsini and others, eds. New York: Wiley, 1987.

International Encyclopedia of Psychiatry, Psychology, Psychoanalysis & Neurology. Benjamin B. Wolman, ed. New York: Aesculapius, 1983–present.

International Handbook of Psychology. Albert R. Gilgen and Carol K. Gilgen, eds. Westport: Greenwood, 1987.

Longman Dictionary of Psychology and Psychiatry. Ed. in chief, Robert M. Goldenson. New York: Longman, 1984.

Mental Measurements Yearbook. Lincoln: Buros Institute of Mental Measurements, 1938–present.

Psychological Abstracts. Washington: American Psychological Assn., 1927–present. Also available on-line through DIALOG.

Psychowave Sourcebook, 1987–88. 2nd ed. Comp. and ed. by Samuel E. Krug. Kansas City: Test Corp. of America, 1987.

Tests: A Comprehensive Reference. 2nd ed. Ed. by Richard C. Sweetland and Daniel J. Keyser. Kansas City: Test Corp. of America, 1986.

Zusne, Leonard. *Biographical Dictionary of Psychology.* Westport: Greenwood, 1984.

PSYCHOLOGY JOURNALS

American Journal of Psychiatry
American Psychologist
Journal of Abnormal Psychology
Journal of Applied Psychology
Journal of Comparative Psychology
Journal of Social Psychology
Psychological Bulletin

B-14 Religion

Encyclopaedia Judaica. 16 vols. New York: Macmillan, 1972. Offers comprehensive information on all aspects of Judaism in the twentieth century.

Encyclopedia of Religion. Mircea Eliade, ed. in chief. New York: Macmillan, 1987.

Encyclopedia of the American Religious Experience. Charles H. Lippy and Peter W. Williams, eds. 3 vols. New York: Scribner's, 1987.

Hardon, John A. *Modern Catholic Dictionary.* New York: Doubleday, 1980.

Hinnells, John R., ed. *The Facts on File Dictionary of Religions.* New York: Facts on File, 1984.

——. *A Handbook of Living Religions.* New York: Viking Penguin, 1984.

Homan, Roger, comp. *The Sociology of Religion; A Bibliographical Survey.* Westport: Greenwood, 1986.

Illustrated Dictionary and Concordance of the Bible. Geoffrey Wigoder [*et al.*] New York: Macmillan, 1986.

The International Standard Bible Encyclopedia. Rev. ed. Gen. ed., Geoffrey W. Bromley. Grand Rapids: Eerdmans, 1979–present.

Mead, Frank S. *Handbook of Denominations in the United States.* New 8th ed. Rev. by Samuel S. Hill. Nashville: Abingdon, 1985.

Melton, J. Gordon. *The Encyclopedia of American Religions.* 2 vols. 3d ed. Detroit: Gale, 1988.

New Catholic Encyclopedia. 17 vols. New York: McGraw, 1967–79.

Oxford Dictionary of the Christian Church. 2nd ed. Ed. F. L. Cross and E. A. Livingstone. London: Oxford UP, 1974.

Religion Index One: Periodicals. Chicago: American Theological Library Assn., 1949–present. Also available on-line from BRS and DIALOG.

Reynolds, Frank E., *et al. Guide to Buddhist Religion.* Boston: Hall, 1981.

Rhymer, Joseph. *Atlas of the Biblical World.* New York: Greenwich, 1982.

Runes, Dagobert D. *Dictionary of Judaism.*Secaucus: Citadel, 1981.

Sacred Books of the East. 50 vols. Ed. Max Muller. Livingston: Orient Book Distributors, 1977–80.

Stutley, Margaret and James. *Harper's Dictionary of Hinduism: Its Mythology, Folklore, Philosophy, Literature, and History.* 1st U.S. ed. San Francisco: Harper, 1984.

Who's Who in Religion. Chicago: Marquis Who's Who, 1975/76–present.

Wilson, John F. and Thomas P. Slavens. *Research Guide to Religious Studies.* Chicago: American Library Assn., 1982.

Yearbook of American and Candian Churches. Nashville: Abingdon, 1973–present.

RELIGION JOURNALS

America
Christian Century
Journal of Biblical Literature
Journal of Jewish Studies
Journal of Religion
Theology Today

B-15 Science

Album of Science. Gen. ed., I. B. Cohen. New York: Scribner's, 1978–present.

American Men and Women of Science. 17th ed. 8 vols. New York: Bowker, 1988. This database is now available for on-line searching through DIALOG Information Services, Inc. and Bibliographic Retrieval Services, Inc.

Annual Review of Information Science and Technology. New York: Wiley, 1966–present. An annual review of developments in science and technology.

Chen, Ching-Chih. *Scientific and Technical Information Sources.* 2nd ed. Cambridge, MA: MIT Press, 1987.

Dictionary of Scientific Biography. Ed. in chief, Charles C. Gillispie. 16 vols. New York: Scribner's, 1970–1980.

Dictionary of the History of Science. Ed. and intro. William F. Bynum *et al.* Princeton: Princeton UP, 1985.

General Science Index. New York: Wilson, 1978–present. A periodical index to scientific information in 87 English-language periodicals. Also available on-line from WILSONLINE and on CD-ROM from WILSONDISC.

Herzenberg, Caroline L. *Women Scientists from Antiquity to the Present: An Index.* West Cornwall: Locust Hill, 1986.

History of Technology. London: Mansell, 1976–present. Annual.

Lincoln, R. J. *The Cambridge Illustrated Dictionary of Natural History.* New York: Cambridge, 1988.

McGraw-Hill Encyclopedia of Science and Technology. 6th ed. 20 vols. New York: McGraw, 1987.

McGraw-Hill Yearbook of Science and Technology. New York: McGraw, 1962–present. Supplements to the *McGraw-Hill Encyclopedia of Science and Technology.*

Parkinson, Claire. *Breakthroughs: A Chronology of Great Achievements in Science and Mathematics, 1200–1930.* Boston: Hall, 1985.

Pure and Applied Science Books. 6 vols. New York: Bowker, 1982. A comprehensive bibliography of more than 220,000 books in science and technology.

Van Nostrand's Scientific Encyclopedia. 7th ed. 2 vols. Ed. Douglas M. Considine. New York: Van Nostrand, 1988.

Walker, Peter, ed. *Chambers Science & Technology Dictionary.* New ed. New York: Cambridge UP, 1988.

The Weather Almanac. Ed. James A. Ruffner and Frank E. Bair. 5th ed. Detroit: Gale, 1987.

SCIENCE JOURNALS

American Scientist
Bulletin of the Atomic Scientists
Nature
New Scientist
Science
Scientific American

B-16 Social sciences

Aby, Stephen H. *Sociology: A Guide to Reference and Information Sources.* Littleton: Libraries Unlimited, 1987.

Annual Review of Sociology. Palo Alto: Annual Reviews, 1975–present.

International Encyclopedia of the Social Sciences. 17 vols. New York: Macmillan, 1968. *Biographical Supplement.* New York: Macmillan, 1979.

London Bibliography of the Social Sciences. New York: Wilson, 1929–present. Annual.

Public Affairs Information Service Bulletin. New York: Public Affairs Info. Serv., 1905–present. Also available on CD-ROM from the publisher.

Smelser, Neil J., ed. *Handbook of Sociology.* Newbury Park: Sage, 1988.

The Social Science Encyclopedia. Ed. by Adam Kuper and Jessica Kuper. London: Routledge & K. Paul, 1985.

Social Sciences Citation Index. Philadelphia: Inst. for Scientific Information, 1973–present. Also available on-line from BRS and DIALOG.

Social Sciences Index. New York: Wilson, 1974–present. An important periodical index. Also available on-line from WILSONLINE and on CD-ROM from WILSONDISC.

Sociological Abstracts. San Diego: Sociological Abstracts, 1953–present. Also available on-line from BRS and DIALOG.

SOCIAL SCIENCE JOURNALS

American Behavioral Scientist
American Journal of Sociology
International Social Science Journal
Journal of Social Issues
Social Forces
Social Research
Society

B-17 Women's studies

Doss, Martha M., ed. *Women's Organizations; a National Directory.* Garrett Park: Garrett Park, 1986.

The Index/Directory of Women's Media. Washington: Women's Inst. for Freedom of the Press, 1975–present.

The International Dictionary of Women's Biography. Comp. and ed. Jennifer S. Uglow. New York: Continuum, 1983.

James, Edward T. and Janet W., eds. *Notable American Women, 1607–1950: A Biographical Dictionary.* 3 vols. Cambridge: Belknap Press of Harvard University, 1971. Begins with an introductory survey of the history of women in America, then presents signed articles analyzing the lives of

American women who have made notable contributions in various fields.

Kramarae, Chris and Paula A. Treichler, with Ann Russo. *A Feminist Dictionary.* New York: Pandora, 1985.

Seager, Joni and Ann Olson. *Women in the World; An International Atlas.* New York: Simon, 1986.

Searing, Susan E. *Introduction to Library Research in Women's Studies.* Boulder: Westview, 1985.

Shortridge, Barbara G. *Atlas of American Women.* New York: Macmillan, 1986.

Tuttle, Lisa. *Encyclopedia of Feminism.* New York: Facts on File, 1986.

Who's Who of American Women. Chicago: Marquis, 1970/71–present.

Women Studies Abstracts. Rush: Rush, 1972–present.

Women's Studies: A Recommended Core Bibliography, 1980–1985. Catherine R. Loeb [*et al.*] Littleton, CO: Libraries Unlimited, 1987.

WOMEN'S STUDIES JOURNALS

Feminist Studies
New Directions for Women
Resources for Feminist Research
Signs
Women's Studies

INDEX

A

Abbreviations, 211–15
Abstract
  in finished form of paper, 194
  student sample of, 244–45
  writing the, 104
Afterword, bibliographic references to, 159
Alphabetizing bibliography entries, 146–48
American Psychological Association (APA)
  footnote style of, 142
  parenthetical documentation style of, 114–22
  reference list style of. *See* Reference List
  sample student paper in style of, 243–64
Annuals. *See also* Reference works
  bibliographic references to, 147, 155, 161
  footnotes for, 127–28
  parenthetical citations to, 111, 113–19
Anonymous authors, 111, 118–19
Anthologies. *See* Collections
Arabic numerals, in parenthetical documentation, 113
Art, reference works on, 241–42
Art works, 165, 170. *See also* Illustrative materials, bibliographic references to
Atlases, 281
Audiovisual room, library, 20
Authors, 115, 149, 154, 162. *See also* Anonymous authors; Corporate authors; Multiple authors; Pseudonymous authors; Single author, bibliographic references to

B

Bible, the
  abbreviations in, 214–15
  bibliographic references to, 170
  footnotes for, 133
Bibliographies, 146–90. *See also* Reference List; Works Cited
  alphabetizing entries in, 146–48
  Modern Language Association (MLA) and traditional styles for, 148–78
  of reference works, 275–76
  working, 34
Bibliography cards, 34–37
Biographical reference works, 283–86
Books. *See also* Bibliographies; Titles of works
  bibliographic references to, 154–60
  books that list other, 274–75
Brochures, bibliographic references to, 172. *See also* Pamphlets
BRS (Bibliographic Retrieval Services), 31
Business and economics, reference works on, 292–94

C

Card catalog, 16
Carrels, 21
Casebooks. *See* Collections
Chapter of a book, bibliographic references to, 156
Charts
  bibliographic reference to, 177–78
  in finished form of the paper, 195–96
Checklist for preparing final draft, 272
Citations
  note, 106–108. *See also* Endnotes; Footnotes

Citations (*continued*)
parenthetical. *See* Parenthetical documentation
Classical works
bibliographic references to, 170–71
footnotes for, 132–33
reference works on, 307–308
Classification systems of libraries, 21–26
Coherence, 89–92
parallel structures in, 90–91
transitional markers in, 91–92
word reference in, 90
Collections
bibliographic references to, 156–57
footnotes for, 128
Compilers, bibliographic references to, 150
Computer programs, bibliographic references to, 166, 185–86
Computers
in libraries, 21
as search tool, 31–34
Congressional publications. *See also* Government publications
bibliographic references to, 175
footnotes for, 130–31
Congressional Record, The
bibliographic references to, 174
footnotes for, 130–31
Consolidation of references, 142–43
Content notes, 139–42, 197
Copy room, library, 20
Corporate authors
bibliographic references to, 147, 154, 181
footnotes for, 127
parenthetical documentation for, 117–18
Corrections, 195
Court decisions. *See* Legal documents or publications
Critical reviews
bibliographic references to, 164
footnotes for, 135
Cutter/Sanborn Author Marks, 23–24

D

Dance, reference works on, 294
Databases
bibliographic references to sources retrieved from, 166, 186
online, 31–32
Dates, 202–203
Decimal outline, 65–66
Dewey Decimal System, 22–23
DIALOG, 31
Dictionaries, 280–81
bibliographic references to, 157
Direct quotations, 73–85
in a book or article used as a source, bibliographic references to, 177
brief, 75–77
documentation of, 112–13
ellipses to indicate omissions in, 81–85
interpolations in, 81
long, 77–78, 87
note cards containing, 43–44, 45
overuse of, 74–75
from poetry, 78–80
punctuation of, 80–81
within another quotation, 80
within a cited work, 112, 129, 157
Dissertations
bibliographic references to, 171
Documentation
parenthetical, 106–39. *See also* Parenthetical documentation
systems used by different disciplines, 108
traditional, 123–29. *See also* Endnotes; Footnotes
types of, 106–108

E

Ecology, reference works on, 295–96
Economics, reference works on, 292–94
Edited collection, footnotes for, 130
Edition
bibliographic references to, 151–58
footnotes for, 129
Editorials
bibliographic references to, 164, 184
footnotes for, 135
Editor(s)
bibliographic references to, 150, 164, 179–80
footnotes for, 130
letters to the. *See* Letters to the editor
Education, reference works on, 296–97
Ellipses to indicate omissions from quotations, 81–85
Emphasis, 93

Encyclopedia(s), 279. *See also* Reference works
  bibliographic references to, 157
Endnotes, 106–108
  bibliographic references to, 171–72
  in finished form of the paper, 197
  format for, 106–107
  numbering of, 124
  placement of numbers of, 124–26
  subsequent references to, 138–39
ERIC (Educational Research Information Center), 32
Ethnic studies, reference works on, 297–99
Evidence, sources of. *See* Sources

F

Films
  bibliographic references to, 166–67, 186
  footnotes for, 136
  guides to, 288–89
Final draft, checklist for preparing, 272
Footnotes, 106–108, 123–43
  for anonymous or pseudonymous authors, 127–28
  author-date style (APA), 142
  author-work style (MLA), 142
  for the Bible, 133
  bibliographic references to, 171–72
  for books, 126–33
  for classical works, 132–33
  for collections, 128
  for *The Congressional Record*, 131
  consolidation of references in, 142–43
  content, 139–42
  for corporate authors, 127
  for double references, 129
  for editions, 129–30
  for films, 136
  in finished form of the paper, 177
  format for, 124
  for government publications, 130–31
  for interviews, 128
  for lectures, 136
  for legal publications, 131–32
  for multiple authors, 127, 133–34
  for multivolume works, 128
  for newspaper articles, 135
  for nonprint materials, 136–38
  numbering of, 122–23
  numbers style for, 143
  for pamphlets, 130
  for periodicals, 133–35
  for personal letter, 138
  placement of numbers of, 124–26
  for radio programs, 136
  for recordings (disc or tape), 137
  for reference works, 129
  for series, 129
  for single authors, 127
  student paper using, 265–71
  subsequent references to, 133–39
  for television programs, 136
  traditional style of, 143
  for translations, 130
Foreign country, bibliographic references to book published in a, 159
Foreign-language books,
  bibliographic references to, 160
Foreign words, 211
Foreword, bibliographic references to, 159

G

Gazetteers, 282
Government publications
  bibliographic references to, 174–76, 187–88
  reference works on, 286–87
Graphs
  bibliographic references to, 177–78
  in finished form of the paper, 195–97, 199

H

High technology, reference works on, 299–300
History, reference works on, 300–301
Hyphenating words, 210

I

Illustrative materials
  bibliographic references to, 177–78
  books of, bibliographic references to, 159
  in finished form of the paper, 198
Indexes
  to microforms, 16, 288
  of periodicals and newspapers, 278–79

Indirect quotations, 85–86
Interlibrary loan, 21
Interpolations, 81
Interviews
bibliographic references to, 165, 167
footnotes for, 138
Introductions
bibliographic references to, 159
to paraphrases or quotations, 109, 111, 113–14, 115
Italics, 208–209
titles in, 205–206

J

Journals. *See* Periodicals

L

Laws. *See* Legal documents or publications
Lectures
bibliographic references to, 165
footnotes for, 136
Legal documents or publications
bibliographic references to, 147, 176, 287–88
footnotes for, 136
Letters. *See* Letters to the editor; Personal letters
Letters to the editor
bibliographic references to, 164, 184
footnotes for, 135
LEXIS, 31
Library, 16–26
audiovisual room of, 20
card catalog of, 16
carrels in, 21
classification systems of, 21–26
computers in, 21
copy room of, 20
layout of, 16–21
main desk of, 19
microform indexes in, 16
microform room of, 20
newspaper racks of, 20
organization of, 21–26
reference room of, 19
reserve desk of, 20
stacks of, 16, 19
typing room in, 21
Library of Congress Classification System, 24–25
Literature, reference works on, 302–305

M

Magazines. *See* Periodicals
Manuscript (typescript), bibliographic references to, 172, 181. *See also* Dissertations
Maps, in finished form of paper, 198
Mead Data Control, 31
Microform indexes, 16, 288
Microform room, library, 20
Modern Language Association (MLA)
footnote/endnote style of, 123–39. *See also* Endnotes; Footnotes
footnote style of, 142
parenthetical documentation style of, 109–113
sample student paper in style of, 218–42
Money, amounts of, 202
Mood, 94–95
Multiple authors
bibliographic references to, 154, 162, 179
footnotes for, 127, 133–34
parenthetical documentation for, 110, 116, 117
Multivolume works
bibliographic references to, 151, 155–56
footnotes for, 128
parenthetical references to, 112
Music
reference works on, 305–307
Musical compositions, bibliographic references to, 167
Mythology, reference works on, 307–308

N

Names of persons, 209–210
Newspaper articles. *See also* Periodicals
bibliographic references to, 161, 163, 184
footnotes for, 135
Newspaper racks, library, 20
Newspapers, reference works on, 276–79
New York Times Information Service, 32
NEXIS, 31

Nonprint materials
bibliographic references to, 165–69
classification of, 25
footnotes for, 136–38
reference works on, 287–90
Note cards
format of, 41
paraphrase, 42–43, 45
personal-comment, 44, 45
quotations in, 43–44, 45
rough draft and, 71
summary, 41–42
Note citations, 106–108
Notes
content, 139–42, 197
incorporation into rough draft, 71–73
Note-taking, 40–46
Numbers (numerals)
Arabic, in parenthetical documentation, 113
connected consecutively, 203–204
for dates, 202–203
page, 153, 193
for percentages and amounts of money, 202
Roman, 204
spelling out, 202
Numbers system
for footnotes, 142
of parenthetical documentation, 122–23
for Works Cited (traditional bibliography style), 189–90

O

OCLC (Online Computer Library Center), 32
Omissions from quotations, ellipses to indicate, 81–85
Online databases. *See* Databases, online
Outline, 59–68
choice of type of, 67–68
decimal notation of, 66
equal ranking of entries in, 61
in finished form of the paper, 192
paragraph, 64–66
parallelism of entries in, 61–62
sentence, 63–64
topic, 62–63
types of, 62–66
visual conventions of, 60

P

Page numbers
in bibliographic references, 153
in finished form of the paper, 193–94
Page reference parentheses, 86–87
Pages of articles, in bibliographic references, 161
Pamphlets
bibliographic references to, 172
footnotes for, 130
Paragraph outline, 64–65
Parallel structures, 90–91
Paraphrase note cards, 42–43
Paraphrases, in rough draft, 71–73
Parentheses, page reference, 86–87
Parenthetical documentation, 106–23
American Psychological Association (APA) style of, 114–22
anonymous authors, 111, 118–19
Arabic numerals in, 113
when authority is not mentioned, 110
awkward placement of references in, 121–22
of corporate authors, 117–18
in-text identification of sources in, 110
introductions to paraphrases or quotations in, 109, 113–14
Modern Language Association (MLA) style of, 109–14
more than one work by the same author, 111
multiple authors, 110, 116–117
multivolume works, 112
numbers system of, 122–23
page reference, for quotation, 87
parenthetical comment, citation as part of, 121
personal communications, 120–21
poetry, 112–13
quotations within cited works, 112
same surname, authors with, 119
single author, 115
specific parts of sources, 120
traditional (footnotes/endnotes), 123–43. *See also* Endnotes; Footnotes
two or more authors, 110–116
two or more works within the same parentheses, 119–20
works in a collection, 112
works without author, 111, 118–19
Percentages, 202

Periodicals
  bibliographic references to (MLA and traditional styles), 160–65
  classification of, 25
  footnotes for, 133–35
  indexes of, 278–79
  in reference list, 160
  reference works on, 276–79
Personal comments, 87–89
  note cards for, 44, 46
Personal communications, parenthetical documentation for, 120–21
Personal letters
  bibliographic references to, 172–73
  footnotes for, 138
Philosophy, reference works on, 308
Plagiarism, 46–49
Plays, bibliographic references to, 173. *See also* Theatrical performances
Poetry
  bibliographic references to, 174
  parenthetical documentation for, 112–13
  quotations from, 78–80
Preface, bibliographic references to, 159
Primary sources of evidence, 38–39
Pseudonymous authors
  bibliographic references to, 155
  footnotes for, 127
Psychology, reference works on, 308–309
Publication facts in bibliographic references, 152
Public documents, bibliographic references to, 174–76. *See also* Government publications; Legal documents or publications
Punctuation of quotations, 80–81

Q

Quotations. *See* Direct quotations; Indirect quotations

R

Radio programs
  bibliographic references to, 167–68
  footnotes for, 136
Readers. *See* Collections
Recordings (disc or tape)
  bibliographic references to, 168
  footnotes for, 130
  guides to, 290
Reference List (APA style), 114–22, 178–89. *See also* Bibliographies
  books in, 179–84
  general order for books in, 178–79
  general order for periodicals in, 184
  nonprint materials in, 185–86
  periodicals in, 182–85
  reports in, 189
  sample references to books in, 185–86
  sample references to periodicals in, 182–85
  special items in, 186–88
Reference room, library, 19
References, consolidation of, 142–43. *See also* Documentation
Reference sources. *See* Sources
Reference works, 274–313
  on art, 291–92
  bibliographic references to, 157
  on books, 274–76
  on business and economics, 292–94
  on dance, 294
  dictionaries, 280–81
  on ecology, 295–96
  on education, 296–97
  encyclopedias, 279
  on ethnic studies, 297–99
  footnotes for, 129
  about government publications, 286–87
  on high technology, 299–300
  on history, 300–301
  on literature, 301–305
  on music, 305–307
  on mythology and classics, 307–308
  on nonprint materials, 287–90
  about people, 283–86
  on periodicals and newspapers, 276–79
  on philosophy, 308
  about places, 281–82
  on psychology, 308–309
  on religion, 309–10
  on science, 310–11
  on social sciences, 312
  on women, 312–13
Religion, reference works on, 309–10
Report paper, 4–5
Reports, bibliographic references to, 177
Reprints, bibliographic references to, 158
Research paper, 2
  finished form of, 192–99
  format of, 2
  reasons for, 3

steps and schedule involved in writing a, 3–4
title of, 59
Reserve desk, library, 20
Reviews. *See* Critical reviews
Revised edition. *See* Edition
Roman numerals, 204
Rough draft
checklist for, 70
coherence of, 89–92
emphasis in, 93
incorporation of notes into, 71–89
personal comments in, 87–89
quotations in. *See* Direct quotations; Indirect quotations
summaries and paraphrases in, 71–73
unity of, 89

S

Science, reference works on, 310–11
Secondary sources of evidence, 38–39
Sentence outline, 63–64
Series
bibliographic references to, 151–58
footnotes for, 129
Shakespeare, William, abbreviations for works of, 215
Single author
bibliographic references to, 115, 149, 154, 162
footnotes for, 127
parenthetical documentation for, 115
Skimming, 37–38
Social sciences, reference works on, 312
Sources, 9, 28–40
evaluating, 39–40
general information, 28–29
in-depth information, 28–29
primary and secondary, 38–39
retrospective and contemporary, 29
selecting, 37–40
single-fact information, 28
topics that can be traced to single, 9
where to look for, 29–31
Stacks, library, 16, 19
Statutes. *See* Legal documents or publications
Style, 95–104
abstract, 104
active voice in, 101–102
conciseness in, 98–99
meaningless words and phrases, 100
objective stance in, 102–103
precision in, 97–98
redundant expressions in, 99–100
sexist language in, 103–104
snobbish diction in, 100–101
Summaries, in rough draft, 71–73
Summary note cards, 41–42

T

Tables
bibliographic references to, 177–78
in finished form of the paper, 195
Tapes. *See* Recordings
Technical subjects, 9
Technology, reference works on, 299–300
Television programs
bibliographic references to, 167–68
footnotes for, 136
Tense, 91–95
Text, in finished form of the paper, 194–95
Theatrical performances, bibliographic references to, 169
Thesis
formulating the, 53–54
definition and function of a, 52–53
placement of the, 58–59
rough draft and the, 70
rules for wording the, 54–57
Thesis paper, 4–5
Titled section of a book, bibliographic references to, 149–50
Title page, in finished form of the paper, 192–94
Titles of articles, bibliographic references to, 160
Titles of works, 204–208
in bibliographic references, 149–50
frequent references to, 208
in italics, 205–206
within quotation marks, 206–207
within titles, 207
Topic outline, 59–60
Topics
to avoid, 8–10
choosing, 8
narrowing, 10–11
Transitional markers, 91–92
Translators
bibliographic references to, 150, 159
footnotes for, 130
Treaties, bibliographic references to, 176

Trivial topics, 10
Typescript. *See* Manuscript
Typing room, library, 21

U

Union lists of periodicals and newspapers, 277
Unity, 89

V

Verbs
  moods of, 94
  tense of, 94–95
Volume numbers. *See* Multivolume works

W

Women, reference works on, 312–13
Word reference, 90
Working bibliography, 34–37
Works Cited (traditional bibliography style), 148–78, 199. *See also* Bibliographies
  address or lecture in, 165
  anonymous author in, 161
  anonymous or pseudonymous author in, 155
  art works in, 165, 170
  authors in, 149, 160
  the Bible in, 170
  books of illustrations in, 159
  chapter or titled section of a book in, 156
  classical works in, 170–71
  collections or anthologies in, 156–57
  computer programs in, 166
  corporate author in, 154
  database source in, 166
  dissertations in, 171
  edited work in, 158
  edition in, 151, 158
  editors, compilers, and translators in, 150
  films in, 166–67
  in finished form of paper, 199
  footnote or endnote citations in, 171–72
  foreign books in, 159
  foreign title in, 160
  general order for books in, 149–54
  interviews in, 167
  introduction, preface, foreword, or afterword in, 159
  legal documents in, 176
  manuscripts in, 172
  multiple authors in, 154, 162
  multivolume works in, 155–56
  musical compositions in, 167
  nonprint materials in, 165–69
  numbers system for, 189–90
  page numbers in, 153, 161
  periodicals in, 160–65
  personal letters in, 172–73
  plays in, 173
  poetry in, 174
  public documents in, 174–77
  publication facts in, 152, 160–61
  quotation within a cited work in, 157
  quotations in a book or article used as a source in, 177
  radio or television programs in, 167–68
  recording (disc or tape) in, 168
  reference works in, 157
  reports in, 177
  reprints in, 158
  sample references to books, 154–60
  series in, 151, 158
  single author in, 154, 162
  special items in, 169–78
  tables, graphs, charts, or other illustrations in, 177–78
  theatrical performances in, 169
  titles of books in, 149–50, 160
  translator in, 159
  volume numbers in, 151

A 9
B 0
C 1
D 2
E 3
F 4
G 5
H 6
I 7
J 8